THE AUTHORS

Woodbrooke College

200 29690

Dr Paul Rogers i   s at
the University of   rial
College, London   op-
ment programme in East Africa. His research interests
are in international resource conflict and strategic studies and he has written over twenty-five papers and
written or edited five books. He was for three years a
member of the Catholic Commission for International
Justice and Peace.

Dr Malcolm Dando is a Lecturer in Peace Studies at
the University of Bradford and was previously Senior
Research Fellow in Operational Research at the University of Sussex. He was educated at the University of
St Andrews and his Ph.D. is in neurophysiology. He has
published over forty research papers specializing primarily in neurophysiology and conflict analysis and also
has a research interest in Civil Defence and the effects of
nuclear weapons.

Dr Peter van den Dungen is a Lecturer in Peace
Studies at the University of Bradford. Dutch by birth, he
studied economics at the University of Antwerp and
international relations at the Johns Hopkins University
in the United States. He took his Ph.D. at the Department of War Studies at King's College, University of
London and his research interests are in the history of
peace research, the politics of disarmament and non-
violence.

AS LAMBS TO THE SLAUGHTER

THE FACTS ABOUT NUCLEAR WAR

Paul Rogers

Malcolm Dando

Peter van den Dungen

Illustrated by Richard Willson

ARROW BOOKS
in association with ECOROPA

341.734

Arrow Books Limited
17 Conway Street, London W1P 6JD

An imprint of the Hutchinson Publishing Group

London Melbourne Sydney Auckland
Wellington Johannesburg and agencies
throughout the world

First published 1981
© Ecoropa 1981
Illustrations © Richard Willson 1981

Set in Linoterm Times by Rowland Phototypesetting Ltd
Bury St Edmunds, Suffolk

Made and printed in Great Britain
by The Anchor Press Ltd
Tiptree, Essex

ISBN 0 09 927270 9

20029690

358.39
355.0217

Contents

Preface   9
Introduction   17
Abbreviations   19

PART 1: READY FOR WAR
1 The Superpowers – the Nuclear Weapons
   of the United States and the Soviet Union   23
2 Britain's Bombs   49
3 Proliferation –
   the Genie out of the Bottle?   66
4 The Slide to Nuclear War   83

PART 2: WHEN IT HAPPENS
5 Target Britain   109
6 Short-term Effects of Nuclear Attack   127
7 Civil Defence in a Nuclear War?   148
8 Long-term Effects of Nuclear Attack   173

PART 3: THE FAILURE OF DISARMAMENT
9 Attempts at Negotiation   201
10 The SALT Talks   219
11 Why the Failure?   236

PART 4: WHAT HAS TO BE DONE
12 Effective Disarmament   251
13 What You can Do   269
   Conclusions   284

The political apathy of people in time of peace indicates that they will readily allow themselves to be led to slaughter later. Because today they lack even the courage to give their signature in support of disarmament, they will be compelled to shed their blood tomorrow.

Albert Einstein

Preface

In the backs of our minds we all know that an uneasy peace exists between the superpowers. We have been told over the last thirty years or so that neither side is likely to attack the other for fear of instant and devastating retaliation. It has been called the balance of terror, and we have become accustomed to living with it. I, for one, have lost little sleep over it: after all, there was little enough I could do about it – it was just one of those bad things in the background, like pollution, or starvation in Africa. And, anyhow, to the extent that anyone could lessen the East–West tensions, well, what do we pay governments to do if it isn't precisely this?

Then last year I happened to pick up a copy of the newly released Home Office publication *Protect and Survive* and, whilst idly turning the pages, it slowly dawned on me that between the lines I was being politely asked if I wouldn't mind accepting the idea that there might shortly be a nuclear war and that, unless I was lucky, I could expect to be killed.

Slowly at first and then with accelerating concern I began asking questions. It didn't take long to realize that the balance of terror is ending. As lambs to the slaughter it seems we are headed for nuclear war.

Gone are the days when the Americans and the Russians backed up their mutual distrust with the threat of lobbing a few missiles over Europe's heads towards each other's capital. Now East and West are mass-producing the tools for global destruction, devising 'handy' nuclear weapons for use by the troops in Europe. Confrontation is drawing nearer, and the possibility of actual war, here in Britain, is now quite real. So this is why we are being steadily conditioned to accept the fact, for a fact is what I now realize it to be, that two-thirds of our population may be killed. It seems that others, too, may have reached the same conclusion: several recent opinion polls have shown that the majority of British people expect a nuclear war within the next ten years.

It was in this context that, on behalf of Ecoropa,* I commissioned from a research team at Bradford University a comprehensive and up-to-date report on the likelihood, nature and probable consequences of nuclear war, and also suggestions for action needed to avoid such a war. They were asked to make this report readily comprehensible to the general public, and it was stipulated that it must be primarily a factual treatment, and that the sources of the facts quoted were to be disclosed. Then they were asked to list what organizations people could join, if, after reading the report, they felt motivated to do something.

This book is their report. It is the first time that much of this information has been made generally available: in fact some of it has never been previously published in Britain.

If this report only enabled us to contemplate our fate, it would serve no useful purpose. It is intended to enable us, through knowledge of the facts, to play some part in influencing events so that the danger of war may be reduced. That it is actually possible for 'the man in the street', you or me, to influence his destiny needs shouting from the rooftops: so many people feel impotent to

---

*Ecoropa is a European group which was set up in 1978 to organize campaigns across Britain and the continent in response to ecological and environmental threats of all kinds. Nuclear war is, of course, the ultimate environmental and ecological catastrophe.

change anything.

Most wars are fought without the combatants being first consulted. There must be a strong case for by-passing governmental reluctance to discuss these matters and for laying the facts before the people whose lives are in the balance so that they can make their own assessment. This is the object of Ecoropa's Campaign for Survival (see the last page of this book) of which this book forms the first step.

But it is inevitable that any questioning of our nuclear defence policy, any pointing out alternatives, any promoting of disarmament or any search for peace will attract official suspicion, since it is held that all moves for peace must be Moscow-inspired as it is in the best interests of the Soviet Union to arrest our momentum in the execution of our defence programme. Indeed, the very word 'peace' has come to have left-wing connotations. It is therefore necessary to make the position of Ecoropa, in commissioning this book and launching the Campaign for Survival quite clear. Ecoropa has no political affiliations, nor is it allied to CND or any other organization. We are simply a group of citizens who, when all is said and done, *want to survive*.

Supporters of Ecoropa include European cabinet ministers, and respected members of the business community, the professions and the Church. We reject the Soviet style authoritarian state in which discussion of defence or anything else is forbidden. We utterly condemn the forcing of the countries of Eastern Europe into the Soviet straitjacket: we deplore the invasion of Afghanistan and watch with utmost concern the events in Poland. But in our rejection of their system we do not overlook the fact that the Soviet citizen is a human being and no less peace-loving than we Western Europeans: neither does he wish to destroy his family or the northern hemisphere any more than his Western European counterpart.

And now, in a book which is primarily factual, I wish to

add some thoughts of my own – perhaps some of my comments may echo yours.

To cadets at a military academy recently, President Reagan was reported as saying, 'The argument, if there is any, will be over which weapons to build, not whether we should forsake weaponry for treaties or agreements.' If he really meant that, then I consider it a moral obscenity. We have slipped a long way since President Kennedy only nineteen years ago said, when signing the Test-Ban Treaty,

This treaty is not the millennium. It will not resolve all conflicts, or cause the Communists to forgo their ambitions, or eliminate the dangers of war. It will not reduce our need for arms or allies or programmes of assistance to others. But it is an important first step, a step towards peace, a step towards reason, a step away from war.

A war today or tomorrow, if it led to nuclear war, would not be like any war in history. A full-scale nuclear exchange lasting less than 60 minutes could wipe out more than 300,000,000 Americans, Europeans, and Russians, as well as untold numbers elsewhere. And, as Chairman Krushchev warned the Communist Chinese, 'the survivors would envy the dead'. For they would inherit a world so devastated by explosions, poisons, and fire that we cannot conceive of its horrors.

Perhaps you have seen a photograph of the utter devastation that was once Hiroshima: an endless desert of debris and burnt corpses. Once seen it cannot be forgotten, yet there are now in the East and West, ready to be launched, an armory of nuclear weapons with the destructive power of a million Hiroshima bombs: enough to make a tomb of every city in the world. Whatever the threat, are you prepared to press the button to unleash one millionth part of such a holocaust? And if not, are you willing to delegate to your political leaders this responsibility? If the price for this hesitation is being 'red rather than dead' perhaps we should look at other ways to maintain our freedom. I am not a pacifist, though I have nothing but respect for those who are; if I believed that

World War III would resemble the last war in its limited (in relative terms) horror, then I would pull the trigger with few misgivings on the Hitler of the day and his supporters.

But the horrors of nuclear war are unspeakable. The mind recoils from their magnitude. Few dare to imagine the survivors, men, women and children – including the remnants of our own families – starving, maimed, stricken with grief, tortured with the knowledge and effects of terminal radiation sickness, scavenging in competition with rats for scraps of contaminated food, deprived of all services; without medicine, shelter or warmth – these poor creatures would indeed envy the dead.

We must not be fooled into thinking that a 'limited' nuclear war in Europe is 'all' we have to fear. The facts, as this book clearly demonstrates, make it so improbable as to be an irrelevant speculation. Britain would certainly become involved, most probably as the battlefield between the US and the USSR. As the former Pentagon strategic planner, Rear-Admiral Gene LaRocque put it, 'We fought World War I in Europe, we fought World War II in Europe and if you dummies let us, we'll fight World War III in Europe.' We could not escape, we could not hide, neither would civil defence save us. It would be the end.

Decisions on defence are made by a few members of the Cabinet: yet they represent the result of heavy 'expert' pressures applied to them by military, technological and manufacturing interests. They also reflect the political doctrines of the party in power and considerable pressure from the United States. Thus we have been committed to the highly controversial £6 billion Trident system. Yet we, the people, who have to pay for such systems and, more importantly, live or die by their consequences, *neither we nor our elected parliamentary representatives, nor even the full Cabinet are consulted.*

Apart from its total denial of the democratic principle –

'We were only carrying out orders.'

the very thing our defence programme should be preserving – what reasons have we to think that those politicians who, in successive Cabinets, have given Britain almost the lowest standard of living in Europe, the highest unemployment, the worst civil violence and who have failed us in so many ways are likely to be any more competent in the field of defence? Do they merit our confidence? I doubt it. When I hear our arms production defended in terms of its contribution to our balance of payments, through sales to the Third World, I feel ashamed and enraged. What kind of morality is this? What form of logic drives the leaders of the superpowers to arm, rather than talk? Are they exemplifying the classic political need to divert attention from crumbling domestic policies by focusing it abroad?

Perhaps we should interest ourselves in our own survival and reject the propaganda of officialdom and the misleading smooth talk such as the Home Office publication *Protect and Survive*. Perhaps through independent education, such as this book provides, we can force our elected representatives to put Britain's defence policy where it belongs, in the public forum.

I believe we have now gone so far down the slippery slope that unless we turn round and, with infinite care, make our way back up again, it will be too late to return. It must be up to each and every one of us who can read, write or speak to fight for his future. We must persuade our leaders to talk from the standpoint of obtaining *positive* results. We must not allow talks to be held for 'cosmetic' purposes, to quieten voices such as ours. The current talks of Helmut Schmidt may be a case in point: we must pay minute attention to ensure that we are not being cynically duped by those whose values are so warped that they favour a continuing escalation of arms.

Of course there are risks with all peace initiatives. But if the alternative is extinction then all the roads towards disarmament must be explored. I do not believe that there is any one right solution. The multilateral disarmers and unilateral disarmers must respect each other and both should encourage the creation of nuclear-free zones leading to a nuclear-free Europe. I hope that everyone who reads this book will join one of the many organizations listed and/or help with the Campaign for Survival to ensure the distribution of some of the tens of millions of leaflets which are needed to inform the people of Western Europe whilst there may still be time.

Inevitably I will be accused of extreme naïvety if I suggest, as I now do, that the one sane action for the superpowers is to cooperate in a joint enterprise to halt the world-wide proliferation of nuclear weapons and to remove, via financial compensation, facilities for their production. Such an action could remove a great danger to world peace and set the scene for a negotiated disarmament between East and West. Many will greet such a proposal with cynicism but it is my firm belief that if (and only if) enough citizens demand this kind of action from their leaders, it could be done.

We have a choice. Either we bear mute witness to all that is leading us inexorably to war – and extinction – or we stand up and do something to prevent it. If we opt for the latter course, this book could make a sound beginning. I have read it and it has affected me deeply.

The father of atomic fission, Einstein, made an appeal in the last week of his life against the development of nuclear weapons. In the final paragraph of the last statement he ever signed he said:

> We appeal, as human beings to human beings: remember your humanity and forget the rest.

> *Gerard Morgan-Grenville*

Introduction

This report is an attempt to present information concerning nuclear weapons, their availability and likely effects, the increasing risk of nuclear war and the failure of attempts at nuclear disarmament. It is primarily a factual account, but we also put forward some proposals for approaches to global nuclear disarmament, proposals which we believe are as realistic as they are necessary.

Although all three of us have worked on aspects of nuclear strategy and disarmament for some time, this is the first opportunity to present such material in the form of a report. We recognize that the problems presented may well appear overwhelming – the catalogue of weapons, their potential effects and the insidious slide towards nuclear war are all enough to test the strongest nerves, and we have found the report disturbing to write. We do feel, though, that the scale and extent of the problem *must* be a subject for informed public debate and hope that the report might facilitate that process.

It has been a collaborative project but, for the record, Parts I and IV were written largely by Paul Rogers, Part II by Malcolm Dando and Part III by Peter van den Dungen.

We would like to thank Helena Wlazlo and our colleagues at the School of Peace Studies, Richard Willson, Richard Evans of Arrow Books, friends and colleagues in London, Brighton, Amsterdam, Stockholm and Washington, our families and especially Gerard Morgan-

Grenville of Ecoropa for help and encouragement. Any mistakes are of course, our responsibility.

Paul Rogers
Malcolm Dando
Peter van den Dungen

16 July 1981 (the 36th anniversary of the first atom bomb test).

Abbreviations

ABM	Anti-ballistic missile
AFAP	Artillery-fired atomic projectile
ALCM	Air-launched cruise missile
ASW	Anti-submarine warfare
BMD	Ballistic missile defences
CEP	Circular error probability
GLCM	Ground-launched cruise missile
ICBM	Intercontinental ballistic missile
IISS	International Institute for Strategic Studies
LOW	Launch-on-warning
LTA	Launch-through-attack
MAD	Mutually assured destruction
MIRV	Multiple independently targetable re-entry vehicle
MRV	Multiple re-entry vehicle
M-X	Missile-experimental
NATO	North Atlantic Treaty Organization
SAC	Strategic Air Command
SALT	Strategic Arms Limitation Treaty
SIPRI	Stockholm International Peace Research Institute
SLBM	Submarine-launched ballistic missile
SOSUS	Sound surveillance system
SSKP	Single shot kill probability
WTO	Warsaw Treaty Organization

Part 1

Ready for War

1
The Superpowers—the Nuclear Weapons of the United States and the Soviet Union

Later in this book we will examine in detail the effects of nuclear weapons and we will include material on the destruction of Hiroshima. For the moment we will concentrate on the nuclear weapons now held by the two major nuclear powers, but as we do, it is essential to try and appreciate the tremendous destructiveness of these modern weapons.

The Hiroshima bomb was equivalent to 12,000 tons of TNT, or 12 kilotons. Some of the larger modern strategic weapons are equivalent to several *million* tons of TNT (megatons) and a very large proportion are at least one hundred times the size of the Hiroshima bomb. By comparison with these weapons that bomb was little more than a toy. Certainly many of the small tactical nuclear weapons intended just for battlefield use are about the size of the Hiroshima bomb.

One country can create a nuclear deterrent force by being capable of delivering some 300 nuclear weapons on another country. At present some countries consider they have a deterrent with even less than this. Yet both the Soviet Union and the United States have more than *twenty times this capacity*. Indeed the degree of 'overkill' has now reached the stage where the world's total nuclear armoury is equal in destructive power to 4 tons of TNT for every man, woman and child on the planet.

THE DEVELOPMENT OF AMERICAN AND SOVIET NUCLEAR WEAPONS

After the first nuclear explosions in 1945, resulting from the Manhattan Project, the United States curtailed the exchange of information about nuclear weapons among its allies and proceeded to develop its own weapons and the means to deliver them. In 1949, though, the Soviet Union successfully tested an atom bomb, but by this time the United States had a moderate-sized nuclear arsenal of over 50 bombs and some long-range bombers capable of reaching the Soviet Union.

By 1951, the Strategic Air Command (SAC) had begun to take delivery of the massive but rather slow Convair B-36 which could reach the Soviet Union from the United States and return without refuelling. Perhaps much more significant, though, was the introduction of the B-47. Made by Boeing, this was a medium range but very fast six-engined jet bomber. It could reach the Soviet Union from bases within 1500 miles, and so the SAC established bases in Morocco and Britain in 1950–51 for the B-47s. Thus Europe became tied in to the American nuclear system at a very early stage.

During the early 1950s the United States also developed much smaller atom bombs, small enough to be delivered by long-range field guns and also deployed on relatively light carrier-borne aircraft. Much more significant, though, was the American testing of the world's first H-bomb in 1952. This thermo-nuclear development involved far greater destructive potential and, much to the surprise of the American government, the Soviet Union followed suit only nine months later.

By the mid-1950s the Soviet Union had developed the medium-range Badger bomber and the long-range turbo-prop Bear bomber which could easily reach the United States. The United States, during the same period, had developed the B-52 Stratofortress, even larger than the Bear.

THIS IS AN
ENDANGERED
SPECIES

The Soviet Union and, to a lesser extent the United States, proceeded to develop interceptors intended to destroy attacking bombers and with the increasing vulnerability of the nuclear bombers both countries began to pay more attention to other delivery systems.

Initially these concentrated on medium- and long-range missiles based on land and on 3 August 1957 a Soviet SS-6 intercontinental ballistic missile (ICBM) made a successful flight. This was some sixteen months before the first full test flight of an American ICBM, the Atlas, and represents the only major strategic weapons development in which the Soviet Union has been ahead of the United States.

Even while the ICBMs were being developed, both sides became concerned about their potential vulnerability, being located on land, and each began to develop the idea of placing them in protected silos. They also commenced work on ballistic missiles fired from submarines and, in 1960, the United States test-fired Polaris, the world's first submarine-launched ballistic missile (SLBM).

Detente – a false hope

By the early 1960s considerable public concern and action over nuclear weapons had developed, caused not least by fears over radioactive fall-out from the extensive atmospheric tests being undertaken, but also by the increasing numbers and kinds of weapons. There followed a period of some fifteen years in which such concern returned to a much lower level. The partial test-ban treaty, SALT negotiations and an easing of East–West tensions all appeared to suggest that the nuclear arms race had slowed down.

In practice this was very far from true. During the 1960s numerous new long-range missiles were tested and many were deployed. The accuracy of these systems increased and, much more significantly, the development began of the first multiple warheads. These consisted of several warheads (i.e. bombs) in the front end of a single missile. Initially there might be three which would spray out over a target, rather like shotgun pellets, the three warheads doing more damage than a single warhead, even though that might be larger. These were called multiple re-entry vehicles (MRV).

Then came the MIRV, or multiple independently targetable re-entry vehicle, in which the several warheads carried by a missile could each be dispersed in such a way as to explode on a different target. Although both countries have such missiles, the United States was the first to produce MIRVed ICBMs and SLBMs and still has a lead in MIRV technology.

As we will see later, the SALT negotiations during the early 1970s did little to slow down the nuclear arms race: they merely channelled it in particular directions. Certainly there was a huge increase in numbers of warheads, both in the strategic and shorter-range systems. In 1970, for example, the United States had 4700 warheads in its strategic arsenals and the Soviet Union had 2100. The total was therefore 6800, but by 1981 this had grown to 9200 American warheads and 6000 Soviet warheads, around 15000 in all, and this was during a decade of relative stability! Moreover, this escalation looks set to continue into the 1980s.

Today's weapons

To understand just what is going on now, and to begin to appreciate the dangers we face, it is necessary to have some information about the current nuclear weapons and the new weapons now being developed by both sides for the 1980s. There is not too much point in giving very detailed descriptions – there are so many weapons systems that it becomes a numbing exercise and, in any case, adequate sources of information are given at the end of this chapter for those who wish to pursue this study further.

For the present though, there is a certain sense in separating the weapons into two types, the strategic and the theatre/tactical systems. The strategic systems are basically for intercontinental use and the theatre and tactical nuclear weapons are supposed to be used in a nuclear war within a continent or even a country. The idea that a war could be limited in such a way is, to say the least, dubious, but there are certainly many different kinds of nuclear weapons which can be delivered over distances of perhaps 500 miles or so and others that are essentially battlefield weapons which may be very small in size, often little bigger than a briefcase, but which can be as destructive as the Hiroshima bomb.

Before we go any further, one has to realize that this separation into, for example, strategic and theatre weapons can be dependent on the country making the judgement. To the United States, an SS-20 missile which the Soviet Union has based in Western Russia and aimed at a target in East Anglia is counted as a theatre nuclear weapon as it cannot threaten the United States. Similarly an American Pershing II missile in Germany will be described by the United States as a theatre weapon. To the Soviet Union, though, the 1000-mile-range Pershing II can reach many highly important targets in the USSR, including many ICBM sites. It is therefore seen as a strategic weapon. To put it bluntly, one person's strategic weapon is another person's theatre weapon.

AMERICA'S NUCLEAR ARSENALS

Strategic weapons

The United States has around 9200 strategic nuclear weapons ranging in size from 40 kilotons to 9 megatons. It deploys them in three ways, ICBMs, SLBMs and long-range bombers. This is termed the *strategic triad* and American policy has been concerned with ensuring that each leg of the triad provides a massive nuclear force. There is, incidentally, a long-standing rivalry between the US Air Force and Navy, with each concerned to maintain its strategic role. What is more important though, is that *each* leg of the triad is undergoing expansion and development at present.

Intercontinental ballistic missiles (ICBMs)

The USA has two kinds of ICBM, the large old Titan and the smaller Minuteman. The Minuteman is being updated continually with new guidance systems and warheads.

Titan II This very large 102-foot-long missile was made by Martin Marietta and can carry a 9-megaton warhead over 9000 miles. It is a troublesome missile and one blew up in its silo in September 1980. The United States currently has 52 Titans. The ten largest Soviet cities have a total population of 21 million and the thirty largest have 37 million (15 per cent of the total Soviet population), and they are highly significant in terms of political, social and economic organization and industrial capacity. The Titan missile force alone could destroy these cities and most of the people in them.

Minuteman This smaller ICBM is made by Boeing and forms the bulk of American ICBMs, 1000 in all, 450 being the Minuteman II carrying a single 1.5 megaton warhead, 125 times the size of the Hiroshima bomb. This force of ICBMs could destroy the 300 largest Soviet cities and towns and kill most of their 83 million inhabitants.

'The prospects for arms control depend upon the achievement of a balance of arms.' General Haig.

In strategic terms, though, the Minuteman III is more important. Until recently most of these had three 200 kiloton warheads each. They were independently targetable and each warhead could be delivered with sufficient accuracy to stand a 50 per cent chance of getting within 300 yards of the target over a range of about 7000 miles (this is termed the circular error probability or CEP). The Minuteman III has now been fitted with the NS-20 guidance system giving an accuracy of 200 yards CEP and, in addition, 300 of the missiles are being fitted with a new warhead, the Mark 12A (presumably the Mark 13 would be unlucky), rated at 350 kilotons. This may appear to be rather dry technical data, but the combination of more powerful warheads and increased accuracy means that the re-equipped Minuteman III poses a threat to Soviet ICBMs, even when they are in protective silos. As we shall see later, this is of the utmost significance in terms of the slide to nuclear war.

M-X (Missile–Experimental) This new ICBM is slightly larger than the Minuteman but can deliver ten of the Mark 12A warheads and will eventually be much more accurate than current systems. It is made by Martin Marietta and 200 will be deployed during the late 1980s, probably in a mobile form to reduce vulnerability to Soviet missiles. The mixture of Minuteman and M-X missiles will, by around 1987 or so, give the United States the ability to destroy the great majority of Soviet ICBMs in their silos.

Small intercontinental ballistic missile (SICBM) Boeing has proposed development and deployment of over 3000 SICBMs each weighing only 10 tons yet capable of carrying a warhead of 500 kilotons. They could be launched from superhard silos or from highly mobile vehicles using ordinary roads.

Submarine-launched ballistic missiles (SLBMs)

All the American SLBMs have been made by Lockheed and there are basically four generations of missile involved.

Polaris Three versions of this, the first SLBM, were produced but only ten Polaris-class submarines are still in service. Each submarine carries 16 missiles and each of the 32-foot-long missiles has a range of under 3000 miles so the submarines have to patrol fairly near Soviet waters. Each missile has three 200 kiloton warheads.

Poseidon This is similar in length to Polaris but weighs twice as much and can deliver up to fourteen 40 kiloton warheads in a MIRVed system, although the usual number is ten. The United States had 31 Poseidon-class submarines but some are being re-fitted with the new Trident missile. Each 16-missile submarine can attack 160 targets and former President Jimmy Carter made the point that the missiles of a *single* Poseidon submarine can destroy every major city in the USSR.

Trident I This missile has already been fitted to three Poseidon submarines and nine more will have them by March 1982. Each has a range of 4600 miles and carries eight 100 kiloton warheads in a MIRV system. At the time of writing, Britain is set to acquire the Trident as a replacement for its Polaris system. The United States is

'No power on earth is stronger than the United States of America today. None will be stronger than the United States of America in the future. This is the only national defense posture which can ever be acceptable to the United States.'

President Nixon addressing a joint session of Congress after the signing of the SALT I agreement.

building a fleet of very large Trident-class submarines, each weighing over 18,000 tons and taking 24 missiles. Such a submarine is approximately eight times the size of a typical World War II submarine. The first, the *USS Ohio*, was launched in 1979 and commenced firing trials in the summer of 1981 and the second, the *USS Michigan*, was launched in April 1980. Each boat costs over $2000 million (£1100 million) and eight are on order initially. The Trident missile is more accurate, carries larger warheads and has a longer range than the Poseidon.

Trident II If the Trident I missile is an advance on earlier SLBMs, then the planned Trident II represents a new generation. Likely to be ready to go into service in 1987 it will have a range of 7000 miles and a payload double the size of Trident I, involving as many as 17 warheads in a single missile. This tremendous firepower is made more significant by the fact that the Trident II missile will be accurate enough to destroy ICBMs in protective silos.

Submarine-launched missiles are popular with military strategists because the submarines are extremely difficult to detect. America keeps more than 20 of its 40 or so missile submarines at sea at any one time. Each of these is separately capable of destroying the major cities of the USSR. They are not yet accurate enough to attack hardened targets such as missile silos but that will come before the decade is out.

Long-range aircraft

The ICBMs and SLBMs were developed partly because the bombers seemed likely to become vulnerable to air defences. It might be supposed, therefore, that bombers are no longer important. This is far from true in the case of the United States. Application of missile and electronic counter-measure technology has allowed the United States to keep a potent bomber force which is now undergoing a quite astonishing expansion in capability.

Boeing B52 Stratofortress 750 of these massive eight-engined jet bombers were built and 340 are still operational together with 230 in reserve or storage. The B52 originally had the strategic function of delivering free-fall H-bombs but this involved overflying the target. To avoid air defences Boeing developed the small Short-Range Attack Missiles (SRAM) which could deliver a 200 kiloton warhead a distance of 100 miles. 1250 SRAMs were built and each B52 can carry 20 of them together with four 1 megaton bombs: *a single B52 carries more explosive power than was used by all the sides throughout World War II.* Boeing have also produced the Air-Launched Cruise Missile (ALCM) which carries a warhead similar to that of the SRAM but can be launched from an aircraft up to 1500 miles from the target and will guide itself with considerable precision. By this means the B52 does not even have to enter Soviet air space. A total of 3418 ALCMs will be deployed initially on approximately 150 B52s starting late in 1982, but the total production run may be 5000 or more. The ALCM will mean the B52 will remain a potent force well into the 1990s.

General Dynamics F-111 The United States has 76 of this smaller but supersonic strategic bomber based in the USA together with another 156 of a medium-range version in Britain. Each can carry up to six SRAMs. The medium-range version can also carry any of seven different free-fall nuclear bombs ranging in yield from 10 to 300 kilotons.

Rockwell International B1 The United States developed a large, expensive, supersonic, strategic bomber in the early 1970s but production was halted temporarily in July 1977. Re-development was suggested by the Reagan administration in June 1981 and the B1 is expected to be built primarily as an ALCM launch platform, carrying 16 internally and a further 14 under the wings. The first will be deployed in 1985. The B1 will use 'stealth' technology, a name given to a variety of techniques used to reduce detection of aircraft by radar. The Defence Advanced Research Projects Agency at the Pentagon is sponsoring designs for a new generation of 'stealth' strike aircraft.

This summary of the American Strategic triad gives some idea of the variety of weapons, the considerable numbers involved and the current escalation. Any one of six different systems could already devastate the population centres of the Soviet Union: Titan, Minuteman II and III, Poseidon, Trident and B52. The degree of overkill is phenomenal yet a new round of escalation is in progress. The M-X missile involves 1400 additional warheads, the ALCMs number 3400 with perhaps only 400 existing missiles being withdrawn, and the Trident submarines involve over 1800 additional warheads.

It all adds up to around 6000 *new* warheads being deployed up to the mid-1980s, taking the American total from 9200 to around 15,000. If we now examine some of the shorter-range systems we find that a similar kind of escalation is in progress there.

American theatre and tactical nuclear weapons

These weapons range in size from nuclear shells only 5 inches in diameter and rated at around one kiloton, to cruise missile warheads sixteen times the power of the Hiroshima bomb. They include many different bombs delivered by aircraft against land, sea and submarine targets, battlefield missiles, ship-to-ship missiles and even atomic demolition munitions intended to prevent enemy advances. These weapons are integrated throughout the

---

'It would be our policy to use nuclear weapons wherever we felt it necessary to protect our forces and achieve our objectives.'

Robert McNamara
US Secretary of Defense, 1961

armed forces of the United States and many NATO countries and involve the air force, army, navy and marines. Examples of the wide variety of weapons will give some idea of the range involved.

Pershing IA A mobile tactical nuclear missile made by Martin Marietta with a range of up to 460 miles and carrying a 400 kiloton warhead. Well over 100 are deployed by the US and West German armies in West Germany.

Pershing II 96 of these will be deployed by the United States in West Germany. Each has double the range of the Pershing IA and will be equipped with a RADAG radar terminal guidance system which compares a radar map of the target area with a stored radar image. This comparison generates course changes in the missile in the last seconds of flight to give it a very high degree of accuracy, certainly accurate enough to destroy heavily protected targets such as control centres and missile silos.

Tomahawk cruise missile This is similar in size, range, speed and destructive potential to the ALCM mentioned earlier but it is being developed in a form which can be launched from mobile land-based vehicles, ships or submarines. It is guided partly by the TERCOM terrain contour matching system in which downward-looking radar in the missile compares the terrain to a digital map in the on-board computer memory, again giving the missile a very high degree of accuracy, also allowing it to fly to its target by a round-about route. The cruise missile is relatively slow, flying at around 500 m.p.h., but is small and difficult to detect. The United States intends to deploy 464 ground-launched cruise missiles in Britain, West Germany, Italy, Belgium and Holland but is also planning to deploy many hundreds on surface ships, where the missile can be fired from dual-purpose launchers available also for the Standard ship-to-ship missile.

Another plan is to use two old battleships, *New Jersey* and *Iowa*, currently moth-balled, as cruise missile launchers, with each taking 320 missiles.

Lance This can deliver a conventional or nuclear warhead up to 75 miles at a speed of 1900 m.p.h. and is in service with the US and many other armies. It can be fitted with the W70-3 enhanced-radiation weapon or neutron bomb, development of which was completed in 1977. Its production was postponed but the Reagan administration is now going ahead with it.

ASROC This is also widely used as an anti-submarine missile carried by surface ships. Built by Honeywell, the US Navy's ASROCS can deliver a 1-kiloton nuclear depth bomb over a distance of 6 miles.

SUBROC This has a similar-sized warhead but is fired from a submarine's torpedo tube, propels itself to the surface, travels up to 35 miles through the air and then delivers a nuclear depth bomb against another submarine.

Genie The United States has anti-aircraft missiles which have nuclear warheads such as the Nike-Hercules, but it even has air-to-air nuclear missiles. The Genie has a range of 6 miles and has a warhead of over 1 kiloton, being intended for use against flights of bombers.

Artillery The United States deploys large numbers of self-propelled guns such as the 155 mm and 203 mm (8 inch) howitzers. These are nuclear-capable and their rounds are termed Artillery-Fired Atomic Projectiles or AFAPs. A major modernization programme is now underway including a new shell, the W79, entering production in 1981, a rocket-assisted projectile which can be fired from the 203 mm howitzer and has a greater range than the existing shells and an enhanced radiation (neutron) warhead. These can be fired at targets over 10 miles away at the rate of one a minute. There are also a group of weapons called 'atomic demolition munitions' which are intended to prevent enemy land force advances by destroying bridges, mountain passes and transport centres. Some may be small enough to be carried by special services units operating in occupied areas.

Nuclear-capable aircraft The United States has a very wide range of strike aircraft able to deliver nuclear weapons. These include the F-4 Phantom, the F-104 Starfighter, the new General Dynamics F-16 and the A-4 Skyhawk, A-6 Intruder and A-7 Corsair, the last three being carrier-based. All of these and the American version of the Harrier jump-jet, can deliver nuclear weapons against land targets. There are also maritime patrol aircraft such as the Lockheed P3 Orion and the Sikorsky SH3 Sea King helicopter which can deliver nuclear depth bombs. These, such as the Mark 57, are quite large – in the range of 5 to 10 kilotons.

The information given here, all from published sources available in the United States and, to a lesser extent, Britain, gives some indication of the extent of nuclear arsenals. At the tactical and theatre level we are talking about as many as 20,000 weapons. It is easy to assume that these are stockpiled weapons but, as the information shows, we are dealing with *a wide range of bombs and missile warheads which are available and ready for use in many different contexts*.

One of the most significant in the case of the United States is the nuclear capability of carrier-based aircraft. The A-6 Grumman Intruder, for example, is an all-weather aircraft which has a combat radius of over 600 miles when backed up by aerial re-fuelling. Moreover this re-fuelling can be provided by tanker aircraft which themselves are launched from a carrier. We therefore have formidable nuclear delivery systems which have independent, mobile bases, the aircraft carriers. Normal deployments are:

Second Fleet (Atlantic)	5 carriers
Third Fleet (Eastern Pacific)	4 carriers
Sixth Fleet (Mediterranean)	2 carriers
Seventh Fleet (Western Pacific)	2 carriers

In addition there are two task forces assigned to the Indian Ocean including the Persian Gulf, each with an aircraft carrier.

THE SOVIET UNION'S NUCLEAR ARSENAL

Strategic Weapons

Figures given earlier indicated that the United States has many more strategic nuclear warheads than the Soviet Union. It also has a much larger number of tactical and theatre warheads and has had, historically, a lead over the Soviet Union in most forms of weapons technology. This should *not* be used as an excuse to dismiss the Soviet arsenal as insignificant. There are at least two significant factors which must be considered.

One is that the long-range missiles developed by the Soviet Union tend to be considerably larger than those of the United States. They have a much greater 'throw-weight' and this means that very large warheads can be carried. The largest Soviet missile warhead is nearly three times as large as that of the United States.

The other is that the Soviet Union has, during the past ten years, succeeded in developing a number of formidable MIRV systems and has, thereby, been able to increase its warheads at a rate even faster than that of the United States. There is also evidence that, like the United States, it has many different development programmes currently under way which will collectively expand its arsenals greatly in the 1980s.

Relative to the American strategic triad, the Soviet Union is far more dependent on its ICBMs, the force of long-range bombers being smaller, slower and older than that of the Americans. The Soviet SLBM force is larger, but considerably less efficient.

Intercontinental ballistic missiles (ICBMs)

There are five types of ICBM in the Soviet forces, the old SS-11s and SS-13s and the much more modern SS-17s, SS-18s and SS-19s.

SS-11 (Sego) This missile was first introduced in 1966 and although it is being replaced by the SS-19 it still forms the bulk of the Soviet ICBM force with 580 currently available. It can carry a single 1 or 2 megaton warhead or three small warheads in a MRV system.

SS-13 Just 60 of the SS-13s are deployed and each has a 1 megaton warhead. Neither the SS-11 nor the SS-13 are very accurate missiles and would be used mainly for attacks against industry and cities together with large military complexes. The combined use of these two missile systems would be sufficient to destroy every city of over 500,000 people in all the NATO countries together with China and Japan.

SS-17 This missile was first deployed in 1975 and carries either one 5 megaton warhead or four 900 or 550 kiloton warheads in a MIRV system. The single warhead, combined with the fairly high accuracy of the missile, is able to destroy protected US missiles, but it is questionable whether the MIRV versions can do this. There were 150 SS-17s deployed in 1980.

SS-18 This is by far the world's largest ICBM and the Soviet Union has 308 deployed, mostly with MIRVed warhead systems involving eight to ten warheads each, ranging from 600 kilotons to 2 megatons. Although these are very large warheads for a MIRVed system, it is doubtful whether they constitute a serious threat to US ICBMs. Other warheads exist for the SS-18, including a massive single warhead variously estimated at 18–25 megatons, although some reports suggest 50 megatons, 4000 times the size of the Hiroshima bomb.

SS-19 Though smaller than the SS-18 this ICBM is considerably more advanced than the SS-11 which it is steadily replacing. It carries a single 5 megaton warhead or a MIRVed system of six 550 kiloton warheads with a CEP possibly as low as 350 yards. While inferior to the US Minuteman III with the latest guidance and warhead, the SS-19 is the most formidable of the Soviet ICBMs in terms of an ability to destroy missiles in their silos.

New ICBMs Four new ICBMs are reported to be under development but these may include developments of existing systems although a new mobile ICBM may also be under way.

The 1398 ICBMs in the Soviet arsenal are, by any account, formidable. While they may be four years or so behind US developments in terms of accuracy, they have a large number of weapons with very large warheads. An example is the SS-18 when fitted with the single warhead. If, as seems most probable, this is rated at about 25 megatons (2000 times the size of the Hiroshima bomb) then the potential damage against industry and conurbations is vast.

While the large warhead SS-18s might be targeted principally on North American and possibly Chinese population centres, one can best appreciate their size with reference to Britain. A 25 megaton warhead exploded as an air burst 30,000 feet over central London would destroy the whole of Greater London, resulting in a main fire zone up to 55 miles across depending on weather conditions. Deaths resulting from just one weapon might total well over five million with further millions of injuries. A single warhead could destroy the whole of the West Yorkshire conurbation, or Greater Manchester, or the Birmingham/Walsall/Wolverhampton conurbation. Just four such warheads would cripple England and kill perhaps ten million people.

Submarine-launched ballistic missiles (SLBMs)

Although the Soviet Union was slower to develop the SLBM than the United States it now has considerably more submarines and missiles. There are three main missile types.

SS-N-6 470 of these are deployed in 29 Yankee-class nuclear submarines. Each is slightly larger than the Poseidon missile but has a shorter range. Each missile either has a single 1 to 2 megaton warhead or a MIRVed system of three much smaller warheads. The SS-N-6 is not at all accurate and would be used mainly against cities.

SS-N-8 This is a very long-range SLBM carrying a single 1 to 2 megaton warhead. 300 missiles are carried by Delta-class submarines and can reach the United States from submarines submerged close to the Soviet Union in Arctic waters.

SS-N-18 This will replace the SS-N-8; 160 have so far been deployed in ten Delta submarines, each fitted with either single or MIRV warheads.

New SLBMs Two new SLBMs are the SS-NX-17 and the very large SS-NX-20. The former are being fitted to Yankee-class submarines but the latter are going into the massive new Typhoon class. Even though this new submarine, first launched late in 1980, is even larger than the American Trident boat, it appears that it will carry 20 missiles rather than 24.

As well as these various missiles the Soviet Union has a number of missiles for launching from submarines or surface ships for use against shipping. These include the new SS-NX-19 200-300 mile range missiles which are carried in the *Kirov*, first of a new class of nuclear-powered battle cruisers. The Soviet SLBM fleet is collectively considerably larger than the American fleet although, as we shall see later, there are considerable deficiencies in operating terms. Even so the Soviet SLBMs could inflict devastating damage on every significant non-Warsaw Pact country in the world.

Strategic bombers

There are two long-range bombers, the turboprop Tu-95 Bear and the jet-powered M-5 Bison. Some 195 of these are still deployed, mainly dating from the late 1950s, but at least a third are now tanker aircraft, trainers or used for maritime patrol. The Bears and Bisons can carry free-fall H-bombs and the Bears can also carry large air-to-surface missiles such as the Kangaroo. Each plane can carry a single missile which is about the size of a small fighter and can fly 400 miles at supersonic speeds carrying a 2 megaton warhead. Even though the strategic bomber force is small by American standards it could destroy every major American city.

Soviet theatre and tactical nuclear weapons

Evidence from the Stockholm International Peace Research Institute (SIPRI) and other sources suggests that the Soviet Union has a smaller arsenal of tactical and theatre nuclear weapons but that these differ in make-up from those of the United States and many of them are both larger and have a longer range. In this category are the missiles such as the SS-20 which cannot reach the United States from the Soviet Union but can reach every part of Europe and the Far East countries such as China and Japan. There are many different weapons, especially if we include aircraft as well as missiles and artillery, so we will restrict ourselves to a description of the more important systems.

SS-4 (Sandal) The 1962 Cuban missile crisis was caused when the Soviet Union attempted to deploy this 1100 mile range missile with its 1 megaton warhead within range of the United States mainland. It is now being replaced in the Soviet Union by the SS-20 but 380 of them are still deployed.

SS-5 (Skean) This is rather like the SS-4 but with double the range. 60 are currently deployed but these too are being replaced by the SS-20.

SS-20 This solid-fuel two-stage missile is 52 feet long, just under 6 feet in diameter and is carried on a tracked launch vehicle capable of rapid reloading. It has a range of 3000 miles and carries a MIRVed system of three 150 kiloton warheads. It is being deployed fairly rapidly with around 200 now in service; up to 40 per cent are believed to be targeted on countries in Asia such as Japan and China.

SS-1b/SS-1c These six-ton missiles are launched from eight-wheeled cross-country vehicles, have a range of up to 160 miles and until recently formed the bulk of the Soviet tactical nuclear missile force although they can also carry conventional warheads. They are being replaced by the new SS-23 with a greater range and accuracy.

SS-12 (Scaleboard) This is similar to the SS-1c but has twice the range and a large 1 megaton warhead. A replacement is being developed.

FROG-7 This missile has a range of over 35 miles and is intended for battlefield use. It is the latest in a long series of FROGs (Free Rocket Over Ground) but was first deployed in 1965 and is now being replaced by the more advanced SS-21.

In addition to these short- and medium-range missiles the Soviet Union has a large number of nuclear-capable strike aircraft. These include the fairly small Su-17, Su-20, Mig-21 and Mig-27 as well as the following more substantial planes from the Tupolev design team.

Tu-16 (Badger) This twin-jet medium bomber was first deployed in 1955 and over 500 of the original production run of 2000 are still in service, many of them for anti-ship attack, carrying nuclear missiles.

Tu-22 (Blinder) This twin-jet medium-range supersonic bomber was developed in the late 1950s but never lived up to design expectations, particularly in terms of range. This is around 1300 miles, but the Blinder-B version can carry the Kitchen stand-off bomb which has a range of 185 miles. Over 100 Blinders are still in service.

Tu-26 (Backfire) This swing-wing supersonic bomber has achieved notoriety amongst Western defence and media circles, the impression being given of a remarkable and formidable plane. It was developed back in the mid-1960s and deployment was slow until 1980, now running at around 30 a year on top of a mid-1980 deployment of 75. It is intended for European, Asian and maritime functions but could reach the United States with aerial re-fuelling. It can be equipped with the Kingfish 375-mile range stand-off missile carrying a 200 kiloton warhead. Thus equipped, the

Backfire is without question a formidable and destructive weapon, but it is instructive to compare it with the American F111. The latter is smaller but only slightly slower and can carry two SRAMs in an internal bomb bay and four more under the wings. With such a load its performance is lowered but, at the same time, it can attack six targets with missiles compared with one for the Backfire.

The Soviet Union relies heavily on missiles for its short- and medium-range nuclear capability, and it is assumed that the two thousand or more nuclear-capable strike aircraft are available primarily for conventional roles. Apart from the missiles and aircraft so far described, the Soviet Union is reported to have some nuclear-capable artillery such as the S-23 180 mm towed gun. It also has surface-to-air nuclear missiles such as the very long-range SA-5 (Gammon) capable of reaching an altitude of 18 miles at a range of 155 miles.

This description of Soviet nuclear weapons demonstrates a considerable degree of development of new weapons in almost every category. It is also probable that the Soviet Union is working on a range of new surface-to-air missiles which can be used against fast low-flying bombers and cruise missiles.

OVERKILL AND ESCALATION

Much of this chapter has been concerned with describing the many different nuclear weapons already deployed and under development by the United States and the Soviet Union. While this might seem rather long and laborious it is a disturbing fact that this kind of information is rarely made available outside the technical literature. Furthermore, it provides the evidence for two factors which are of crucial significance.

Overkill As must now be obvious, each country has a nuclear arsenal far in excess of anything required for deterrence. Any one of the three main kinds of American or Soviet ICBMs is deployed in sufficient numbers to destroy the major population centres of the opposing bloc. In addition, each country has many thousands of warheads which can be delivered by SLBMs, the United States has a vastly powerful long-range bomber fleet and the Soviet Union could destroy all the large population centres of Europe, China and Japan without using *any* of its ICBM or bomber forces.

Escalation Even though each side has a huge capacity for waging nuclear war, each is still developing new weapons and numbers are actually being increased. The rate of increase in the case of strategic warheads is quite staggering, *possibly as high as 50 per cent in the period 1980 to 1985 alone*.

Many people imagine that each side has a sizeable number of strategic weapons, that this number is more or less constant and there is a stable balance of power. As we have seen, this is far from the truth for the numbers are many times more than are appropriate for deterrence postures and we are in the process of escalation. We will discuss later in this book the manner in which new weapons systems are more suited to nuclear-war fighting than deterrence but it is first appropriate to examine the other nuclear powers and the risks of the spread of nuclear weapons to other countries.

'Nothing could have been more obvious to the people of the early twentieth century than the rapidity with which war was becoming impossible. And as certainly they did not see it. They did not see it until the atomic bombs burst in their fumbling hands.'

H. G. Wells
The World Set Free 1914

REFERENCES

Stockholm International Peace Research Institute (1980). *World Armaments and Disarmament: SIPRI Yearbook 1980*. Taylor & Francis, London.

International Institute for Strategic Studies (1980). *The Military Balance 1980–81*. IISS, London.

Rogers, P. (1981). *A Guide to Nuclear Weapons*, Peace Studies Papers No. 5. School of Peace Studies, University of Bradford.

Polmar, N. (1976). *Strategic Weapons: An Introduction*. Macdonald & Jane, London.

Richardson, D. (1981). 'World Missile Survey', *Flight International*, 30 May 1981, pp. 1607–52.

Stockholm International Peace Research Institute (1978). *Tactical Nuclear Weapons: European Perspectives*. Taylor & Francis, London.

Pretty, R. T. (Ed.) (1980). *Jane's Weapon Systems 1980–81*. Jane's, London.

Taylor, J. W. R. (Ed.) (1980). *Jane's All the World's Aircraft 1980–81*. Jane's, London.

Foss, C. F. (1976). *Jane's World Armoured Fighting Vehicles*. Macdonald & Jane, London.

Taylor J. W. R. and Swanborough, G. (1979). *Military Aircraft of the World*. Ian Allan, London.

Taylor, M. J. H. (1980). *Missiles of the World*. Ian Allan, London.

Bowman, M. W. (1980). *U.S. Military Aircraft*. Arms and Armour Press, London.

Bonds R. (Ed.) (1979). *The Soviet War Machine*. Hamlyn, London.

Brown H. (1981). *Department of Defense Annual Report Fiscal Year 1982*. US Government Printing Office, Washington D.C.

Jones, General D. C. (1981). *United States Military Posture for FY 1982*. US Government Printing Office, Washington D.C.

Bertram, C. (Ed.) (1981). *Strategic Deterrence in a Changing Environment*. Gower and Allanheld Osmun.

Douglass, J. D. Jnr. (1976). *The Soviet Theatre Nuclear Offensive*. US Government Printing Office, Washington D.C.

International Institute for Strategic Studies (1981). *Strategic Survey 1980–81*. IISS, London

Van Cleave, W. R. and Cohen, S. T. (1978). *Tactical Nuclear Weapons: An Examination of the Issues.* Macdonald & Jane, London.

Fiscal Year 1981 Arms Control Impact Statement (1980). US Government Printing Office, Washington D.C.

2
Britain's Bombs

Two common assumptions about Britain's nuclear weapons are that they consist just of the Polaris submarine fleet and are independent of other countries. *Both are wrong*. Britain has developed a wide range of nuclear weapons over the past thirty years, they are integrated into NATO and they would involve Britain in a nuclear war in the early stages of any major conflict.

BRITAIN'S NUCLEAR CAPABILITY

Immediately after the destruction of Hiroshima and Nagasaki, and with the ending of the war, the United States administration developed a reticence about sharing the fruits of the war-time research efforts. The McMahon Energy Act, passed by the US Congress, controlled the exchange of information on the design of nuclear weapons with other countries and gave the United States a temporary nuclear monopoly. Britain then proceeded to develop its own nuclear weapons programme and tested an atom bomb on 3 October 1952 in Australia at Monte Bello.

By the late 1950s Britain had gone on to develop its own hydrogen bomb (first tested in 1956) and also three V-bombers (Valiant, Vulcan and Victor) which could carry nuclear weapons over distances sufficient to threaten the Eastern European members of the Warsaw Pact and much of the western part of the Soviet Union.

The V-bombers were relatively high performance aircraft which could fly at just below the speed of sound and could deliver free-fall nuclear bombs from altitudes of up to 55,000 feet. In 1962 the Vulcan Mark II entered service, being equipped with the Blue Steel 'stand-off' air-to-surface missile designed to be capable of delivering a nuclear warhead to a target when launched from the aircraft over 220 miles away.

The Valiant bombers lasted only nine years before being grounded because of metal fatigue problems, but in the mid-1960s the RAF had around 160 Vulcan and Victor bombers making up Britain's deterrent force. Already, though, they were thought to be incapable of penetrating Soviet air defences, even when equipped with the Blue Steel missile, so Britain attempted to acquire the 1100-mile range Skybolt air-launched missile, then under development in the United States. However, Skybolt ran into technical and financial trouble and was cancelled by Kennedy's Defense Secretary, Robert McNamara, leaving Britain with the problem of finding a replacement for the V-bombers. Britain eventually opted for a submarine-based system following an offer from President Kennedy to supply both Polaris missiles and technical help with the design of the submarines.

Polaris

Britain's first Polaris submarine was *HMS Resolution* which was launched in September 1966 and began its first patrol in June 1968, and three further submarines were built: *Renown, Repulse* and *Revenge*. The original plan had been to have five submarines, enabling at least two to be on patrol at any one time, but the fifth submarine was cancelled by the Wilson government in February 1975. Each of the four Resolution-class submarines has a displacement of 7500 tons and is powered by a Rolls-Royce pressurized water-cooled reactor giving a submerged speed of 25 knots. Each submarine carries 16 Polaris A3 missiles with a range of over 2500 miles, the

'Don't worry, we're knocking hell out of them in return.'

missiles being fired from vertical launch tubes. There are also six 21-inch torpedo tubes in the bow.

Although the submarines were built in Britain, the Polaris missiles themselves were built by the Lockheed Missiles and Space Company. The warhead system on the Polaris missile is British, having been developed at the Atomic Weapons Research Establishment at Aldermaston in Berkshire, a centre with a staff of 5000 and an annual budget of £100 million. The system consists of a multiple re-entry vehicle which delivers three H-bombs to a single target, each having a destructive capacity of 200 kilotons, sixteen times the size of the Hiroshima bomb.

The Polaris warheads are *not* independently targetable, so each missile is suitable for attacking just one large target or else a cluster of targets very close together. Appropriate targets would be, for example, Moscow, Leningrad or another large city region. The three warheads on each missile have a shotgun effect, landing within about ten miles of each other.

The real significance of this is that the British Polaris system is intended as a *counter-city* weapon, designed to destroy industry and people. It is *not* a *counterforce* weapon in that it is of little use in attacking military targets except in the rare cases where these are heavily concentrated as, for example, with major naval bases.

An attack pattern from the 16 missiles on one Polaris submarine might be:

City	Population (million)	Missiles
Moscow	7.2	4
Leningrad	4.0	2
Kiev	1.6	2
Kharkov	1.3	1
Gor'kiy	1.2	1
Kuybyshev	1.1	1
Sverdlovsk	1.0	1
Minsk	0.9	1

Tbilisi	0.9	1
Rostov	0.8	1
Volgograd	0.8	1
Total	20.8	16

A single submarine would be expected to kill 10 to 15 million people. It is perhaps easier to appreciate the power of such a system if we envisage an attack on Britain. A *single Polaris submarine* could place four missiles with 12 warheads on London and one missile with three warheads on each of Birmingham, Manchester, Glasgow, Belfast, Cardiff, Swansea, Edinburgh, Newcastle, Leeds, Liverpool, Sheffield and Bristol, thereby killing or injuring perhaps 20 per cent or more of the population of the country.

Each Polaris submarine patrol lasts 12 weeks but 4 weeks of this consist of trials and only 8 weeks consists of being on station or *en route* to the patrol station. The submarines also have to undergo an 18-month re-fit every 3½ years, so that it is not normally possible to have more than two boats on station at one time, and often only one is available.

This is widely used as an argument for having five boats but this conveniently leaves out the fact that a Polaris boat does not have to be on station to fire its missiles.

Patrols can be extended, firing can be undertaken *en route*, and it is even possible for Britain's Polaris boats to fire their missiles when at their base at Faslane near Glasgow. A recent report indicates that this can take 25 minutes to set up. Needless to say, it makes that part of Scotland particularly vulnerable to Soviet attack.

Chevaline

Soon after the Polaris missile submarines came into service there were suggestions that the Soviet Union was developing an anti-ballistic missile system to defend Moscow and its surrounding area, including some ICBM sites. The most important single target for Britain's Polaris missiles was Moscow, and the idea of an apparently independent deterrent depended on the ability to destroy Moscow, especially in view of the centralized nature of Soviet political organization.

The new Soviet Galosh anti-ballistic missile system was held to damage this 'Moscow criterion' of being able to destroy the capital city, and work was speeded up on a more advanced warhead for Polaris, the Chevaline programme. The point worth noting is that the purpose of the Chevaline programme was to preserve the ability of Britain's Polaris missiles to destroy Moscow. It is wrong to suggest that the missiles were or are aimed just at military targets. Britain's deterrent is basically a counter-city weapon and will remain so after the Chevaline programme is completed. Its use would involve the deaths of many millions of people in the Soviet Union.

The Chevaline programme was developed during the 1970s with the approval of successive governments, or rather small groups of ministers acting in secret. Its total cost is now estimated at over £1000 million and it was due to enter service in 1979. That date has now been put back three years so, if the Trident programme goes ahead, the immensely expensive Chevaline warhead will only be in service for eight years before being replaced by Trident!

Like the Polaris warhead the separate Chevaline components are not independently targeted. However, the whole of the front end of the missile can be manoeuvred in space so as to confuse the radar system controlling anti-ballistic missile defences. It may have six 40 kiloton warheads but a combination of three warheads plus many decoys is more likely. Whatever the combination the essential point is that Chevaline, like the earlier Polaris warhead, is basically a counter-city weapon.

Trident

By 1977, advocates of the independent British deterrent were calling for replacement of the Polaris system in view of the expected deterioration of the boats by the early 1990s. After considerable debate about submarine-launched missiles, cruise missiles and new bombers, the Conservative government took the decision to replace the Polaris boats with a new generation of Trident submarines. This decision, made early in 1980, has caused considerable controversy and is particularly important in terms of British defence policy. It is therefore worth examining in detail, not least because it involves a remarkable and largely unnoticed increase in Britain's nuclear arsenal.

After Lockheed had developed the Polaris missile for the US Navy in the early 1960s, it went on to produce a missile of similar length but slightly larger width, the Poseidon. The Poseidon missile was about twice the weight of the Polaris and most of the US fleet of missile submarines is still equipped with it. Each Poseidon missile carries ten warheads and while it can fit into a Polaris launching tube, most of the submarines now in service were designed for Poseidon.

After the Poseidon missile came the third generation of American submarine-launched missiles, the Trident Mark I (D4). This will not fit into the early Polaris submarines but will fit the later Poseidon boats. It has a considerably longer range than the Poseidon missile and can deliver eight 100 kiloton warheads to different targets.

The United States has had the Trident missile in service since July 1980, having retro-fitted it to Poseidon boats. As we have seen, it is also building a new generation of very large Trident submarines, each carrying 24 missiles.

In addition to the Trident Mark I, Lockheed is working on a Mark II missile. This is designed to fit into the new

Trident submarines but is too large to go into existing Poseidon and Polaris boats. It will have a range of nearly 7000 miles, a high degree of accuracy and some reports indicate it could carry 17 independently targeted warheads in an advanced manoeuvrable re-entry vehicle capable of eluding ballistic missile defences.

The Trident Mark II is, to all intents and purposes, one of a new generation of missiles. It will almost certainly be accurate enough to destroy ICBMs even when protected in silos, especially if it is armed with the very efficient Mark 12A warhead now being fitted to the American Minuteman III and due to be used on the new M-X missile.

This digression becomes significant when we apply this information to the British decision to opt for Trident. At the time of writing (July 1981) it is not clear precisely what system the British are going to opt for. What is clear is that even the smallest system involves a huge increase in the ability to destroy targets.

As mentioned earlier, each of Britain's existing Polaris missiles can attack just one target, because its three warheads are not capable of independent targeting. The smallest force of Trident missiles would, like Polaris, be 64, with 16 missiles on each of four boats. Remember though, that each missile can carry eight *independently targetable* warheads. Thus even this system increases the targeting ability by a factor of eight! We are told repeatedly that Britain has an adequate independent deterrent, yet the new system will be very considerably larger than Polaris.

This, though, is the minimum. In the minutes of the House of Commons Defence Committee published in January 1981, the senior civil servant at the Ministry of Defence responsible for policy and planning, Michael Quinlan, stated that it was intended to purchase around 100 missiles for four craft, with extra being required if a fifth craft were ordered. If only 16-tube craft are to be built then the basic requirement is for 64 missiles plus some extra for test-firing and spares. An initial order of 100 missiles suggests that Britain will build stretched craft carrying 20 or 24 missiles. His comment on the fifth craft suggests that this is also being considered. Five craft with 24 tubes each carrying a missile with eight warheads give us a total of 960 warheads in all, a fifteen-fold increase in targeting capacity over Polaris!

Even this is far from being the full extent of the possible increase in warheads. Since Britain is building entirely new submarines it makes very little sense, from a conventional economic standpoint, to build craft which can be fitted with the Trident Mark I but have launching tubes too small to take the Trident Mark II. After all, the submarines will not come into service until 1990, some twelve years after Trident Mark I entered service in the US Navy and probably four years after the initial deployment of even the Mark II version.

It follows, therefore, that the new submarines will at least have the capability of taking the more advanced missile. Here, though, we are dealing with an even more formidable missile re-entry system, believed capable of delivering 17 separate warheads, each to different targets. We are left then with a maximum potential for Britain of five boats with 24 missiles, each with 17 warheads. This gives us a total of 2040 warheads with a collective targeting ability over thirty times as great as Polaris.

This is the maximum and would involve a total programme far more expensive than the presently quoted £6000 million. But we have already seen that even the smallest Trident programme involves a huge escalation of targeting ability, certainly large enough to involve every large city in the Soviet Union. Perhaps the most significant point however, is that these British submarines and their missiles are not counted in with the American missiles in the SALT negotiations. The Soviet Union is thus faced with an escalation which is out of the control of SALT and made worse, as we shall shortly see, by French plans to MIRV *their* submarine-launched missile fleet as well. *Britain's Trident decision is, without question, a major boost to the global nuclear arms race.*

BRITAIN'S OTHER BOMBS

The replacement of the Polaris missiles with Trident is not the only way in which Britain's nuclear capability is being expanded in the early 1980s. Throughout the armed forces there are tactical and theatre nuclear weapons and in several cases there is a considerable expansion of weapons systems in progress.

Army

The British Army is equipped with several kinds of tactical nuclear weapon intended for deployment in North Germany. There are, for example, 12 launchers for the Lance tactical nuclear missile equipping a regiment. This missile has a range of up to 75 miles and carries a warhead in the low kiloton range. The launcher is re-usable and, based on normal usage of seven missiles per launcher, the British Army probably has at the very least around 60 missiles available.

The most important artillery weapon is the massive 25 ton howitzer, the American M110, which can fire atomic projectiles over 12 miles at a rate of one a minute. Sixteen of these, together with 50 of the smaller M-109 155 mm howitzer equip four artillery regiments. The Army also has a small stock of atomic demolition munitions, intended to destroy bridges, major transport interchanges and other strategic complexes in order to delay an enemy advance, although some ADMs may be small enough to be transported into occupied territory.

A further 69 of the M-109 howitzer are entering service, commencing in 1981. Both the M-110 and the M-109 are self-propelled guns but a new towed howitzer, the Anglo/German/Italian FH70 155 mm gun is also nuclear-capable and will be deployed by the British Army.

The artillery and missiles which have been described

can all fire conventional high-explosive as well as nuclear munitions. What is significant, though, is that the army in Germany has a wide range of nuclear-capable delivery systems and these are being increased in number.

Royal Air Force `

When the RAF handed over responsibility for the strategic deterrent to the Royal Navy in 1970, it retained a commitment to the use of nuclear weapons in a future conflict. This commitment currently involves over 200 nuclear-capable aircraft of four types, expanding to over 300 during the 1980s. The aircraft are as follows:

Hawker Siddeley Vulcan The Mark II version of this medium bomber first entered service with the RAF in July 1960. Forty-eight aircraft are now deployed in a low-level penetration bombing role for use from their bases at Scampton and Waddington in Lincolnshire, supported by Victor tanker refuelling aircraft. The Vulcan's combat radius can be as high as 2875 miles with aerial re-fuelling and it can carry a 1-megaton British-made H-bomb.

Hawker Siddeley Buccaneer This two-seat strike aircraft was originally developed for the Navy and is capable of delivering conventional and nuclear weapons over a combat radius exceeding 1100 miles. There are now five squadrons totalling 60 aircraft in service although the Buccaneer has had problems of metal fatigue which have limited its serviceability. Three of the squadrons are based at Honington in Suffolk and in Germany and are assigned to strike roles in Central and Eastern Europe. Two more squadrons are assigned to maritime strike roles, especially in the North East Atlantic and are based at Lossiemouth in North East Scotland.

Sepecat Jaguar This small single-seat aircraft is described as a light tactical support aircraft but is known to be

nuclear capable. It is a much more recent design than the
Vulcan or Buccaneer, having first entered service with the
RAF in 1972. Seventy-two aircraft are currently based at
Coltishall near Norwich and at two bases in Germany.

British Aerospace HS Nimrod The Nimrod is based on
the airframe of the old Comet IV airliner and is deployed
by the RAF in several roles, the most significant being
a long-distance maritime reconnaissance and anti-
submarine role. It carries American-built nuclear depth
bombs for anti-submarine purposes and there is a total
inventory of 46 aircraft, progressively undergoing modernization from Mark I to Mark II. Some 27 are currently
in service and with squadron based at St Mawgan in
Cornwall and three stations at Kinloss in North East
Scotland.

In addition to this range of nuclear-capable aircraft *the
RAF is in the early stages of an enormous expansion
programme associated with the Panavia Tornado*, the
so-called Multi-Role Combat Aircraft. This very expensive two-seater aircraft has been developed by an Anglo-
German-Italian consortium and the Royal Air Force
intends to deploy a total of 385 Tornados over the next
decade. Of the total inventory some 220 will be the
so-called interdictor-strike or GR Mark I version, and
another 165 will be the F Mark II air defence variant. It
was originally anticipated that the strike version of the
Tornado would replace the Vulcan and Buccaneer aircraft, so that 108 of the old aircraft would be replaced by
220 of the new. It is now known that the RAF plans to
keep on the two squadrons of Buccaneer aircraft assigned
to maritime roles, so that the deployment of the Tornado
represents a considerable increase in the RAF's nuclear
strike capability. Even without aerial re-fuelling the Tornado has a combat radius of around 1000 miles and is
capable of approaching targets at very low level and high
speed.

The Tornado is extremely expensive. The cost of the RAF's 385 aircraft was estimated in the 1981 Defence White Paper to be £4875 million. This excluded development costs of around £800 million and the cost of armaments, spares, servicing etc. Taken altogether the cost of each of the strike version of the Tornado is likely to be around £20 million. *At 1981 costings it is probable that the RAF's Tornado programme is actually more expensive than the Trident programme!*

What is all the more remarkable is that the RAF has succeeded in increasing its bombing capability considerably, and that includes its nuclear capability. There have been frequent indications that the RAF regards the Tornado as a basis for a strategic nuclear delivery system, should the Navy's Trident programme be cancelled. The most likely option would be to use the Tornado as a launching aircraft for a cruise missile. This might possibly be of American origin or else might be developed by British Aerospace which already has experience of cruise missile technology with anti-ship missiles.

The significance of this is considerable. Since the Trident decision was announced early in 1980 there has been considerable criticism levelled against it. The criticism has come from two quite different sources. One has been the increasingly effective and well organized disarmament movement which sees Trident as a major escalation in Britain's nuclear role. The other source has been from within the defence community, arguing that Trident is unnecessarily large and expensive. This line of argument usually maintains the need for an independent strategic nuclear force for Britain but argues for an alternative to Trident. Such an alternative might be ground-launched or submarine-launched cruise missiles, but the strongest candidate would be an air-launched system.

We are therefore left with the possibility that the Trident programme might be cancelled but replaced by a Tornado/cruise missile system. This could be given the appearance of a downgrading of Britain's strategic forces in order to quieten the disarmers, but could in reality involve the development of a new generation of weapons.

Royal Navy

The Navy's strategic role has already been examined but its nuclear capability extends well beyond this. The role of the Royal Navy within NATO is primarily one of anti-submarine activities in the North East Atlantic. To fulfil this role the Navy has a fleet of nuclear attack submarines and also uses a wide range of surface ships almost invariably equipped with helicopters. These include destroyers, frigates and the new anti-submarine carriers.

What is somewhat surprising and, incidentally, rarely appreciated outside the armed forces, is that the helicopters employed on these duties are actually nuclear capable, being equipped with British nuclear depth bombs. By implication a large number of surface ships therefore carry nuclear munitions for their helicopters. According to a recent NATO report the Navy provides

five squadrons of Sea King helicopters, two flights of Wessex, 25 flights of Wasps and 18 flights of Lynx, all of which are capable of operating from warships at sea and delivering British nuclear depth bombs.

The total number of nuclear-capable helicopters is thus well over 60. Moreover it is going to increase over the next three years if two more of the large anti-submarine carriers come into service.

The first such carrier is *HMS Invincible* which entered service in 1980. It will be followed by *Illustrious* and probably *Ark Royal*. With the phasing out of the large, old and very expensive aircraft carriers such as *Eagle*, it appeared that the Navy's maritime air role would be restricted to anti-submarine purposes using helicopters. The decision to build these carriers allowed the Navy to retain its commitment to fixed-wing aircraft in the form of the Sea Harrier jump-jet. In addition to ten nuclear-capable Sea King helicopters, each of the new carriers will have eight Sea Harriers.

The Sea Harrier is a single-seat fighter/strike/reconnaissance aircraft and has a combat radius of 480 miles when used as as strike aircraft. As well as the new aircraft carriers the Harrier may be carried on other ships. Perhaps its most significant feature is that it is now known to be nuclear capable. What is remarkable, though, is that it is intended to be used with free-fall atom bombs, not nuclear depth bombs. The significance of this is that such munitions are not appropriate for any kind of maritime role. They are suitable for attacks against land targets. Thus the idea that the new carriers are purely anti-submarine ships is nonsense. Against the odds the Navy has succeeded in maintaining a number of nuclear-capable strike aircraft!

The purpose of such a function is not clear, given the Navy's primary role of anti-submarine warfare in the North East Atlantic but nuclear-capable strike aircraft would, presumably, be used in the event of a conflict in Northern Europe. It is certainly clear that the carriers are seen as having a useful versatility.

With persistent reports of severe cuts in the Navy's establishment of surface vessels, there appeared to be a possibility that the third of the aircraft carriers, *Ark Royal*, would be mothballed immediately after its launching in the summer of 1981. At the launch ceremony on 2 June, however, the British Defence Secretary, John Nott, declined to confirm this, commenting, 'I would only say that I do see a future and important use for a carrier such as *Ark Royal*.' He added, 'this might be in wider out of area activities in support of our allies, and in particular of

---

'So I repeat in all sincerity as a military man I can see no use for any nuclear weapons which would not end in escalation, with consequences that no one can conceive.'
Lord Louis Mountbatten, 1979

the US.' Taken with the knowledge of the ship's considerable nuclear capability, this is a further indication of the expansion of Britain's extensive commitment to nuclear weapons.

CONCLUSIONS

This description of Britain's extensive and varied nuclear weapons systems reveals several remarkable and largely unrecognized features. The most obvious one is that the Trident programme involves an immense increase in Britain's strategic nuclear armory, even though the current Polaris missiles are said to constitute an adequate deterrent. Moreover, the Trident programme means that Britain is very much an integral part of the global nuclear arms race and we should expect the Soviet Union to respond to this escalation. At the very least it is likely to involve further deployment of missiles such as the SS-20.

As well as Trident, it is obvious that tactical and theatre nuclear weapons are integrated throughout Britain's defence forces. The fundamental significance of this is that in a major conventional conflict involving the Soviet Union, Britain would be involved in any early nuclear escalation.

REFERENCES

Stockholm International Peace Research Institute (1980). *World Armaments and Disarmament: SIPRI Yearbook 1980*. Taylor & Francis, London.
International Institute for Strategic Studies (1980). *The Military Balance 1980–81*. IISS, London.
Rogers, P. (1981). *A Guide to Nuclear Weapons*, Peace Studies Paper Number 5. School of Peace Studies, University of Bradford.
Smith. D. (1980). *The Defence of the Realm in the 1980s*. Croom Helm, London.
Baylis, J. (Ed.) (1977). *British Defence Policy in a Changing World*. Croom Helm, London.

Freedman, L. (1980). *Britain and Nuclear Weapons*. Macmillan, London.

Statement on the Defence Estimates 1981 (1981). HMSO, London.

Ministry of Defence (1981). *Britain and NATO*. Ministry of Defence, London.

Taylor, J. W. E. and Swanborough, G. (1979). *Military Aircraft of the World*. Ian Allan, London.

Taylor, M. J. H., (1980). *Missiles of the World*. Ian Allan, London.

Wheeler, B. C. (1979). *Air Forces of the World*. Ian Allan, London.

Nott, J. (1981). *Decisions to Modernize UK's Nuclear Contribution to NATO Strengthen Deterrence*, NATO Review, April 1981. Brussels.

3
Proliferation—the Genie out of the Bottle?

The number, size and variety of the nuclear weapons deployed by the United States and the Soviet Union is so large that the smaller arsenals of other countries seem unimportant. But we have already seen that Britain has many different kinds of nuclear weapons and is increasing its arsenal rapidly. The same is true of France and China and there are clear signs of an acceleration in the proliferation of nuclear weapons to many other countries.

What now faces us is the transition of the world to a general nuclear-armed condition. It is dangerous to underestimate the capability of countries like Britain, France and China to deploy nuclear weapons. They set the pattern for other countries to follow *and by expanding their own nuclear forces they encourage further escalation.*

FRANCE

Although France remains a signatory of the North Atlantic Treaty it does not integrate its forces into NATO but persists in maintaining independent conventional and nuclear forces. Its nuclear forces involve strategic, theatre and tactical weapons and new developments are currently in progress at every level.

France began to develop its own nuclear weapons soon after the end of the Second World War and conducted its first atom bomb test near Reggan in the Sahara on 13 February 1960, thus becoming the world's fourth nuclear power.

Attempts to elicit American aid in developing nuclear missile delivery systems were unsuccessful so France began a programme to develop land-launched and submarine-launched missiles (SSBS – Sol-Sol Balistique Stratégique and MSBS – Mer-So Balistique Stratégique).

Deployment of such systems was anticipated by the end of the 1960s but this left a gap which was filled by deployment of small numbers of the supersonic Mirage IV-A bomber. Some of these are still in service. France also has a tactical missile, the Pluton, and a further missile is under development. The full range of France's nuclear forces is considerable but can be summarized as follows:

SSBS (S-2) This two-stage solid-fuel missile carries a 150 kiloton warhead and can reach most parts of European Russia. Two squadrons of the S-2, totalling 18 missiles, became operational in 1971 and 1972, both housed in underground silos. One squadron has now been replaced with the S-3 and the other will be replaced shortly.

SSBS (S-3) This missile is made by Aerospatiale and is similar in size to the S-2. It has a longer range and carries a much larger warhead, rated at around 1 megaton. The two SSBS squadrons are located in silos 3 to 8 km apart in the Plateau d'Albion in Haute Provence.

SSBS-X French concern that the silo-based missiles might become vulnerable to Soviet attack has led to the development of a large new mobile missile with an intended range of around 1800 miles and fitted with a 150

kiloton warhead. This could be transported along ordinary roads and, it is claimed, would thus be invulnerable
to a surprise attack. It is hoped to deploy this missile from
1985 onwards.

MSBS (M-20) The French missile-carrying submarine
force consists of 80 missiles in five submarines with a
further submarine under construction. The M-20 has a
range of 1800 miles and carries a single 1 megaton warhead.

'In France, for example, the modernisation of our *force de
frappe* should allow us to achieve an important escalation,
our capacity being capable of ensuring over 60 million dead
besides wounded.'

Rapport de la Commission des Finances No. 1976, annex 56
October 1980

MSBM (M-4) This much more advanced three-stage missile was first test-fired in the Pacific in December 1980. It is double the weight of the M-20 and has a range of 2500 miles. It will be fitted initially to the sixth submarine in the French fleet, *L'Inflexible*, but all the other five submarines will, in due course, be adapted to carry it as well. The most significant point about the M-4 is that it carries a MIRVed warhead. The details of this are not yet known but it may have several warheads each rated at around 150 kilotons. As with the British Trident development it involves a considerable increase in targeting capacity and is not covered by the SALT negotiations.

Dassault Mirage IVA This relatively small medium-range supersonic bomber was developed in the 1950s but its deployment was delayed until 1964. France maintains six squadrons totalling 33 aircraft. Each can be equipped with conventional bombs or a single free-fall H-bomb rated at 70 kilotons, five times as large as the Hiroshima bomb.

Tactical nuclear-capable aircraft France has 80 Jaguar, 30 Mirage IIIE and 36 aircraft-carrier-based Dassault-Breguet Super Etendard strike aircraft, all capable of delivering nuclear weapons.

Pluton This is a mobile tactical nuclear missile developed by Aerospatiale to replace the American Honest John missile which previously equipped French forces. The Pluton was first test-fired in 1969 and deployment commenced in 1974, the current total being 30 missiles. It is fired from a launch vehicle based on a modified tank chassis, has a range of up to 75 miles and carries a single nuclear warhead rated at between 15 and 25 kilotons.

Hades This is the appropriately named successor to Pluton intended to be deployed in the 1980s. It will be similar in size and weight but with double the range.

Enhanced Radiation Weapon (neutron bomb) There have been persistent reports that France is developing its own neutron bomb. Indeed one may have been tested in June 1980 and deployment could start as early as 1983.

This list of weapons adds up to a formidable and expanding arsenal. France has persisted in its efforts to develop as a nuclear power. It has not been a party to test-ban treaties nor to the SALT negotiations. While linked in with NATO policy it represents an independent, almost maverick phenomenon in international nuclear politics. Any effective moves to curb the nuclear arms race will have to involve a fundamental change in French attitudes, a change which is likely to be particularly difficult to achieve.

CHINA

If the continued expansion of the French nuclear armory is significant, then the situation in China is doubly so. Ever since the Sino-Soviet split in the early 1960s China has presented two kinds of military problems for the Soviet Union. Firstly there is an immense military capability contained in the Chinese army and secondly this capability is rapidly being matched by a growing arsenal of nuclear weapons.

After the initially cool relations between China and the Soviet Union following the Chinese Revolution in 1949, co-operation increased during the 1950s and extended to detailed technical and military co-operation which included nuclear technology. In 1957 the Soviet Union agreed to extend this co-operation further but by the early 1960s relations had cooled greatly.

Even after this split, China had the technical capacity to develop its own nuclear weapons and the first device was exploded in a desert testing site in Sinkiang on 16 October 1964, the same day, incidentally, that Khrushchev was removed from power in the Soviet Union.

Over the next fifteen years, and in spite of the considerable internal upheavals, the Chinese sought to develop a number of nuclear weapons and delivery systems. These included bombers based on Soviet designs, intermediate and long range ballistic missiles and even the development of submarine-based systems.

B5 (Ilyushin IL-28 Beagle) This aircraft is a relatively short-range light bomber. China has some 400 B5s operational and production is continuing at the Harbin State Aircraft Factory. It has a crew of three, a range of 1350 miles and can carry a load of 4500 lbs.

B6 (Tupolev Tu-16 Badger) This was originally due to be produced under licence from 1959 onwards but after the Sino-Soviet split the Chinese embarked on the considerable task of copying the Russian version, with deployment starting in 1968. Production continues at the Sian State Aircraft Factory and there are about 80 currently in service. The B6 has a range of 4000 miles enabling it to reach all of the Soviet Union east of the Urals. Extensive tests have been undertaken with air-dropped nuclear weapons at the Lop Nor testing site using this bomber.

CSS-1 This old missile first came into service nearly fifteen years ago but it can deliver a 15 kiloton warhead, slightly larger than the Hiroshima bomb, over a distance of 1100 miles. There are still about 50 deployed.

CSS-2 This much more formidable missile has a range of at least 1500 miles and can deliver an H-bomb warhead in the range of 1 to 3 megatons. Such a missile could reach most of the Soviet Union east of the Urals and there are believed to be between 65 and 85 deployed at present.

CSS-3 This was the first Chinese attempt to build an ICBM but has been of limited success. It is a multi-stage missile with a range of nearly 4000 miles which can carry a warhead similar in size to the CSS-2 to any part of the Soviet Union, but only four have been deployed.

CSS-X-4 With this new missile China becomes the third country to have effective ICBMs. The rocket has been used extensively in China's space programme to put satellites into orbit. In addition it was tested in the ICBM form in May 1980 and is now believed to be in full production. It will have a range of 7500 miles, *bringing Europe, Asia and North America within range* and will carry a huge 5 to 10 megaton warhead.

Submarine-launched missiles China has a single conventionally powered 'Golf' class missile-carrying submarine which has not yet been fitted with its complement of six missiles. A nuclear-powered submarine has now been completed and was reported in early 1981 to be undergoing sea trials. Both submarines should eventually be fitted with a missile now under development which is broadly similar to the Polaris missile.

These weapons add up to a considerable nuclear capability but this must be considered in the context of China's conventional forces. These currently amount to some 4.5 million, involving an army of 3.6 million, an air force of half a million and a navy of just under 400,000. This compares, incidentally, with Soviet armed forces of 3.6 million, just over half of whom are in the army.

We are not, of course, comparing like with like, in that the Soviet weapons, both conventional and nuclear, are superior. But the Chinese forces are still formidable and their existence ties down a large part of the Soviet conventional and nuclear forces. Usual estimates are that between 25 and 40 per cent of Soviet forces are assigned to Eastern

Asia, with 450,000 men actually along the Chinese border alone.

A report from the Peking Institute for International Strategic Studies was made public in June 1981 and this indicated a Chinese view that the Soviet Union could not destroy all of China's nuclear weapons in a first strike and that any land invasion of China by the Soviet Union would require military forces larger than all of those of the Soviet Union.

The rising power of China is a factor in nuclear politics which is easily and conveniently forgotten by Western analysts when arguing about the balance of power between the West and the Warsaw Pact. As with France, China's nuclear weapons are not covered by SALT and, to the Soviet Union, represent an added threat. That threat may eventually be directed elsewhere but recent developments, such as the US decision in July 1981 to supply lethal weapons to China, suggest continued opposition to the Soviet Union. This is certainly supported by an assessment of Chinese capabilities by the US Joint Chiefs of Staff published early in 1981.

China possesses a relatively small and comparatively unsophisticated strategic offensive force which, nevertheless, serves as a credible nuclear deterrent to the Soviet Union. An innovative deployment strategy poses severe targeting problems for any potential aggressor. Survivability of some portion of the ballistic missile force is virtually guaranteed through launch unit mobility, hardened storage for launchers, concealment practices and dispersal in mountainous terrain. If the Soviets launched a nuclear attack on China, they would do so knowing that they would suffer significant damage in retaliation.

INDIA

On 17 May 1974 India exploded a small nuclear device in the desert region of the State of Rajasthan. The device was similar in size to the Hiroshima bomb, modest indeed by modern standards. Over the last few years the Indian

Government has persistently denied reports that the country is developing a general nuclear capability. Even so, many observers find it very difficult to accept this denial, especially in view of India's difficult relationship with Pakistan.

India does have a number of aircraft which could be nuclear capable. These include 60 Canberra light bombers and 50 of the home-produced Hindustan Aeronautics HF-24 Marut, intended as a fighter/ground attack aircraft and capable of carrying a 4000 lb bomb load, considerably heavier than a moderate-sized nuclear weapon. India also has a vigorous space programme which has involved the construction of some quite impressive rockets. The first Indian-built satellite was the Aryabhata which was launched by a Soviet Intercosmos rocket from Volgograd in the USSR in April 1975. Since then, though, India has built its own launcher, the SLV-3, produced at the Vikram Sarabhai Space Centre and intended to launch satellites weighing up to 85 lbs. There are plans for a much larger rocket, the ASLV, which could carry a pay-load of 320 lbs. Such rockets seem intended for non-military use but their development involves the acquisition of experience and technology which could be used in a military context.

If countries such as Pakistan and Iraq prove able to produce their own nuclear weapons then India should be able to develop a nuclear weapon arsenal with little difficulty.

ISRAEL

According to official records, just six countries have nuclear weapons. While there are many more which seem likely to acquire them in the next two decades, others either have, or can readily construct, nuclear weapons now. These are Israel and South Africa, the former being the more advanced in this regard.

Israel has long maintained that it would not be the first

country to introduce nuclear weapons into the Middle East. This is a somewhat misleading statement as there is little doubt that American and possibly Soviet ships and planes armed with nuclear weapons have been in the area of the Middle East.

A more interesting statement was that of Israel's President Katzir on 1 December 1974, when he announced that Israel 'has the potential' to make a nuclear weapon, 'and if we need it we will do it'. Since then there have been persistent if unconfirmed reports that Israel has had nuclear weapons since the early 1970s.

One of the more authoritative of these was a report in a Boston newspaper in 1975 by William Beecher on his return from a visit to Egypt and Israel. Mr Beecher had previously held the post of Deputy Assistant Secretary of Defense (Public Affairs) at the Pentagon for two years and he said that in 1974 Israel had ten atom bombs.

A reasonable consensus of current opinion would be that Israel has an arsenal of 20 to 30 nuclear weapons, is probably producing them at the rate of two or three a year and may well be attempting to develop thermonuclear weapons. The work is likely to be located primarily at the Dimona Nuclear Research Centre south-east of Beersheba in the Negev Desert.

What is certainly true is that Israel, equipped with a wide variety of modern strike aircraft, has a number of potential delivery systems. These include some 130 F4 Phantoms, 30 Mirage IIIs and 80 of the home-produced Kfirs. The Israeli Army is equipped with the American Lance surface-to-surface missile which could be fitted with a nuclear warhead and Israel also has two significant home-produced missiles. These are the Gabriel and the appropriately named Jericho.

Gabriel On 21 October 1967 a number of Soviet-built SS-N-2 (Styx) cruise missiles were launched from Egyptian patrol boats in Port Said harbour at the Israeli destroyer *Eilat* some 15 miles away. The *Eilat* was hit and sunk. In order to provide a counter-weapon the Israelis completed the development of the Gabriel ship-to-ship missile and commenced deployment in 1970. The most recent version of the Gabriel has a maximum range of just under 30 miles.

It is 11 feet long and travels at just under the speed of sound carrying a conventional 400 lb warhead. It is possible that the Gabriel could be equipped with a nuclear warhead, but what is more significant is that it demonstrates the ability of the Israelis to produce their own substantial missiles. A number of countries including Argentina, Taiwan and South Africa have bought the Gabriel.

Jericho (MD-660) Far less is known about this missile but the indications are that it is a surface-to-surface missile with a range of just under 300 miles. This two-stage missile has solid-fuel motors and is launched from a mobile ramp. It can probably be fitted with conventional or nuclear warheads and is roughly comparable to the American Lance missile.

SOUTH AFRICA

The position with regard to South Africa is rather less clear although a consensus of opinion would be that South

'Before the end of this century, a score of nations could possess nuclear weapons. If this should happen, the world that we leave our children will mock our own hopes for peace. The level of nuclear armaments could grow by tens of thousands, and the same situation could well occur with advanced conventional weapons. The temptation to use these weapons, for fear that someone else might do so first, would be almost irresistible.'

Jimmy Carter
Address to the UN General Assembly, 4 October 1977

Africa either has nuclear weapons or could assemble them rapidly, that is in weeks or at the most months rather than years. There is evidence of a South African interest in nuclear-tipped artillery shells. The South African air force has a variety of nuclear-capable aircraft including Canberra, Buccaneer and Mirage III jets. In addition the South African Navy has 12 fast attack craft fitted with the Israeli Gabriel missile, with six more on order. Close collaboration with Israel has long been a feature of South African policy.

POTENTIAL NUCLEAR POWERS

Many countries such as Canada, Australia and the Netherlands could have developed their own nuclear weapons if it was their policy to do so. What is much more significant is the list of countries which might adopt such policies and could have the technical ability, with or without co-operation from other countries, to do so over the remaining years of this century. It includes Pakistan, Iraq, Brazil, Argentina, Egypt, Libya, South Korea and Taiwan.

Such proliferation is closely linked with the development of civil nuclear power and the risks involved have recently been discussed by Frank Barnaby, a physicist and former director of the Stockholm International Peace Research Institute. One method of producing plutonium for use in constructing nuclear weapons is to run a civil nuclear reactor in such a way as to enhance the production of plutonium-239 of potential weapons grade. This is highly inefficient in terms of optimizing the generating potential of the power station, but this would not, of course, be the prime purpose.

Most civil nuclear power stations utilize uranium as the normal fuel and the plutonium is produced as an inevitable by-product, although not with a concentration of plutonium-239 high enough to be suitable for making a bomb. The concentration can be increased to this level by limiting the burn-up of the uranium fuel. There are, of course, considerable technical problems, but these would not be beyond the capability of either a technically advanced country or else a country or group with adequate financial resources.

The table gives an indication of the number of thermal reactors operating in 1977 and an indication of those under construction or planned. Some of those planned may never be built, whether due to political disturbances, as in Iran, or as a result of concern about nuclear power since the problems at the Three Mile Island plant near Harrisburg.

Thermal nuclear reactors

	Reactors in operation (March 1979)		Reactors in operation, under construction or planned	
	No.	Total power output (MW(e))	No.	Total power output (MW(e))
Argentina	1	345	3	1,505
Austria			1	692
Belgium	3	1,665	8	6,483
Brazil			3	3,116
Bulgaria	2	837	4	1,677
Canada	10	5,465	24	15,217
Cuba			2	880
Czechoslovakia			11	4,541
Finland	2	1,080	5	3,160
France	11	6,860	34	29,495
FRG	11	8,076	34	35,916
GDR	2	816	12	4,896
Hungary			4	1,632
India	3	602	8	1,689
Iran			8	8,982
Israel			1	600
Italy	4	1,382	8	5,242

	Reactors in operation (March 1979)		Reactors in operation, under construction or planned	
	No.	Total power output (MW(e))	No.	Total power output (MW(e))
Japan	20	13,239	32	23,019
Korea	1	564	5	3,598
Mexico			2	1,308
Netherlands	1	447	1	447
Pakistan			1	600
Philippines			1	621
Poland			2	816
Romania			1	440
South Africa			2	1,843
Spain	3	1,073	19	15,991
Sweden	6	3,700	12	9,442
Switzerland	3	1,006	10	7,833
Taiwan	2	1,208	6	4,923
Thailand			1	600
Turkey			1	620
UK	22	6,230	32	12,408
USA	67	51,183	202	200,931
USSR	12	6,669	31	23,269
Yugoslavia			1	632
TOTAL	186	112,447	532	435,064

(Source: SIPRI)

But the table does indicate the large increase in numbers of reactors and the many different countries involved.

According to Barnaby:

Plutonium *could* also be obtained clandestinely from a plutonium-production reactor, acquired specially for the purpose. A small reactor with a power of about 40 megawatts of electricity could produce enough plutonium-239 annually for two 20 kiloton atomic bombs. The components for such a small reactor can be easily and secretly obtained on the open market for a cost of less than $20 million. The reactor and a small chemical reprocessing unit to remove the plutonium from the reactor fuel elements could be clandestinely constructed and run by, say, the military.

It is worth noting that even in 1976 a total of 16 non-nuclear weapons states, or rather supposedly non-nuclear weapons states, had research reactors, including Argentina, Israel, Pakistan, South Africa, Thailand and Turkey.

Barnaby also points out that an alternative way of producing a nuclear weapon is to use uranium which has been enriched so that more than 40 per cent of it is made of uranium-235. Pakistan and South Africa have both constructed small enrichment plants and countries with substantial uranium reserves include Algeria, Argentina, Brazil, Gabon, India, Niger and South Africa.

As nuclear power programmes expand, then the production of plutonium increases and its control becomes more difficult. As Barnaby concludes:

Nuclear materials are being produced in an increasing number of countries. So far, a total of 100,000 kg of plutonium has been accumulated from civilian nuclear-power reactors. At present, about 230 power reactors are generating about 120,000 megawatts of electricity (MW (e)) in 22 countries (enough to produce about 30,000 kg of plutonium a year); another 230 or so power reactors are under construction. By the year 2000, reactors generating about 600,000 MW(e) may be operational and about *150,000 kg of plutonium produced a year – enough to make roughly 30,000 bombs of the Nagasaki type*. The spread of reactor-grade plutonium is the most immediate nuclear-weapon proliferation threat. [Our italics].

In case anyone doubts the connection between civil and military nuclear programmes, the most relevant example is that of Britain. In December 1945 the British Cabinet took the decision to build an atomic pile capable of producing enough plutonium to make fifteen bombs a year. The reactor was built at Windscale, alongside a reprocessing plant, and went critical late in 1950, producing enough plutonium by 1952 for Britain to test its first bomb. As Britain's nuclear weapons programme accelerated, the decision was taken to combine plutonium production with electricity generation for civil use and eight Magnox reactors were built during the mid-1950s, four at Calder Hall next to Windscale and four more at Chapelcross in Scotland. They were all small 50 MW (e) reactors intended to produce plutonium for military purposes but were heralded in the press as nuclear power stations and evidence of the value of the 'peaceful atom'. Their real military purpose went almost entirely unnoticed!

CONCLUSIONS – THE THREAT OF PROLIFERATION

As we have seen, France and China each have an impressive array of nuclear weapons and delivery systems and the development of such capabilities is underway in a number of other countries. Whatever one's view on the theory of nuclear deterrence between the two superpowers, it is difficult to imagine such a mechanism having any chance of giving stability in a world with twenty or thirty nuclear powers. At the same time it is hardly appropriate for countries such as the United States, the Soviet Union or Britain to decry such developments when they themselves are involved in an immense nuclear arms race.

Proliferation is one of the major factors leading towards an increased risk of nuclear war but it is difficult to see any way in which it can be brought under control unless as part of a general commitment to nuclear disarmament by the world's major nuclear powers. Only then would they be in a position where action to halt proliferation would be acceptable to the world community.

REFERENCES

Stockholm International Peace Research Institute (1980). *World Armaments and Disarmament: SIPRI Yearbook 1980.* Taylor & Francis, London.

International Institute for Strategic Studies (1960). *The Military Balance 1980–81.* IISS, London.

Polmar, N. (1979). *Strategic Weapons: An Introduction.* Macdonald & Jane's, London.

Rogers, P. (1981). *A Guide to Nuclear Weapons*, Peace Studies Paper No. 5. School of Peace Studies, University of Bradford.

Richardson, D. (1981). 'World Missile Survey', *Flight International*, 30 May 1981, pp. 1607–52.

Pretty, R. T. (Ed.) (1980). *Jane's Weapon Systems 1980–81.* Jane's, London.

Taylor, J. W. R. and Swanborough, G. (1979). *Military Aircraft of the World.* Ian Allan, London.

Taylor, M. J. H. (1980). *Missiles of the World.* Ian Allan, London.

Jones, General D. C. (1981). *United States Military Posture for FY 1982.* US Government Printing Office, Washington D.C.

Barnaby, F. (1981). *The Nuclear Arms Race,* Peace Studies Papers No. 4. School of Peace Studies, University of Bradford.

Stockholm International Peace Research Institute (1979). *Nuclear Energy and Nuclear Weapon Proliferation.* Taylor & Francis, London.

Bunyard, P. (1981). *Nuclear Britain.* New English Library, London.

4
The Slide to Nuclear War

A common perception of current nuclear weapons is that a balance of terror more or less exists which, through deterrence, prevents nuclear war. All that is necessary is that the United States is able to keep up with the Soviet Union in terms of weapons technology and so maintain its ability to deter the Soviet Union by being able to strike back after an attack, with devastating results.

Whether this notion of a stable deterrent was ever tenable is dubious, but we are concerned here with the several factors which are eroding any question of deterrence stability. The principal factors are:

1 The size of the arsenals.
2 Their current and future rapid growth.
3 The proliferation of nuclear weapons.
4 The development of new and accurate weapons suited to fighting global nuclear war, as distinct from deterring it.
5 The integration of nuclear weapons throughout the defence forces.

Three of these will be reviewed briefly as they have already been introduced, but the latter two will be examined in more detail. Collectively these factors suggest that we are entering an era of great danger.

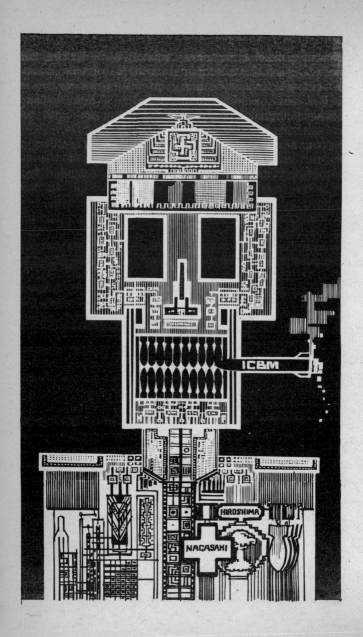

THE SIZE OF THE ARSENALS

When President Carter stated that a single Poseidon submarine, with its 16 missiles and 160 warheads, could destroy every major city in the Soviet Union, he was simply giving a graphic illustration of a more general outlook attributed to, among others, President Kennedy's Secretary of Defense, Robert McNamara. He had concluded that minimum deterrence needed 400 warheads sufficient in size to destroy two thirds of Soviet industry and one quarter of the Soviet population.

Both countries exceeded this kind of nuclear capability before 1960 and now have arsenals dozens of times the size necessary for such a function. Even allowing for possible vulnerability of land-based missiles and long-range bombers, the American SLBM force alone has at sea at any one time submarines sufficient to meet McNamara's deterrence requirement seven or eight times over.

In terms of size of arsenals alone it is impossible to relate them to deterrence policy. Even in the case of Britain and France, these countries will have an SLBM force in the 1990s which will be far larger than required for deterrence. The nuclear arms race appears no longer to be related to deterrence, if indeed it ever was.

THE GROWTH OF THE ARSENALS

If the size of the superpowers' nuclear arsenals makes no sense, then neither does the current rate of growth. Several examples have been given, the most notable on the American side being the 3400 ALCM warheads being deployed with the long-range bombers of the Strategic

'What in the name of God is strategic superiority? What is the significance of it politically, militarily, operationally at these levels of numbers? What do you do with it?'
Henry Kissinger, July 1974

Air Command during the early 1980s and the 2000 warheads involved in the M-X programme. These two alone increase American arsenals by some 50 per cent, and there are further increases in hand for SLBMs and shorter-range weapons. The MIRVing of Soviet ICBMs and SLBMs continues and there is also a significant expansion of theatre systems such as the SS-20 and Backfire bomber.

Apart from the risks involved in increasing the size of the arsenals, this process rather makes nonsense of the Strategic Arms Limitation Treaty negotiations. We shall see later the way in which SALT has channelled arms developments in particular directions but it is apparent from these figures that SALT overall has failed to limit the numbers of weapons.

PROLIFERATION

It is necessary to stress once more the three aspects of proliferation that decrease stability. One is the existence of three major nuclear powers quite apart from the United States and the Soviet Union. While it is true that they are small compared to the two superpowers, it is not true at all that they are insignificant. Each has greater destructive potential than would be required to devastate the major cities of the Soviet Union or Europe and each is presently increasing its nuclear armaments; yet each is, to some degree, independent.

The British Government persistently claims that it is desirable to have an alternative centre of nuclear decision-making in the West, and that this will enhance deterrence by inhibiting the Soviet Union as they will be less sure of Western reaction to crisis. It could be argued more strongly that this is, if anything, destabilizing – that the most stable system is one of two nuclear powers facing each other and that if one of them is facing, in addition, smaller nuclear powers, then it will feel obliged to escalate at an early stage in a conflict.

Certainly from Soviet viewpoints the existence of Britain, France and China in an opposing role is highly undesirable, more so in view of the escalation of the nuclear arms of each of these countries. This is more worrying to the Soviet Union in terms of the fitting of MIRV warheads to British and French submarine-launched missiles, and the development of Chinese ICBMs.

The second factor in proliferation is the development of independent nuclear states in two of the most unstable regions of the world, the Middle East and Southern Africa. By its action against the Baghdad reactor in 1981 Israel showed itself ready to take pre-emptive action against nuclear developments in neighbouring states, yet it almost certainly has a substantial nuclear capability of its own. While its conventional superiority in the region remains effective for the present, this might not persist and there can be little doubt that Israel would willingly use nuclear weapons if it was losing a conventional war.

The pressure of political change in Southern Africa is likely to increase conflict, and the mineral resources of the region inevitably result in any conflict having international significance. This is, of course, true of the Middle East so that the international involvements make it most unlikely that a regional conflict in either area that involved nuclear weapons could be contained.

THE DEVELOPMENT OF WEAPONS FOR NUCLEAR WAR-FIGHTING

There is growing agreement among independent analysts such as members of the Stockholm International Peace Research Institute, and even some acceptance within Western military circles, that trends in weapons developments are rapidly de-stabilizing deterrence and are greatly increasing the risk of nuclear war.

By the time the United States had developed a nuclear armory sufficient to cause massive damage to an opponent, in the mid-1950s, it was faced with a Soviet Union without that capability but with very large conventional forces. The Secretary of State in the Eisenhower administration in 1954, John Foster Dulles, spoke of a doctrine of 'massive retaliation' whereby the United States would respond to Soviet attacks with the destruction of Soviet cities and industry.

By 1960 the Soviet Union had its own considerable nuclear armory and the policy of the United States evolved into an attempt to deter at any level of attack by appropriate means, not necessarily nuclear. This 'graduated response' approach involved consideration of limited nuclear war, but ran counter to Soviet thinking which regarded it as inevitable that low-level use of nuclear weapons would inescapably escalate to strategic conflict.

The notion of massive retaliation, though, was also breaking down as the United States and Soviet reliance on long-range bombers in the late 1950s involved a risk of vulnerability to anti-aircraft defences. Both countries were therefore involved in developing long-range missiles which could not be intercepted, and by the early 1960s each had a number of intercontinental ballistic missiles in addition to bombers and each was developing SLBMs as well. By these means, the United States, for example, believed that the Soviet Union could be deterred by the threat of retaliation after attack. This is summarized in the recent report of the UN Secretary-General,

A Comprehensive Study on Nuclear Weapons
(12 September, 1980):
The concept of deterrence implies that beyond a certain level of expected damage, States will prefer peace to war. In the mid-1960s, former United States Secretary of Defence Robert McNamara stated that unacceptable destruction would require one-fourth to one-third fatalities to the population of a large industrialized nation and destruction of half to two-thirds of the entire industrial capacity. Likewise, Mr McNamara has illustrated the United States' capacity for 'assured destruction' by

'I feel secure if you feel secure.'

stating that the United States, even after suffering a first strike, could then in a second strike have destroyed two-fifths of the Soviet Union's population and 70 per cent of its industry.

This doctrine of *mutually assured destruction* (with the appropriate acronym MAD) persisted into the 1970s although there was always flexibility of approach with US targeting policy allowing for many different kinds of attack. Essentially, though, the weapons technology of the 1960s and early 1970s involved an ability to retaliate after a massive surprise first attack, and a key to such a policy was having land-based missiles in heavily protected silos and maintaining a force of hopefully invulnerable ballistic missile submarines. This does not explain, of course, the large numbers of missiles involved, far more than required by MAD, but what is more significant is the increased concern with attempting to overcome the invulnerability of the opposing nuclear armory to destruction in a first strike.

While each country maintains that its strategic nuclear forces are for deterrence, each is also working towards producing weapons *which can fight and possibly 'win' a strategic nuclear war by means of a pre-emptive or disarming first strike.* This trend is central to the increasing risk of instability and, indeed, part of the slide to nuclear war. It is essential to look at it in some detail, and it involves considering new missile systems, anti-submarine warfare, anti-ballistic missile defences and the future role of long-range bombers.

New missile systems

To protect land-based ICBMs from destruction by surprise attack they are housed in heavily protected underground silos and can only be destroyed by adjacent nuclear explosions. ICBMs are now becoming accurate enough to do this. In addition, ICBMs can now deliver a number of independently targeted warheads, so that a force of, say, 500 missiles each with four warheads could attack 1000 missiles in their silos with two warheads aimed at every enemy silo. Over the past twenty years the accuracies of American and Soviet ICBMs have increased considerably, as also have the accuracies of their SLBMs. As well as showing the progressive improvements in accuracy the table on page 92 shows the continuing lead of the United States, usually four to seven years ahead of the Soviet Union. Against this the Soviet Union has been able to deploy missiles with larger warheads, although this does not entirely counteract the United States' advantage in accuracy.

Improvements in accuracy are continuing and during the 1980s missiles will be deployed which combine sufficient destructive power and accuracy to threaten silos with a very high degree of probability. This is measured by Single Shot Kill Probability (SSKP) which takes into account warhead power and accuracy. An SSKP of 0.8 means that a single warhead has an 80 per cent chance of destroying a missile in its silo, and two warheads fired at one silo will have a kill probability of around 94 per cent (allowing for the possibility of one warhead knocking out the other – a phenomenon known as fratricide!).

None of the multiple warhead missiles mentioned in the following table have any effective counter-silo potential but the world's first counter-silo missile system is now in operation, the Minuteman III fitted with the new 12A warhead. By 1980 all 550 of the Minuteman III missiles had been fitted with the NS-20 guidance system giving them Circular Error Probabilities of 600-700 feet compared with the previous CEP of 900 feet. Furthermore, 300 of the Minuteman IIIs will, by 1982, have been fitted with the very advanced IZA warhead of 350 kilotons compared with the old Mark 12 which was 200 kilotons. The combination gives the missile a SSKP of 0.72, considerably better than anything the Soviet Union has deployed at present. The table on page 93 summarizes, probable future developments.

The figures must be treated with some caution, and

Accuracy of existing missiles

Class	Missile	Date of first deployment	CEP (feet)
US/ICBM	Titan II	1962	3,000
	Minuteman II	1966	1,800
	Minuteman III*	1970	900
US/SLBM	Polaris A3	1964	3,000
	Poseidon C3*	1971	1,800
	Trident C4*	1981	1,500
USSR/ICBM	SS-7	1961	9,000
	SS-9	1965	3,000
	SS-17*	1975	1,800
	SS-18 (mod 1)	1974	1,500
	SS-19 (mod 1)*	1975	1,200
USSR/SLBM	SS-N-6	1969	6,000
	SS-N-8	1972	3,000

*Denotes MIRV system.

those given in brackets are tentative, but they illustrate a general trend towards increasing vulnerability of silo-based ICBMs. The United States will shortly have 900 warheads each with an SSKP of over 70 per cent. By 1986 or so it will have nearly 3000 warheads with SSKPs over 90 per cent and with Trident II it will have, by the end of the decade some 6000 such warheads. On the Soviet side present indications are 4000 warheads with SSKPs over 80 per cent by the mid-1980s.

There are responses to this trend such as developing mobile ICBM systems, improving the strength of the silos and attempting to develop ballistic missile defences, but against this a new generation of guidance systems is now in progress which involve terminal guidance using radar or laser sensing which enables warheads to be placed with accuracies believed to be around 50 feet CEP.

Future trends in missile accuracy (primary source: Daggett)

Class	Weapon	Initial deployment	Warheads (No & KT)	CEP (ft)	SSKP	Missiles	Warheads
US/ICBM	Minuteman III	1982	3 × 350	600	.72	300	900
	Minuteman III	1985	3 × 350	300	.98	300	900
	M-X	(1986)	10 × 350	300	.98	200	2,000
US/SLBM	Trident I	1981	8 × 100	1,500	.10	176	1,408
	Trident II	(1988)	14 × 150	300	.92	216	3,024
USSR/ICBM	SS-17	1979	4 × 550	1,500	.25	100	400
	SS-17	(1984)	10 × 600	600	.83	200	2,000
	SS-19	1979	6 × 550	1,500	.25	310	1,116
		(1984)	6 × 550	600	.81	(360)	(2,160)
USSR/SLBM	SS-N-18	1979	(3 × 1MT)	3,000	(.15)	160	480

The problem remains that technological developments are providing the military with weapons which might be thought capable of disarming the missile capabilities of opponents. Under circumstances of major crisis involving conventional conflict escalating rapidly to tactical and theatre nuclear conflict, *the temptation to make an attempted disarming first strike would be appallingly high*. The alternative would be to risk the opponent doing likewise.

A strategy in response to this could be one of launch-on-warning (LOW) or launch-under-attack (LUA). In each case the missiles of a country are *pre-programmed* to ensure that a proportion of the arsenal (perhaps 25 per cent) is launched *automatically* on warning of an attack or when an attack has commenced. The latter is risky because most missiles might be disabled and the former is clearly more certain of success.

The central problem is that such a response *does not involve human intervention*. It may deter an opponent from attempting a disarming first strike but carries the risk of an accidental launching through systems error, (what has been described as an 'automated Armageddon'). The adoption of LOW systems now seems highly probable as ICBM capabilities against silos increase.

In summary, improvements in missile accuracy now threaten silos and will increasingly do so in the 1980s to the point that either side might believe it can disarm the ICBMs of its opponent. Even if the evidence is based only on test launchings, if one side *believes* it can achieve this aim, then under conditions of crisis it may attempt to do so. There remain, however, the questions of SLBM invulnerability, ballistic missile defences and the use of the other leg of the triad, the long-range bomber.

Anti-submarine warfare (ASW)

In 1981 the United States had 41 ballistic missile submarines. Britain had four and their targeting was integrated with that of the United States. France had five, but in a quasi-independent force. The Soviet Union, though, had slightly over 60 submarines and the immediate assumption is that this gives that country a considerable superiority.

Further examination shows this to be far from true. Recent evidence from SIPRI suggests that the United States is considerably more successful in maintaining ballistic missile submarines on station, keeping some 20 of its boats available for use at any one time, together with one or two of Britain's fleet. SIPRI suggests that the Soviet capability is far more limited, being around 12 submarines out of a larger total fleet. Even this may be an overestimate. Both the United States and the Soviet Union normally have a proportion of their boats undergoing refits but it appears that the Soviet Union has a very poor record of patrol capability. Thus the 1980–81 edition of *Strategic Survey* (published in May 1981) says:

Of the 31 US ballistic-missile submarines currently operational, about 20 (with about 3200 warheads) are generally at sea at any one time, and these are regarded as invulnerable to current Soviet anti-submarine warfare capabilities. On the other hand the Soviet Union generally maintains only 7 to 10 such boats permanently on station, and they are continuously monitored by US ASW forces.

The Soviet Union has a relatively limited anti-submarine capability, including 46 nuclear-powered attack submarines, whereas the United States had 74 and Britain a further 11. In addition, the United States has three important advantages:

Geography American ballistic missile submarine bases on the US mainland and overseas (such as Holy Loch in Scotland) are adjacent to the open sea. The Soviet bases near Murmansk and Vladivostok involve their boats passing relatively narrow stretches of water before reaching the oceans, and this enhances American and NATO efforts to detect and track them.

Sound Surveillance System (SOSUS) This is an elaborate, passive hydrophone system deployed off the east and west coasts of America, the west coast of Britain and elsewhere, which is reportedly able to locate Soviet submarines to within a 55-mile circle.

Mobile Acoustic Systems The United States has a considerable lead over the Soviet Union in terms of helicopter-based dipping sonars, sonar buoys and guided torpedoes. Taken with SOSUS for initial detection this adds up to an impressive ASW ability.

Against the American ASW superiority the Soviet Union is now deploying much longer-range SLBMs which means that some of its submarines can patrol areas some 5000 miles or more away from the United States in Arctic waters close to the Soviet Union. In broad terms the United States still has the advantage and under crisis conditions might well risk a missile attack to destroy the large numbers of Soviet boats at port and a concerted ASW operation to attempt to destroy those at sea.

Ballistic missile defences

In the early 1970s both the United States and the Soviet Union developed ballistic missile defences based on interceptor missiles carrying nuclear or even thermonuclear warheads which were intended to detonate near enough to incoming warheads to destroy them. The American system consisted of long- and short-range Spartan and Sprint missiles but it proved of limited capability and was disbanded in 1977. The Soviet Galosh system had 64 missiles and associated radar and protected Moscow and nearby ICBM bases. Half of these missiles have been removed but there are reports of replacement missiles which can both loiter and change course.

Both countries are engaged in expensive and intensive research and development efforts to provide ballistic missile defences. The United States has already reached the point where it could deploy the Low Altitude Defence System (LOADS) to protect 150 Minuteman IIIs by 1983–4. Any larger system would be in defiance of the Anti-Ballistic Missile Treaty but there are pressures on the Reagan administration to do this, just as SALT II remains unratified.

Work is also in progress on the more exotic weapons such as lasers and particle beams. These are unlikely to have any use against incoming missiles until well into the 1990s, but their use against satellites is another matter. Both countries are dependent on satellites for warning of attack and for communications. Deployment of successful anti-satellite systems during the mid or late 1980s could represent a breakthrough which would invalidate many other strategic advantages of an opposing power.

Long-range bombers

Although there are occasional reports of new Soviet long-range bombers under development, there is little concrete evidence yet available. On the American side there have been two major developments. One is the production of the air-launched cruise missile (ALCM) and its deployment from 1982 on B52s. This weapon gives the United States an immense advantage over the Soviet Union in this respect, providing some 3400 new warheads which can be delivered without the need for the bombers to penetrate Soviet air space. Furthermore, the development of a new penetration bomber, the modified B1 using stealth technology, and the plans for a completely new bomber for the 1990s, demonstrates a continuing commitment to a triad which has all three components capable of inflicting truly massive damage.

Conclusions

The conclusion of this section on the slide towards nuclear war-fighting is that both of the superpowers are currently engaged in a massive nuclear arms race which is resulting in weapons and defence systems aimed at the fighting and winning of a nuclear war.

If a situation of extreme international tension develops and this escalates rapidly to involve nuclear weapons, then the possession of strategic nuclear-war-fighting weapons will ensure the escalation to strategic conflict forthwith. While the United States is more likely to be in the position to make a disarming first strike it matters little that this should be so.

Whichever side perceives that it is at a disadvantage will be under tremendous pressure to use its strategic weapons at a very early stage in any conflict, while those weapons are still intact. If it fails to do this, it risks their loss, together with the effects of perhaps thousands of megatons of groundburst detonations. If it succeeds it will suffer grievously but if it has attacked its opponent then it will not be 'defeated'. *It will lose but so will its opponent.*

INTEGRATION OF NUCLEAR WEAPONS

The developments in weapons represent perhaps the greatest increase in the risk of nuclear war, but almost as important is the integration of nuclear weapons into the organization and policies of the nuclear powers. It should be clear from the descriptions of nuclear weapons given in earlier chapters that we are not just dealing with ICBMs and other long-range systems. The artillery, short-range tactical missiles, atomic demolition munitions, tactical free-fall bombs, nuclear-capable helicopters, nuclear-tipped anti-aircraft missiles and nuclear-tipped ship-to-ship missiles collectively represent the fundamental integrating of nuclear weapons into military organization. The small size of some nuclear weapons, below 0.5 kilotons, coupled with increased destructive power of conventional explosives such as fuel-air mixtures *means that the borderline between nuclear and non-nuclear weapons is becoming extremely tenuous*. Deployment of the enhanced radiation weapon or neutron bomb intended for use against armoured attacks serves to encourage this trend, and the increased commitment to chemical weapons does likewise.

NATO has a policy of flexible response and is prepared to be the first user of tactical nuclear weapons in the event of it being unable to contain an assault by conventional means. On the Soviet side it must be emphasized that evidence of military thinking suggests that nuclear weapons would be used on a large scale at an early stage in a conflict.

The overriding danger is that the demarcation is no longer clear. Given the widespread deployment of tactical nuclear weapons, 11,000 in Europe alone and around 40,000 world wide, *it is now scarcely plausible to envisage a major conflict that does not 'go nuclear'*. Possession of weapons at relatively low command levels cannot be made completely stable by even the most impressive control procedures. *In time of war the decisions will most likely rest with individual field commanders*. Any such person, whether on land or sea, who is faced with defeat, will be under extreme pressure to use tactical nuclear weapons, whatever control procedures have been employed.

Escalation is similarly all too easy to comprehend. Use of nuclear shells may meet with a response delivered by air or by medium-range tactical missiles. This in turn can only be contained by nuclear strikes against air bases and missile-deployment areas, with consequent retaliation and so on.

Recent deployment decisions, and also reports of American plans for dealing with casualties from a European theatre war, suggest that the United States strategists may believe there is a possibility of containing a war at the stage of a European conflict even though Europe would be devastated. There is a central illogicality about this in that a European war is, to the United States, a theatre war but to the Soviet Union it is a strategic war. Any conflict involving significant nuclear strikes on the

western parts of the Soviet Union will inevitably occasion the use of long-range weapons. Under conditions of uncertainty over first-strike capabilities this escalation to a strategic war will be rapid.

HOW A NUCLEAR WAR MIGHT START

The targeting policy of the United States and the outlook of Soviet strategic analysts both indicate that nuclear war-fighting, as distinct from deterrence, has been an attitude present on both sides for many years. The current trend is towards elevating this attitude to a position of much greater importance, and this trend is aided by the new generations of weapons and the integration of tactical and theatre nuclear weapons into the armed forces. We would argue, therefore, that the overall risk of nuclear war is growing rapidly but it is also possible to suggest, more precisely, how it might start.

One serious possibility is that it could start by accident. There have been persistent reports of false alarms affecting American missile-surveillance systems, including a major alert in November 1979 and another early in 1980.

We do not know whether there have been similar alerts on the Soviet side but cannot rule this out. No humanly engineered system is totally proof against error of malfunction and there is always a risk that conflict will begin by accident.

This risk is substantially increased if either side adopts a policy of launch-on-warning (LOW), seeking to fire off a part of its missile arsenal automatically following an indication of enemy attack. As we have seen, LOW is an almost inevitable response to the risk of a disarming first strike. There is already reported to be an option for LOW in the American targeting plan and there have been indications that the Soviet Union may be adopting similar tactics.

Even if we leave aside accidents involving strategic weapons there is the risk that, with over 40,000 tactical nuclear weapons, a command system could go wrong and a nuclear attack start. If this were to occur under conditions of international tension it is highly probably that escalation would follow.

The handling of nuclear weapons can never be foolproof and there have been many examples of accidents involving them. On 17 January 1966, a B52 carrying four H-bombs collided with a tanker aircraft during re-fuelling over Spain and both aircraft crashed near Palomares. One bomb was recovered from the land and one from the sea after a two-and-a-half-month search, but the other two bombs broke up in the crash and the resultant cleaning-up operation involved removing 1400 tons of contaminated soil and vegetation.

Almost exactly two years later on 21 January 1968 another B52 crashed near Thule Air Force Base in Greenland. This was also carrying four nuclear weapons and the clean-up operation involved removal of 4000 tons of ice, snow and water.

Four months later the United States submarine *Scorpion* sank with the loss of ninety-nine crew in the Eastern Atlantic. The *Scorpion* was carrying anti-submarine tor-

pedoes with nuclear warheads. On 19 September 1980, a
Titan II ICBM exploded at a base near Little Rock in
Arkansas, killing two people and throwing the *9 megaton*
warhead over 300 feet from the silo. Fortunately the
warhead did not explode.

There have been reports of at least six accidents involving Soviet nuclear weapon-carrying submarines in the
past fifteen years and in at least one of these there are
suggestions that nuclear-tipped torpedoes were lost.

There have not so far been any reports of accidental
launches of nuclear missiles but an extraordinary episode
occurred in the Caribbean in July 1981. A US Navy
destroyer involved in exercises near the Virgin Islands
accidentally fired a Harpoon anti-ship missile. This long-
range sub-sonic missile was then detected heading in the
direction of a cruise liner some sixty miles away and
aircraft from the carrier *Dwight D Eisenhower* were
launched to try and intercept it. In the event the missile
disappeared, presumably into the sea. The Harpoon is a
substantial missile, 15 feet long and weighing nearly half a
ton. It carries a 500 lb high-explosive warhead and is not a
nuclear missile. An accidental launch of such a missile is
remarkable, the more so because many of the naval
destroyers and cruisers which are armed with the Harpoon also carry the ASROC missile which *does* have a
nuclear warhead.

The episode gives cause for concern that a risk of
accidental nuclear-missile launches does exist and as
numbers of weapons and of countries with nuclear
weapons grows, then the risk increases. That an
accidental nuclear holocaust would be the supreme irony
would, in turn, be of little comfort to the victims.

A probable source of a nuclear exchange would be the
development of a major conventional conflict involving
NATO and Warsaw Pact armed forces, probably in
Europe. This could escalate from very small incidents,
perhaps little more than border skirmishes, but as conflict
proceeded, then whichever side was losing would have

little alternative but to escalate. Both sides have clear policies to 'go nuclear' if they cannot avoid defeat by other means, and from there escalation would be very rapid, probably involving theatre weapons and then strategic arsenals within hours.

Away from Europe there is the increasing risk that a small or new nuclear power could employ nuclear weapons in a regional conflict. The Middle East and Southern Africa are the two most likely areas of conflict. The former would be particularly dangerous as both sides are likely to be, to some extent, the client states of superpowers. Whichever side was losing would be likely to involve the relevant superpower and from there the escalation would proceed.

More generally there is the increasing risk of conflict over resources. American concern over the need for a Rapid Deployment Force relates closely to its perceived need to safeguard resource supplies for its own use. As the industrialized nations become increasingly dependent on third world countries for resource supplies, so the risk of superpower conflict starting in the third world grows. In a world of increasing nuclear weapons proliferation the prospects would be bleak.

Finally there is the growing risk of a disarming first strike with one side *believing* that it might destroy the great majority of an opponent's strategic nuclear arsenal. Whether it could actually do so is, to say the least, debatable, but the point is that if the perception is there, the reality is less important. We have to remember, too, that we are not necessarily talking about a completely cold-blooded disarming first strike, coming 'out of the blue' at a time of low tension. What we are considering is how a nation with very accurate ICBMs might react under conditions of considerable tension, possibly involving conventional conflict. Under such circumstances the attacking country may accept that it will receive some damage, perhaps ten per cent loss of life of its own population, yet still go ahead with an attack. Of course the various intermediate weapons would, meanwhile, destroy most of Western and Central Europe, but that would be of relatively little importance to the superpowers.

CONCLUSION

A section such as this must make depressing reading because it is concerned with a series of issues which, collectively, offer appalling prospects. We have seen that the arsenals of the two major nuclear powers are immense, *far larger than could possibly be justified by any theory of deterrence*. We have also seen that these arsenals are currently increasing at a quite horrifying rate, *a possible 50 per cent increase by the mid-1980s*.

Furthermore there has been the description of the nuclear weapons of Britain, China and France, three countries with formidable if smaller armories which are all engaged in their own escalation. Beyond these there is already a process of proliferation in progress and this involves two of the most tense regions of the world and is likely to spread to several other countries during this decade.

Perhaps least appreciated yet most worrying is the trend in new weapons and in integration of nuclear armaments throughout the military structure of the major powers. *The combination of these factors leads towards the conclusion that nuclear war is not just possible or even probable but, on present trends, is becoming almost inevitable.*

' . . . the nearest thing to doomsday that one could possibly imagine, I am sure, that at the end of the world – in the last millisecond of the earth's existence – the last man will see what we have just seen!'

George Kistiakowsky
Comment on the first atomic bomb explosion
16 July 1945

REFERENCES

Stockholm International Peace Research Institute (1980). *World Armaments and Disarmament: SIPRI Yearbook 1980.* Taylor & Francis, London.

International Institute for Strategic Studies (1980). *The Military Balance 1980–81.* IISS, London.

Barnaby, F. (1981). *The Nuclear Arms Race*, Peace Studies Papers No. 4. School of Peace Studies, University of Bradford.

Rogers, P. (1981). *A Guide to Nuclear Weapons*, Peace Studies Papers No. 5. School of Peace Studies, University of Bradford.

Daggett, S. (1980). *The New Generation of Nuclear Weapons.* Institute for Policy Studies, Washington D.C.

Aldridge, R. C. (1979). *The Counterforce Syndrome.* Institute for Policy Studies, Washington D.C.

Bertram, C. (Ed.). (1981). *Strategic Deterrence in a Changing Environment.* Gower and Allanheld Osmun.

United Nations Secretary-General (1980). *Comprehensive Study on Nuclear Weapons.* UNO, New York.

International Institute for Strategic Studies (1980). *Strategic Survey 1980–81.* IISS, London.

Part 2

When it Happens

5

Target Britain

In this chapter we will examine the possible involvement of Britain in a nuclear war in terms of the kind of attack which the country is likely to experience. To do this we have first to examine the strategic nuclear policies of the United States and the Soviet Union. By doing so we will be able to get some idea of the kind of attack to which we might be exposed. The relevance of US policy is that it is likely to parallel Soviet policy in some basic respects and has the dubious advantage to us that a fair amount of information about it is available.

UNITED STATES AND SOVIET STRATEGIC NUCLEAR POLICY

A common misconception about American strategic nuclear policy is that it has recently changed from a targeting of population centres (as part of an essentially deterrent policy) to one of military targets. Carter's Presidential Directive 59 is cited as evidence for this, but in practice the United States has had detailed and complex targeting plans for military as well as non-military targets for many years. What is true, especially of the current administration is that there appears to be an increasing belief in the use of nuclear weaponry for fighting a war. In other words, while the capability has been there for some time, the political will is now leaning increasingly in that direction.

American targeting policy is codified in the classified

Single Integrated Operational Plan (SIOP), broad details of which are occasionally published in reputable technical journals. From a list of about 70 targets in 1949 the total number has grown to some 40,000 in the current SIOP-5 plan, introduced in January 1976 but subject to up-dating. SIOP-5 includes more than 15,000 economic-industrial targets, more than 20,000 military targets, centres of political leadership and probably targets outside of the Warsaw Pact countries. The idea of 40,000 targets for fewer than 10,000 warheads is not nonsensical for one warhead might destroy a number of different targets and SIOP-5 also involves a number of different options.

This very fact is indicative of a commitment to nuclear war-fighting – the idea that alternative attacks may be postulated over a number of hours, days or even longer. Certainly US targeting is likely to involve attempts to disarm Soviet nuclear capabilities or these together with conventional military capabilities. Other options might be attacks to aid Chinese military action, known in the trade as 'kicking the door in'!

Overall, the United States has developed a range of options which are, it believes, an enhancement of deterrence by demonstrating a willingness to engage in strategic nuclear conflict at a variety of levels. It can be argued, however, that such a trend is fundamentally destabilizing due to the difficulty or even impossibility of controlling any major nuclear exchange. Even a counter-force strike aimed just at destroying ICBMs, strategic bombers, missile submarines and associated communications could involve a loss of life approaching twenty million people on either side. Any such attack would involve retaliation by the surviving nuclear weapons systems against a broad range of targets – in other words general nuclear war.

Yet US targeting policy appears to envisage a controlled strategic nuclear exchange falling short of all-out destruction. We must remember, though, that under the actual conditions of nuclear war-fighting there would be a

Airstrip One

very high degree of disorder, with decisions being taken after the loss of many command and control personnel, with disruption of communications by electro-magnetic pulse and other effects and on the basis of highly confused reports of damage already experienced. The inevitable and overwhelming tendency under such conditions would, in our view, be for surviving political and military authorities on both sides to go for rapid use of most of the remaining weapons systems. In other words *we do not believe that a strategic nuclear exchange can be limited.*

Nevertheless, the very fact that trends in US targeting policy appear not to recognize this view is alarming. The move towards a concentration on nuclear war-fighting is likely to make arms control far more difficult because the presentation of different options in a targeting programme requires increased numbers of nuclear weapons in the strategic armory.

Turning to Soviet strategic nuclear strategy, the writings of Soviet military authorities that have been available in the West suggest that the basic approach of Soviet strategists has traditionally been one of integration of nuclear with conventional weapons. The concern over thresholds of use of tactical nuclear weapons has been less obvious, indeed almost absent from Soviet thinking, and the presumption has been that any major conflict with NATO and China would inevitably 'go nuclear'.

The recent limited modification of this view has concerned the possibility of localized wars involving tactical nuclear weapons but Soviet strategists appear not to consider that a nuclear exchange arising from a general conflict would be contained. A recent paper by Desmond Ball says that,

Despite some improvements in the capabilities for control, Soviet doctrine still seems to be that in the event of a nuclear exchange the Soviet forces would be used massively against a range of targets – nuclear forces, other military forces, the military-industrial base and, almost certainly, the US and NATO military, political and administrative control centres.

The most significant point is that Soviet doctrine appears to be to use nuclear weapons on a massive scale immediately a conflict escalates to strategic nuclear weapons. The attitude is one of strike early – and strike hard.

Post-war considerations

As we shall see later when examining the long-term effects of nuclear war, strategists are not just concerned with the actual war, because targeting takes into account the post-war situation, and by 'post-war' we can be talking of fifty years or so.

The government officials of either of the superpowers who are involved in strategic analysis will obviously accept that in a strategic nuclear exchange their own country will suffer grievous damage. There will be a range of possibilities but they must assume that there is a high risk that their country will be crippled by the immediate and long-term effects of the nuclear exchange. This might mean loss of a large part of the population and most of the industry. The ultimate aim, though, must still be for that country to 'win' the war – that is that it must emerge eventually as the stronger and more powerful country.

In the context of the superpowers, though, the country must emerge *after* a nuclear exchange as the most powerful country in the world. What would it profit the Soviet Union or the United States for them to defeat the other but then become secondary to China, Japan, Western Europe, Latin America or even India. We must assume that targeting policy takes into account such eventualities and the logical outcome of such a line of reasoning is that

---

'I do not think it at all likely that a limited nuclear exchange would remain limited.'

Harold Brown, US Secretary of Defense,
11 January 1977

such potential post-war rivals must be contained. Thus targeting policy must not just involve the destruction of the economic structure of the opposing power, but also the control – i.e. partial destruction – of countries not involved in the conflict! We should presume, therefore, that a nuclear exchange would be truly global.

THE NATURE OF AN ATTACK ON BRITAIN

It is obviously not possible to say with certainty what would be involved in a Soviet nuclear attack on Britain: presumably the Soviet planners have a number of options. Yet from a knowledge of the weapons available, attitudes towards a post-war power struggle and the significance of Britain in strategic terms, it is possible to sketch in some of the probable features of an attack. There are four features which make Britain an opponent of significance to the Soviet Union.

– Britain is a major centre of strategic nuclear forces with two submarine bases at Holy Loch and Faslane. It also plays a major role in supporting other strategic weapons systems.

– The United States and Britain maintain large numbers of medium-range nuclear weapons in Britain.

– The country would act as the major centre for receiving, maintaining and supplying North American reinforcements to a conflict in Europe.

– Britain is a medium-sized but significant industrial power which might have to be disabled to prevent any post-war threat.

Apart from over 6000 strategic warheads the Soviet Union has several medium-range missiles including the SS-4, SS-5 and SS-20. These latter give a total of around 1000 warheads although perhaps one third are reserved for other regions such as South-East Asia. There are over

800 medium-range bombers including the supersonic Blinder and Backfire and more than 2000 shorter-range strike aircraft such as the later versions of the Fitter and Fencer and the Mig-21s and Mig-27s. A large proportion of these might be assigned to Western European targets. There are large numbers of submarine-launched missiles of which the shorter-range SS-N-6 could include a portion assigned to targets in Britain. Finally the strategic ICBMs cannot be presumed to be targeted just on the United States. Some of the smaller ICBMs could certainly be used against Britain. This point may be controversial but, as we will see, the significance of UK targets and the options open to targeters suggest that any doubt is misplaced.

Exercises involving possible nuclear attacks on Britain are held each year and a major exercise, Square Leg, in September 1980 involved an attack of around 130 warheads with a total force of more than 200 megatons. On the infrequent occasions when the Home Office staff discuss the extent of possible attacks it is in terms of a 200 megaton assault in line with Square Leg. In practice, though, *this seems an extremely low figure* and one which we find very difficult to take seriously. It represents less than three per cent of Soviet medium- and long-range warhead systems and less than five per cent of megatonnage, and this for a country with a unique concentration of targets.

Targets in Britain can, for convenience, be listed under a number of headings. We will not pretend that the following lists are comprehensive; they should be taken as examples – representative of the probable pattern of destruction.

Strategic bases

The US Navy base at Holy Loch near Glasgow normally serves up to ten Poseidon submarines, rather more than *one quarter* of operational US missile submarines; the neighbouring Royal Navy base at Faslane serves four

Polaris submarines and will be expanded to cope with four or five larger Trident submarines. Each base has an associated nuclear weapons store, at Glen Douglas and Coulport respectively, and the British submarines undergo refits at the naval dockyard at Rosyth, across the Firth of Forth from Edinburgh. Communications with the British Polaris boats are handled from a transmitting facility near Rugby.

These six places would be immediate and major targets and would be expected to receive multiple warheads involving ground and/or air bursts. In addition we should expect a pattern of bombing of the Clyde estuary to catch any submarines making emergency escape to the Atlantic. As we will see later there are particularly dangerous effects from larger nuclear explosions over or in seawater. The warheads aimed at these targets would be large, possibly 2 megatons each, and as the targets are crucially important each would have at least two aimed at it to ensure its destruction. As has been mentioned earlier, missile submarines *can* launch their weapons given some notice, perhaps twenty-five minutes, and any general nuclear attack would have the elimination of these facilities as a top priority.

Theatre nuclear bases

Britain has a large number of RAF and USAF bases from which medium-range bombers and shorter-range strike aircraft would fly to attack Warsaw Pact countries and armed forces. Other bases house fighter aircraft and there are many bases to which military aircraft would be dispersed during a time of conflict.

Some of the more important targets would be the Vulcans at Scampton and Waddington in Lincolnshire and the Buccaneers based at Honington in Suffolk, and at Lossiemouth in Scotland. Jaguar strike aircraft are based at Coltishall near Norwich and Nimrod anti-submarine aircraft are located at Kinloss in north-east Scotland and St Mawgan in Cornwall. All these would be targets for ground and air-burst weapons. The former would be to destroy hardened defence structures and aircraft hangars, while the latter would be detonated above and adjacent to the bases to destroy aircraft which have attempted to take off.

A similar kind of attack pattern would apply to bases such as Marham near King's Lynn which has Victor K2 tanker aircraft for aerial re-fuelling of the bombers, and Cottesmore some forty miles to the west near Peterborough which is the first base in Britain for the new Tornado strike aircraft. Fighter bases would also come under early attack, as part of a policy of 'defence suppression' designed to disable any attempts to destroy Soviet bombers and strike aircraft. This would certainly involve more than one detonation on the Lightning and Phantom bases at Binbrook and Conningsby in Lincolnshire, Wattisham in Suffolk and Leuchars in Central Scotland. The air base for the tactical strike aircraft, the Harrier, at Wittering near Peterborough would be a target as would the naval air station at Yeovilton in Somerset.

Major transport bases such as Brize-Norton in Oxfordshire and Lyneham in Wiltshire would be destroyed, as would many other airfields to which planes could have been dispersed, these being as far afield as Valley on Anglesey and Manston in Kent.

The United States Air Force has more than twenty bases in Britain of which the more important would be targets for massive attack. These include the bases housing the F111 medium-range supersonic bombers – Lakenheath in Suffolk and Upper Heyford in Oxfordshire, the Fairchild Thunderbolt base at Bentwaters in Suffolk and significant transport and support bases such as Mildenhall and Woodbridge in Suffolk and Alconbury in Cambridgeshire.

Probably most crucial of all would be the new cruise missile bases at Greenham Common in Berkshire and Molesworth in Cambridge when they become operational. While many of the missiles would, presumably, be dispersed at a time of conflict, a surprise attack would, in all likelihood destroy some, especially if a pattern bombing of the area within perhaps a twenty mile radius of each base was undertaken.

As well as these and many other air bases, an attack would involve the naval bases and dockyards such as Devonport and Portsmouth and the larger army camps including Aldershot and Catterick. Significant nuclear research and production establishments such as Aldermaston and Burghfield near Reading and the ordnance factory in Cardiff would be destroyed, probably with added contamination from released nuclear material, and many defence research establishments such as Porton Down and Portland would be hit.

Command, control and communications

Still staying with the more strictly military aspects of targeting we can add a wide range of communications and control facilities. An obvious candidate would be the Ballistic Missile Early Warning Station at Fylingdales near Scarborough in North Yorkshire. Like the submarine bases this would probably be attacked using low-trajectory missiles from Soviet submarines, such an attack pattern giving the minimum warning. Other targets include communications centres such as Edzell in Central Scotland, Menwith Hill near Harrogate and Chicksands in Bedfordshire and the submarine monitoring station at Brawdy on the Pembrokeshire coast.

In terms of command and control it goes without saying that Central London has numerous defence-related targets and there are a number of major command facilities for British and NATO posts at Northwood (Navy and NATO), Portsmouth (Navy and NATO), High Wycombe (RAF and NATO), Wilton (Army), Brampton (RAF), and Dunfermline (Navy and NATO). District Army Headquarters are at Bulford, Aldershot, London, Colchester, Brecon, Shrewsbury, York, Preston, Edinburgh and Lisburn. Probably all of these would be subject to ground-burst attacks.

The fifty or so bases listed here represent just some of the military targets which would be attacked and such an attack should be assumed to involve at least double that number of warheads. Many of the warheads would not, of course, land on target. Some would fail at launch and others might fail on discharge from the MIRV portion of the missiles. Others might suffer guidance failures and could detonate anywhere in Britain or indeed outside Britain.

In addition to these land targets there would be attacks on surface ships and on submarines in the waters around the coast of Britain. Fall-out from some of these attacks would be likely to affect Britain.

Quasi-military targets

Even if we continue to restrict ourselves to the direct military context we have to add a large number of civil facilities which would be significant in a conflict. These must include all major civil airports as they are capable of taking military transports and bombers. Places such as Heathrow, Gatwick, Luton, Stanstead, Prestwick, Manchester, Birmingham and many other airports would fall into this category and there are also scores of smaller airports which could take smaller dispersed military aircraft. The more important targets would probably be assigned to missiles and the less important probably to free-fall nuclear bombs delivered by medium-range bombers.

Other quasi-military targets would include the more important ports and ship-building towns such as the London docks, Dover, Southampton, Avonmouth, Cardiff, Swansea, Birkenhead, Liverpool, Belfast, Barrow, Greenock and the Clyde (again!), Aberdeen, Leith, Tyneside, Teesside, the Humber ports, Harwich, Felixstowe and Tilbury.

Targets of post-war significance

On the assumption that the Soviet Union experiences considerable damage and loss of life in a nuclear war, it must fight that war in such a way as to ensure that its opponents and even potential opponents are crippled even more. This will apply particularly to potential military capabilities but also to general industrial, communications and political organization. The major states of Western Europe are collectively as important as the United States and a large part of the Soviet nuclear forces will have to be directed at their political, economic and industrial base. If the damage to the Soviet Union in a nuclear war is assumed by their strategic analysts to be sufficient to set the country back at least fifty years then they would have to ensure that potential rivals suffer an even greater set-back. . . .

This would be achieved by destruction of the major political, commercial and industrial centres with emphasis on manufacturing industries especially those concerned with armaments. Such is the nature of the modern armaments industry that this takes in virtually every industrial centre of any size. Subsidiary targets would be those dispersed localities such as power stations and oil refineries which support such activities. Many of these targets would have already been assigned warheads because of more direct military importance but we should anticipate attacks on, for example, the following places.

(a) Political, commercial and industrial centres would include London, Edinburgh, Cardiff, Belfast, Bristol, Swansea, Coventry, Birmingham, Wolverhampton, Leicester, Norwich, Derby, Stoke, Sheffield, Manchester, Stockport, Bolton, Preston, Leeds, Bradford and Glasgow. The ports, of course, are already covered.

(b) Energy resources would be particularly significant and would include refineries and petro-chemical com-

Условные обозначения

● Аэродром (авиабаза)

⚓ Военно-морская база (пункт базирования)

▭ Склад

⫿⫿ Радиолокационный пост раннего обнаружения

△ Узел связи

Керкуолл

Тёрсо

Элгин
Инвернесс

Абердин

СЕВЕРНОЕ

Арброт
Сент-Андрус

МОРЕ

Фолкерк
Фаслейн
Холи-Лох
Ротсей Глазго
Ферли
Кэмпбелтаун Престуик
Розайт
Эдинбург

Лондондерри

Ашингтон
Ньюкасл-Апон-Тайн
Сандерленд

Белфаст
Карлайл

Файлингдейлс-Мур

Дуглас

Барроу-Ин-Фернесс

Йорк

Лидс
Гулль

Холихед
Ливерпуль
МАНЧЕСТЕР
ШЕФФИЛД

ИРЛАНДСКОЕ
МОРЕ

Стаффорт
Ноттингем

БИРМИНГЕМ

Ипсвич

Суонси
Суиндон
ЛОНДОН

Кардиф
Бристоль
Чатем

Саутгемптон
Дувр

Брайтон
Портленд Портсмут

Пензанс Плимут
Дартмут

ПРОЛИВ ЛА-МАНШ

A Soviet map, published in 1980, showing military locations, both British and American, in Britain plexes such as Grangemouth, Teesside, Stanlow/Ellesmere Port, Milford Haven, Fawley and the Thames estuary. North Sea oil facilities in Scotland, North East England and East Anglia would be attacked, as would the major coal mines in, for example, Yorkshire, Central Scotland and the East Midlands. Larger power stations such as Drax, Eggborough and Tilbury would be potential targets – destruction of just five large 2000 MW power stations would reduce total generating capacity by nearly twenty per cent.

(c) Communications centres would be targeted specifically if not already included in other attack plans. Some emphasis would probably be placed on major bridges such as the Severn and Forth Bridges. An attack on the former could cut the M5 as well as M4 and an attack with a large warhead on the Rosyth naval dockyard could also destroy the Forth road and rail bridges. Other targets would be rail centres such as Crewe and Doncaster, the latter significant because a single detonation could destroy a rail junction, power station and the town with its engineering works and also cut the A1(M) and M18. The M5/6 interchange near Birmingham and the M61/62/63 interchange near Bolton would also be potential targets.

Targeting options

The discussion of targets given so far is a long way from being the only approach. There are a number of different options and it is instructive to consider some of them.

One of the most significant would be an attack on nuclear power stations and associated production facilities. It has been argued that a country such as the Soviet Union might refrain from such an action because the fall-out load would combine with much of the reactor contents and could be dispersed over Europe and the Soviet Union. There is certainly some truth in this, but much of the damage could be localized to Britain and Western Europe by using relatively small ground-burst weapons if these could be placed with some precision. By limiting the contamination in the upper atmosphere in this way, fall-out might be restricted largely to 500 miles or so from a particular nuclear reactor.

The Square Leg exercise postulated attacks on some nuclear power stations and they certainly make very tempting targets, a kind of collective Achilles heel for a country such as Britain. This is especially so because Britain's nuclear power plants have been built almost all round the coast of the country, so that whichever way the wind was blowing there would be considerable contamination! The most severe case would be Windscale, involving a number of reactors including the Calder Hall plant and extensive reprocessing facilities and storage ponds and silos. The prospect of dispersal of that radioactive load is appalling.

Another targeting option is to use relatively few very

'Well, gentlemen, are we agreed that twenty million dead and thirty million injured is acceptable? Right, last one through the airlock's a sissy.'

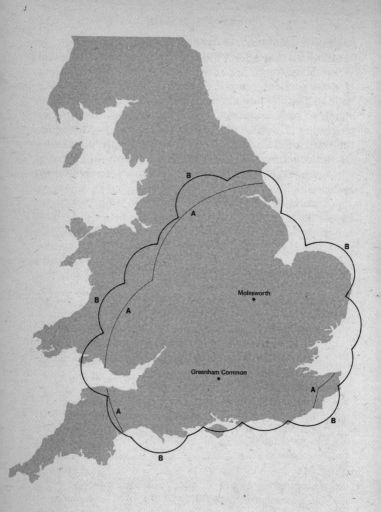

Pre-emptive attack against deployed cruise missiles.
*Missiles are to be deployed up to 100 miles from the two bases
(circles marked A). A pattern bombing attack with twenty-four 25
megaton air bursts gives overlapping zones of serious fire risk
with outer boundaries marked B.*

large warheads. As indicated earlier, it is commonly assumed that the Soviet Union has not targeted ICBMs on Western Europe. This is far from being a warranted assumption, for several Western European countries have a sufficient density of potential targets to lend themselves to such an attack. A single SS-18 fitted with a 25 megaton warhead would be a useful vehicle for destroying the strategic facilities on the Lower Clyde and would also destroy much of Glasgow. Such a warhead could destroy London, the West Midlands, Greater Manchester or West Yorkshire.

A further development of this option relates to cruise missiles deployed in Britain. These are due to be based at Molesworth and Greenham Common but, given warning of conflict, would be dispersed on mobile launchers throughout much of England and eastern Wales. Virtually the only way to destroy *all* these missiles before they were launched would be to use a pattern bombing attack on the deployment areas with very large warheads – 25 megatons or larger. Some 24 warheads could create a zone of major fire risk *covering the whole deployment area of most of England and Wales*. Careful use of additional warheads could ensure the destruction of most other targets in the area. In the process, of course, the country would be destroyed and loss of life would be almost

---

'And when it is all over what will the world be like? Our fine great buildings, our homes will exist no more. The thousands of years it took to develop our civilization will have been in vain. Our works of art will be lost. Radio, television, newspapers will disappear. There will be no means of transport. There will be no hospitals. No help can be expected for the few mutilated survivors in any town to be sent from a neighbouring town – there will be no neighbouring towns left, no neighbours, there will be no help, there will be no hope.'

Lord Louis Mountbatten, 1979

complete. Such an attack would still involve the use of less than fifteen per cent of Soviet strategic and theatre nuclear megatonnage.

CONCLUSIONS

This discussion must be considered to be no more than an introduction. It should be taken together with the next chapters which consider the effects of nuclear weapons and the current state of civil defence preparations. The list of targets given here does suggest, though, that government estimates of 200 megaton attacks are of dubious validity. We should expect any attack to be much larger.

REFERENCES

NATO (1978). *Facts and Figures*. NATO, Brussels.

Ministry of Defence (1981). *Britain and NATO*. Ministry of Defence, London.

Wheeler, B. C. (1979). *Air Forces of the World*. Ian Allan, London.

International Institute for Strategic Studies (1981). *Strategic Survey 1980–81*. IISS, London.

Lee, C. (1981). *The Final Decade*. Hamish Hamilton, London.

Ball, D. (1981). 'Counterforce Targeting: How New? How Viable?' *Arms Control Today*, Volume II, No. 2, February 1981.

Goodwin, P. (1981). *Nuclear War – The Facts on Our Survival*. Ash & Grant, London.

Laurie, P. (1979). *Beneath the City Streets*. Granada, London.

United Nations Secretary-General (1980). *Comprehensive Study on Nuclear Weapons*. UNO, New York.

New Statesman (1980). Serial articles on home defence exercises, September–November 1980. London.

Stockholm International Peace Research Institute (1980). *World Armaments and Disarmament: SIPRI Yearbook 1980*. Taylor & Francis, London.

6
Short-term Effects of Nuclear Attack

In the previous sections we reviewed the nuclear arsenals now available for use, the ways in which a large-scale nuclear war might come about, and the kind of attack Britain would probably suffer. We now turn our attention to the short-term effects of such an attack (that is up to about a month after the attack). We will attempt to illustrate the devastating nature of these effects through a series of concrete case studies. Before we do that, however, we must briefly review the characteristics of nuclear weapons.

A CHANGE OF SCALE

The power of a bomb is measured in terms of the number of tons of TNT that would be needed to produce the same-sized explosion. It is very important to grasp the scale of the effects that we are dealing with in regard to nuclear weapons. The authors of the Stockholm International Peace Research Institute's book *Arms Uncontrolled* put the pertinent facts clearly.

. . . The first nuclear bombs were 1000 times more powerful than the largest conventional bombs ever made. And the first thermonuclear bombs were 1000 times more powerful than the first nuclear bombs. There was therefore a million-fold increase in the destructive power of weapons in the space of a decade. A single thermonuclear weapon could now be made so powerful as to exceed in explosive power that of all the explosives used by all the combatants during World War II.

A 1-kiloton weapon, therefore, has the power of 1000 tons of TNT, and a 1-megaton weapon has the power of 1,000,000 tons of TNT.

It may help to have a different example of such a change of scale. Imagine concentrating on this paragraph for ten seconds, a thousand seconds, or a million seconds. Can you guess what the differences would be? Ten seconds gives you time to read the paragraph, 16.6 *minutes* gives you rather too long a period of study, but a million seconds is *11.6 days*. The general point is that we are not accustomed to dealing with changes of this scale, particularly if they come about with the speed of the development of nuclear weapons.

THE MAIN CHARACTERISTICS OF NUCLEAR WEAPONS

The bombs which fell on Hiroshima and Nagasaki in 1945 were based on the break-up (fission) of atoms of uranium and plutonium respectively. The uranium and plutonium used spontaneously breaks up and emits small particles called neutrons. When a sufficient (critical) mass of such material is brought together enough of these neutrons hit and break up other atoms for a chain reaction of fissions to occur. This releases enormous amounts of energy. The power of such weapons can be thousands of times that of conventional bombs, but problems of bringing sub-critical masses of material together limits the practical size possible.

In thermonuclear weapons a fission bomb is used to create conditions under which fusion (joining-up) of different forms of hydrogen can occur. Fusion releases even more energy for the same weight of charge. Moreover, it is possible to use neutrons produced in the fusion process to initiate more fissions in the common form of uranium. There is no limit, apart from convenience, to the possible size of such thermonuclear weapons. It should be noted, however, that the blast damage caused by nuclear weapons does not increase in direct proportion to increasing size of bomb. Military planners therefore often prefer to use a number of small warheads which in total cause more damage than an equivalent megatonnage delivered in one warhead.

All nuclear explosions at or near ground level produce energy in roughly the following percentages:

35 as light and heat,
45 as blast and shock,
 5 as initial nuclear radiations,
and 15 as residual nuclear radiations from fission products.

Light, heat, blast and shock are caused by conventional explosives. Only nuclear explosions cause nuclear radiation. Initial nuclear radiations are radiations which occur within a minute of detonation. These are important in smaller nuclear weapons; but in larger weapons the other bomb effects are so strong near the point of detonation that people are almost inevitably killed by these anyway if exposed to the radiation effect. The initial radiations are powerful and can cause material they hit to become radioactive. Residual nuclear radiations are radiations emitted after one minute. These come from the 'fall-out' which is discussed below. Most nuclear radiation in thermonuclear weapons comes from the fission processes, and commonly this is taken to produce fifty per cent of the weapon's power.

If a nuclear weapon is exploded high enough in the air for the fireball caused by the detonation *not* to come into significant contact with the surface it is said to be an *air burst*. As little of the energy is used at the surface directly below the detonation, most of it is available to spread out from the explosion. On the other hand, if a significant part of the fireball *does* come into contact with the surface, energy is used in large amounts near the point of detonation. A *ground-burst* weapon, for example, produces a crater around the point of impact. Naturally, therefore, there will be less energy available to spread destruction out away from the explosion (blast damage ranges being reduced by thirty per cent, and thermal radiation ranges by fifty per cent in Home Office publications).

Such ground bursts also have another major feature. Soil taken up in the fireball attaches to the radioactive bomb products. This leads to large amounts of radioactive 'fall-out' coming directly back down to the earth from the bomb cloud. The distribution of such fall-out is dependent on the prevailing weather conditions, but is usually assumed to form an elongated plume downwind from the point of the explosion. The fall-out is heaviest near the explosion and tails off progressively downwind as the cloud empties its larger particles. Much of the residual radioactive material from surface bursts does not, however, fall directly back to earth. It therefore forms a delayed and far more widely-distributed dangerous fall-out later. The same is true for radioactive material from an air burst, although part of this may be brought down from the bomb cloud by rain or snow. The fall-out pattern for water surface bursts or shallow underwater bursts is more complex. Yet, heavy fall-out can result from such bursts. We must note in particular that bursts in sea water can lead to fall-out with heavy induced radiation from the sodium of the sea water.

In summary, we can say that nuclear weapons differ from conventional weapons firstly because of the size of the effects. Secondly, it is clear that the thermal radiation from a nuclear explosion is much greater than from conventional explosions. Thirdly, only nuclear weapons produce nuclear radiation. Finally, it is becoming more widely known that an electromagnetic pulse is emitted from nuclear explosions. This can seriously damage electronic equipment (for example in ground communication systems).

NUCLEAR RADIATION AND ITS EFFECTS ON PEOPLE

Nuclear radiation from these weapons takes a variety of forms – alpha and beta particles, gamma rays and neutrons. These different forms of radiation have different characteristics and different effects on body tissue. For our purposes here it is sufficient to note that there is a measure called the rem (roentgen equivalent man) which provides a direct indication of the biological dose of radiation. In this chapter we will not deal with the long-term danger from delayed fall-out or that from contact or ingestion of radioactive material. We will just concentrate on what is called 'whole body' radiation from gamma rays coming (from a distance) from fall-out. Some very easy rules can help us to understand the effects. The intensity of the radiation decays in relation to the inverse of the square of the distance from the source. Thus, if the distance is doubled the radiation intensity is cut by a quarter (also placing dense material between the body and the source cuts radiation more than the same thickness of air). Additionally, radiation intensity decays over time in the relationship of decay by a factor of ten as time lengthens by a factor of seven. Thus, a radiation level of

100 rem per hour from the complete fall-out will drop to 10 rem per hour after seven hours and to 1 rem per hour after two days. Clearly, with such rules it is possible to gain an overall idea of what dosages of radiation people are likely to receive in different fall-out and sheltering conditions.

What then are the short-term medical effects of such radiation? We can summarize in the following way for radiation received quickly. If from 1 to 50 rems are received there are no observable medical symptoms at the time. From 50 to 200 rems, less than half of the people exposed will vomit soon after exposure and most will exhibit no further symptoms. From 200 to 450 rems more than half the people will vomit soon after exposure, and be ill for several days. Following a period of one to three weeks of apparent recovery, more than half these people will experience loss of hair followed by a moderately severe illness due mainly to damage to the blood-forming tissues of the bone marrow. More than half the exposed people will survive. From 450 to 600 rems there will be the same effects as for 200 to 450 rems, but in a more severe form. The initial illness is longer, the latent period shorter, and the complications more difficult. Less than half will survive. Above 600 rems the effects are even more rapid and death is probable. At levels of above about 1000 rems the person dies rapidly and nothing can be done. Treatment of these short-term effects, where it is possible, is difficult and expensive. It will not be generally available after an attack.

The types of effect we must keep in mind

It is common to find people concerned only with the effects of blast damage from nuclear weapons, whilst it is quite clear that equal weight should be given to the much less easily measurable medical, economic, social or ecological consequences of an attack.

Given that we have to take this broad view, it is

important that we recognize the major uncertainties in the estimates that we are able to make. This very important issue has been reviewed in the United States Congress Office of Technology Assessment's Study on *The Effects of Nuclear War*. In their opinion there are *three levels* of uncertainty. First, there are uncertainties because of the assumptions we have to make about the attack: size of bomb, location of targets, weather and so on. Second, there are uncertainties about effects that *will* take place, but whose magnitude cannot be calculated. These include the effects of fires, the shortage of medical care, and the extent to which economic disruption will magnify economic damage. Finally, there are effects which *may* occur, but whose likelihood is as incalculable as their magnitude. These include the possibility of a long economic decline, political disintegration, epidemics and ecological disasters.

With that in mind we will turn our attention to a series of case studies of increasing severity of attack. At the end of the chapter we will then return to the implications for Britain of the kind of attack we are likely to suffer.

A small weapon air-burst on a single city

Hiroshima lies near the southern end of the main Japanese island of Honshu. In 1945 it was a busy city and port, and a major military base. The city was built on a flat delta and divided by many river branches which ran through it into the sea. Hills lie to the north east and north west of the delta and the city limits extended up to the hills to encompass about twenty-six square miles. However, only about thirteen square miles were built-up. The four square miles of residential, commerical and military buildings which formed the centre of the city contained about three-fifths of the total population.

Personal accounts of the effects of the atomic bombing on the people of Hiroshima and Nagasaki have been given in many publications – from John Hersey's *Hiroshima* through to the recent *Unforgettable Fire*. It is most important to read these books carefully for, as Lawrence McGinty put it in his recent *New Scientist* book review 'Memories to remind us':

> . . . the vision of nuclear war that heads of state and military strategists conjure up is a lie . . . to tell the truth would be to make pacifists of us all, or at least to convince us that a nuclear war is such a disgusting inhumanity that no political advantage is worth having if it can be won only at the risk of nuclear obliteration . . . that's why . . . these books will change your life. Both of them – *Unforgettable Fire* and *Children of Hiroshima* – tell a truth that few can reveal: what it is like to be a victim of nuclear war. . .

What follows, then, is to be seen as a supplement to such essential reading.

According to the 1977 International Review Symposium, *Call from Hibakusha of Hiroshima and Nagasaki* the bomb that was air-burst over the centre of Hiroshima had the power of about 12,000 tons of TNT. By the end of 1945 it had caused the death of 140,000 of the 350,000 people in the city on that day (though both of these figures are uncertain because of the chaos and destruction).

The official British Home Office and Air Ministry report was written a few months after the bombings by people who had spent the war studying destruction. Its 'tone' is entirely different from later Home Office publications. For example, the authors comment early on, that,

> 'We, the citizens of Hiroshima, ever mindful of this cruel experience, clearly *foresee* the extinction of mankind and an end to civilization should the world drift into nuclear war. Therefore we have vowed to set aside our griefs and grudges and continuously pleaded before the peoples of the world to abolish weapons and renounce war so that we may never again repeat the tragedy of Hiroshima.'
>
> Takeshi Araki, Mayor of Hiroshima
> 6 August 1976

. . . no civilian defence services in the world could have met a disaster on this scale, and these services were in fact over-whelmed. On August 6th, the authorities in Hiroshima were making preparations to meet what they believed to be a threatened incendiary attack: *they were not prepared for a holocaust.* [Our emphasis]

As the air-raid warning system did not work properly, most people in Hiroshima were going about their normal business when the bomb detonated. The British investigators reported that people saw a 'blinding white flash in the sky'. They were then hit by thermal radiation which caused, 'severe burns on exposed skin', at 1500 yards and, 'mild burns on exposed skin,' at 2½ miles. These figures emphasize that besides the blast power and nuclear radiation, nuclear weapons produce much more thermal radiation than conventional bombs.

The blast from this small weapon spread out as a shock front (with its associated high winds) in a manner which, it was estimated, would have 'damaged British houses beyond repair' at 1 mile and produced 'major damage' at 1½ miles. Additionally, the team thought that the initial radiation would have been sufficient in itself to kill 50 per cent of the people exposed at a range of ¾ mile.

Despite more recent equivocation about the possibility of fire-storms after nuclear attacks, the United States' main report is quite clear:

. . . Practically the entire densely or moderately built-up portion of the city was levelled by blast and swept by fire. A 'fire-storm' . . . developed in Hiroshima: fires springing up almost simultaneously over the wide flat area around the centre of the city drew in air from all directions: the inrush of air easily overcame the natural ground wind. . . . The 'fire-wind' attained a maximum velocity of 30 to 40 miles per hour 2 to 3 hours after the explosion. The 'fire-wind' and the symmetry of the built-up centre of the city gave a roughly circular shape to the 4.4 square miles which were almost completely burnt out.

The fire-storm produced a second problem. In the 1977 International Symposium it is reported that,

Generally, fire-storms are accompanied by rain because . . .
moisture is considered to condense around the particles of
carbon and other matter produced by the fire, when they come
into contact with the cold air above. In fact, a considerable
amount of radioactive 'black rain' fell in Hiroshima over a wide
area . . .

The original observers, however, were struck above all by
the scale of the casualties. The British report suggests a
death rate of 95 per cent out to ¼ mile from the explosion,
85 per cent from ¼ to ½ mile, 58 per cent from ½ to ¾,
and 35 per cent from ¾ to 1 mile. Naturally, with this scale
of fatalities, a very large percentage of the families involved were affected by death or injury. Some idea of the
scale of deaths can be gained from the simple comparison
given in the British report:

. . . For comparison, the number of those killed by air attack
during the whole war in London was 30,000, and the number of
those killed throughout Great Britain, including London was
60,000.

The effect of the explosion did not stop with destruction of
buildings and deaths and injuries. The main United States
report shows how the medical services were effectively
eliminated:

. . . Of more than 200 doctors in Hiroshima before the attack,
over 90 per cent were casualties and only about 30 physicians
were able to perform their normal duties a month after the raid.
Out of 1780 nurses, 1654 were killed or injured . . . . Only three
out of 45 civilian hospitals could be used, and two large Army
hospitals were rendered unusable . . .

Such devastation bit deep into the normal organizations
required for a city to function. As another detailed United
States report notes:

The report of the Medical Division on the effects of the atomic
bomb leads to certain definite conclusions. The public health
and sanitary aspects of Hiroshima and Nagasaki as a result of
atomic bombings varied little from the effects of demolition and

incendiary raids seen in other Japanese cities. From a purely medical aspect, however, there was a very wide difference in the . . . psychological reaction of the general population. . . . The psychological effects were evident by the mass exodus of the people to outlying areas with little regard for care of the casualties, the complete apathy of the population, the inability of the public authorities towards restoration of sanitary facilities and the supply of an adequate and safe water supply.

All of this, it must be stressed, is in regard to a single small bomb on a city which was rapidly given significant help from outside.

We will return to the medical consequences of this bombing in a later chapter. On looking at the original scientific reports there are perhaps two comments by the British investigators which best convey the effect of this bomb:

. . . Such figures could be multiplied and become meaningless: the reader who finds them so may prefer a summary analogy. This is that the scale of destruction expected would be that which would befall a model town built to the scale of Gulliver's Lilliput, 1 inch to the foot, if there were exploded above it a bomb more than twice as large as the largest British 'blockbuster', which with its case weighed about six tons.

and,

. . . some tribute should be paid to isolated feats of restoration. . . . *Nevertheless, the larger impression which both cities make is of having sunk, in an instant and without a struggle, to the most primitive existence* . . . [Our emphasis]

Enough, then, of kiloton weapons. Let us now turn to larger weapons.

What would be the effect of a 1 megaton ground burst on a modern city?

No one (as yet) has dropped a 1 megaton weapon on a city. It is necessary, therefore, to attempt to transpose knowledge of weapon effects gained from tests to see what might happen to a city. Many such analyses have been carried out by governments and, as we shall see, some of the results have been made public.

First, we need to get a general idea of the power of megaton weapons. A 1 megaton ground-burst would emit enough initial radiation to kill 50 per cent of people exposed at a distance of 1½ miles. This, however, would be irrelevant because of the lethal effect of the massive blast and heat at that distance from the detonation. Exposed people would, in fact, have their skin charred out to 5 miles and houses would be at least moderately damaged at the same range. The Home Office states that on a clear day there would be a 'main fire zone', from 1½ to 5 miles out from the detonation point. The ground-burst weapon would produce a 100-foot-deep crater 1100 feet across (in clay) with a large lip of soil piled up around it. Furthermore, there would also be a large area in which there would be very dangerous levels of radiation from the fall-out. It is clear that we are dealing here with a different order of events even from the devastation of Hiroshima.

We can gain a vivid picture of how different these effects are from those at Hiroshima if we briefly review the study of the possible effects of a 1 megaton ground-burst on Detroit, Michigan made by the Office of Technology Assessment in *The Effects of Nuclear War*. Detroit is a major transport and industrial centre with a metropolitan population of about 4.3 million people. In order to simplify the analysis it was assumed that the attack took place at night, without warning, and that only Detroit was attacked. The weapon detonated at the civil centre and the usual circles for 12, 5, 2 and 1 lbs per square inch (psi) of blast over normal pressure were calculated.

Surrounding the 1000 foot crater would be an area out to 0.6 miles in which nothing would be recognizable. Only at 1.7 miles (the 12 psi limit) from the point of detonation would any significant structures begin to be seen. Of the

70,000 people in this region almost none would survive. If the attack occurred during the day the same fate would befall 130,000 people.

In the next (5 psi) region, between 1.7 and 2.7 miles out, typical multistorey buildings would have all their walls blown away and individual houses would be destroyed. Only towards the outer edge of the ring would even heavy industrial plant be functional. Debris would clog the streets and even at the edge of this region few vehicles would remain useful. On conservative estimates, half of the 250,000 people would be killed and most of the rest injured.

In the 2 psi band from 2.7 to 4.7 miles from the point of detonation, large buildings would have lost windows and door frames. Low residential buildings would be, at least, severely damaged. Casualties amongst the 400,000 people would be 20,000 dead and 180,000 injured. There would be substantial debris in the streets, but many trucks and cars would be functional. This, however, is the region of most severe fire hazard. Perhaps five per cent of the buildings would be initially ignited. Fires would spread for at least twenty-four hours, and ultimately destroy half the buildings (but there is great uncertainty in such estimates).

The outer 1 psi band from 4.7 to 7.4 miles would show light damage to commercial structures and moderate damage to residences. Of the 600,000 people few would die, but about 150,000 would be injured. Fire ignitions would be comparatively rare and survivors perhaps in a condition to deal with them.

In total then, 220,000 people would be killed and 420,000 injured. The sensitivity of such calculations to variations in the assumptions is well illustrated here by the possible effects of thermal radiation. On a winter night perhaps one per cent of the population might be directly exposed. On a summer evening there could be 25 per cent exposed. Given the power of the thermal radiation it is not surprising that this could double the fatalities.

Casualties from fall-out were not included in the analysis. Those who did not evacuate or find adequate shelter in affected areas could receive very dangerous levels of radiation. It is also clear that many of the injured would have double or triple types of injury (radiation plus burns, burns plus mechanical wounds, radiation and burns and wounds). Such injuries are more dangerous than single injuries because burns stress the blood system, radiation affects blood formation, and mechanical injury introduces infection. All these effects could therefore act in conjunction.

The prognosis for the injured would, in any event, be bleak. The nearly half a million people injured would present an insuperable problem with *complete* facilities available. In the Detroit example 55 per cent of the total 18,000 hospital beds would be destroyed inside the 5 psi ring, and another 15 per cent severely damaged in the 5 to 2 psi ring. Thus, some 5000 beds would be available – sufficient for 1 per cent of the estimated injured. The size of the problem is indicated by the fact that in 1977 there were about 1½ million hospital beds available in the USA, and, of these, about 1000 to 2000 were for specialist treatment of burns.

The authors of the Office of Technology Assessment study show contours for a 7-day accumulated radiation dose assuming a 15 mph wind. The 90 rem outer contour is about 250 miles long, the 300 rem contour 150 miles long, the 900 rem contour 80 miles long and the 3000 rem contour 30 miles long. Decay to acceptable peacetime levels would take 3 years in the outer contour and 8 to 10 years in the inner contour. *Home Office information to the public about fall-out dust remaining dangerous for 'some days' should be judged against this kind of information.*

What would be the effect of an attack deliberately aimed at oil refineries?

As we have learnt to our cost in recent years, oil is vital to the economies of the developed world. Oil refineries are also vulnerable installations, and capacity is concentrated. The USA refines about 17.9 million barrels per day of crude in 288 refineries. The USSR refines about 11.0 million barrels in 59 refineries (figures for the late 1970s).

In the Office of Technology Assessment Study mentioned previously, an independent analyst designed a Soviet attack on the USA under two conditions: that only ten strategic nuclear delivery vehicles were to be used, and economic damage was to be maximized. No account was taken of civilian casualties. The Defence Department then worked out the consequences.

MIRVed missiles were used to maximize damage per missile. Thus, eight 1 megaton warheads were assumed for each of ten SS-18 ICBMs. This attack could therefore hit eight targets in each of ten 'footprints' (areas over which the IRVs could spread from each missile). Essentially, the attack struck the 77 largest-capacity refineries and the three remaining warheads double-targeted the largest refineries in relevant footprints.

The 80 warheads destroyed 64 per cent of the United States petroleum-refining capacity in this simulated attack. Additionally, as the weapons were large and air burst and refineries are near major urban centres, the attack also killed five million people (though the assumptions that produced this casualty figure look optimistic). Naturally, the attack also caused much other economic damage. For example, many complex petrochemical production plants are located in major ports. Thus, both petrochemical production and port facilities were damaged in the strike. The authors tried to imagine what the effects might be on the ground:

. . . Fires at refineries could not be extinguished because of intense heat, local fallout, an inadequate supply of chemicals to use on petroleum fires, and roads blocked by rubble and evacuees . . . firestorms or conflagrations might begin, in this case supported by thousands of tons of gasoline . . .

In the British context one is left to reflect on the vulnerability of, say, Fawley or Milford Haven.

Even such a small attack on the United States would leave it with only one third of its refining capacity, and major damage to its ports – which could well restrict importing. The government would have to ration. Many jobs would be directly at risk. Many people would have great difficulty in getting to work. The effects would spread to land values and small businesses. The post-attack society would be radically changed, and the study shows that a similar attack by the United States on the Soviet Union would be just as damaging.

We will find later (Chapter 8) that heavier attacks could easily be designed to remove almost all the refining capacity, and that the same could be done for many other industries.

What would happen if a nuclear power station was attacked with a nuclear weapon?

The recent Israeli attack on Iraq's nuclear power station near Baghdad has highlighted a possibility that has begun to trouble many people in recent years. Clearly, an attacker could target nuclear power stations and eliminate power-generating capacity with an enhanced fall-out 'bonus'.

Fetter and Tsipis have looked carefully at the problem in their article on 'Catastrophic Releases of Radioactivity'. They comment,

. . . the detonation of a weapon on a reactor is many times more damaging than the detonation of a weapon on the ground. The nuclear attack turns the reactor into a devastating radiological weapon.

They proceed to examine the case in which a 1megaton thermonuclear weapon is detonated on a 1 gigawatt (1000 megawatt) nuclear reactor. They conclude that the effect (even on conservative assumptions) is far worse than for the bomb alone:

. . . The area in which the dose would remain 2 rem per year for a year is 25,000 square miles, or 20 times larger. An area of 180 square miles would continue for more than a century to expose any occupant to a dose of at least 2 rem per year. Such an area would be a permanent monument to the catastrophe.

This, it must be emphasized, is the effect of *one* bomb on *one* reactor. Britain has twenty-two operational nuclear plants, most with twin reactors.

THE REALITY OF NUCLEAR WAR

Most reasonable human beings will, no doubt, be hoping that the catalogue of horrors given in these case studies will stop here. Yet, we have to take the illustrations one stage further to grasp the reality of modern war. The plain fact is that *none* of these examples conveys what general nuclear war will really be like. Frank Barnaby, the Director of the Stockholm International Peace Research Institute, put the matter quite simply in his study on *The Nuclear Arms Race*. He stated that,

All the major cities in the Northern Hemisphere, where most nuclear warheads are aimed, would be destroyed (on average, *each* is targeted by the equivalent of some 2000 Hiroshima bombs).

Clearly, we must go on to give an idea of what such an attack on a city would be like (and we are not, of course, dealing here with an attack on a single city but a major attack which would prevent outside assistance becoming available). Once again it is possible to give an official study as an example. In 1979 the United States Arms Control and Disarmament Agency issued a report on the *Effects of Nuclear War*. One section deals with 'Effects of General Nuclear War'. The scenario assumed strategic forces as in a SALT II agreement, and a Soviet strike on US strategic forces, military bases and industry, followed by a similar US attack on the USSR. We will review the attack on Moscow.

The severity of the attack on Moscow was such that *60 warheads* came down on it with, in total, about *1400 times* the tonnage used on Hiroshima. Peak overpressures were such that nothing was left standing in downtown Moscow, and the 5 psi overpressure contour covered 85 to 90 per cent of the total urban housing. It was assumed that fires would burn out almost all of this area. Additionally, if the weapons were all ground-burst.

. . . Almost the entire city is covered by [maximum dose contours of] more than 5000 rems and, in some parts of the city, the dose is above 30,000 rems. . . . Clearly, no human being exposed to the kind of radiation dose that would exist in Moscow could survive. People in the area who were very well sheltered could have some chance if they stayed inside for several months.

In total, the study concludes that in the short term, each side loses from 25 to 100 million dead, from 65 to 90 per cent of industry is destroyed, their 200 largest cities are destroyed, and 80 per cent of all cities of over 25,000 people are attacked by at least one weapon. The Director of the authoritative Stockholm Institute spells out the same kind of message:

Most of the urban population there (Northern Hemisphere) would be killed by blast and fire, the rural population by radiation from fallout.
Many millions of people in the Southern Hemisphere would be killed by radiation.

This is what we are really talking about in our discussions of modern nuclear war.

CONCLUSIONS: IMPLICATIONS FOR BRITAIN

In Chapter 5 we argued that if a nuclear war started there was every reason to expect that Britain would be hit very heavily. Given our strategic position and the variety of targets here, it would be stupid of the Russians *not* to attack us heavily. Additionally, their military doctrine suggests that is exactly what they would do if war came.

It often appears that 'official' estimates are that Britain would suffer an attack weight of about 200 megatons. In this regard it is interesting to note what Lewis said (in his well-known article, 'Prompt and Delayed Effects of Nuclear War') of such an attack on a much larger target:

. . . a well-planned American attack of even 200 equivalent megatons could still promptly kill a fifth of the USSR's population and destroy more than two-thirds of its industry . . .

In our opinion, of course, there is no reason to accept that the attack *would* be limited to 200 megatons, but for the sake of illustration let us use that figure for the present. What kind of effects would the rapid delivery of that level of megatonnage have on Britain?

The facts outlined in this chapter can leave little room for doubt – the country would be devastated. We will go into the details in the next chapter, in particular when we examine what the Home Office expects to happen. The overall picture is simple enough to grasp – destroyed cities, millions of dead and injured, and refugees beginning to attempt to cope with an utterly changed world.

Whilst there are no official estimates available to us, the literature is full of suggestions on the casualties. These give us an idea of the *scale* of the total effects to be expected. Try to imagine a Britain which almost overnight had its population reduced to 20 million, 12 million or even 5 million people!

Even now some readers may have difficulty in accepting the argument put forward here. They might find it helpful to reflect on the reasons why some men – Mountbatten, Carver, Zuckerman – who are no strangers to military matters, have spoken out so loudly against nuclear weapons in recent years.

It is also worth noting that, whilst we have stuck to the official reports here, Peter Goodwin in his recent book *Nuclear War: The Facts on Our Survival* has, in his more detailed treatment, attempted to relate the Office of

Technology Assessment study to our position in Britain. Thus, for example, in regard to the attack on oil refineries, he shows that the 20 British refineries could have their capacity reduced by more than two-thirds by an attack with just 12 warheads. In regard to a large-scale attack he comments,

If an available arsenal of some 140 weapons were to be launched against Britain, it is clear . . . that the future existence of civilisation in Britain would be seriously in question.

He, in fact, concludes that this level of attack would leave about 16 million survivors in the short term. But he then continues,

. . . If a significant proportion of the available Warsaw Pact nuclear arsenal available for use against Britain were ever actually used, the chances that *anybody* would see again civilisation as we now know it, must be regarded as truly remote.

Goodwin, we must emphasize, is a physicist who makes it quite clear that he is only interested in presentation of the facts. That has also been *our* aim, and our conclusion is the same as his.

REFERENCES

Arms Control and Disarmament Agency (1979). *The Effects of Nuclear War*. State Department, Washington D.C.

Barnaby, F. and Huisken, R. (1975). *Arms Uncontrolled*. Stockholm International Peace Research Institute, Sweden. Harvard University Press.

Barnaby, F. (1981). *The Nuclear Arms Race*, Peace Studies Papers No. 4. School of Peace Studies, University of Bradford.

Broad, W. J. (1981). 'Nuclear Pulse (1): Awakening to the Chaos Factor', *Science*, 212, pp.1009–12.

Clarke, R. (1978). *Britain and Thermonuclear War: The Chances of Survival*, Ph.D. thesis. University of Lancaster.

FEMA Attack Environment Manual (1980), Chapter 5. *What the*

Planner Needs to Know About Initial Nuclear Radiation. Federal Emergency Management Agency, Publication CPG 2-1A5, Washington D.C.

Fetter, S. A. and Tsipis, K. (1981). 'Catastrophic Releases of Radioactivity', *Scientific American* 224 (4) pp.33–9.

Glasstone, S. and Dolan, P. J. (1980). *The Effects of Nuclear Weapons.* United States Department of Defense and Department of Energy. Published by Castle House, Tunbridge Wells, UK.

Goodwin P. (1981). *Nuclear War: The Facts on Our Survival.* Ash and Grant, London.

Hersey, J. (1946). *Hiroshima.* Penguin, London.

Home Office and Air Ministry (1946). *The Effects of the Atomic Bombs at Hiroshima and Nagasaki.* Report of the British Mission to Japan. HMSO, London.

Home Office (1980). *Nuclear Weapons.* HMSO, London.

Japan Broadcasting Corporation (1981). *Unforgettable Fire.* Published by Wildwood House, London.

Japan National Preparatory Committee (1979). *Call from Hibakusha of Hiroshima and Nagasaki*: Proceedings of the International Symposium on the Damage and After-Effects of the Atomic Bombing of Hiroshima and Nagasaki, 21st July – 9th August 1977, Tokyo, Hiroshima and Nagasaki. Pergamon Press, Oxford.

Lewis, K. N. (1979). 'The Prompt and Delayed Effects of Nuclear War', *Scientific American* 241 (1) pp. 27–39.

McGinty, L. (1981). 'Memories to remind us', *New Scientist*, 11 June, p.704.

Office of Technology Assessment (1980). *The Effects of Nuclear War.* Congress of the United States. Published by Croom Helm, London.

United States Strategic Bombing Survey (1946). 'The Effects of Atomic Bombs on Hiroshima and Nagasaki', *Pacific War*, No. 3. United States Government Printing Office, Washington D.C.

United States Strategic Bombing Survey (1946). 'The Effects of Atomic Bombs on Health and Medical Services in Hiroshima and Nagasaki', *Pacific War*, No. 13. United States Government Printing Office, Washington D.C.

7

Civil Defence in a
Nuclear War?

We started Part 2 of this book with a description of the kind of attack which we think Britain would suffer if a nuclear war with the Soviet Union actually occurred. In the last chapter we tried to give an impression of what such an attack would mean for people here. We now turn to the much debated question of the potential value of Civil Defence in such circumstances.

For simplicity we will attempt to look first at what can be done. We will do this by examining Civil Defence in some other countries. We will then turn to what has been done here. This will lead us, finally, to a detailed examination of what the Home Office actually expects to happen in a nuclear attack.

We must begin, unfortunately, with a word of caution. To put it at its mildest, there is a widespread feeling that the Home Office has been somewhat optimistic about the effects of nuclear weapons in the publications it has produced for the general public.

Much criticism has been directed at *Protect and Survive*, but the more recent *Domestic Nuclear Shelters* is just as worrying. If we recall the facts set out in the last chapter (radioactive contamination lasting years), it does seem at best careless to make, without any qualification, statements such as, '. . . Fallout dust remains radioactive for some days after the explosion – and can, in certain circumstances, still be dangerous after several weeks.' or '. . . But with air-burst weapons there is no dangerous radioactive fallout – since the fireball does not touch the ground no earth is sucked up.'

Whilst it must be acknowledged that condensing technical material for a non-scientific audience is difficult, and the odd mistake is surely possible, there is reason to suspect that an over-optimistic gloss has been pervasive. In particular, as we shall see later, Home Office material produced for official purposes exhibits a contrasting stark realism.

CIVIL DEFENCE IN SWITZERLAND

Given the characteristics of nuclear weapons, there are very few options available to any government in regard to Civil Defence policy. We will look first at Switzerland, which is widely acknowledged to have one of the best Civil Defence systems in the world. This will allow us to examine one clear-cut option for the general public – in-place blast sheltering. Before we discuss that policy, however, we need to understand the context in which it is set.

Switzerland has a long history of neutrality. This is not in any way a 'soft-option' policy. Although Switzerland has a fine record in regard to attempting to mitigate the effects of war (the Red Cross) and in attempting to assist the disarmament process, its neutrality is *armed* neutrality. In fact, as the Swiss official documents make clear, the aim is to maintain their full and free independence. They see neutrality as the best means of achieving that aim. Civil Defence, along with foreign policy, the armed forces, economic policy and so on, fits into this hard-headed concept.

It is no surprise, therefore, to find that the Swiss feel that they must be prepared for a possible nuclear attack, or at least from the side-effects (radioactivity, stray missiles) of a European nuclear war. In such circumstances they reject the idea of evacuation of the urban population. Their policy is based on the concept of a designated place

'It says "If you know of a better 'ole don't go to it."'

in a blast shelter *for everyone.* Whilst they accept that their shelters are inadequate near a nuclear explosion, they feel that their 1 atmosphere (14.7 pounds per square inch) overpressure standard would protect people from blast at a range of 1.6 miles from a 1 megaton explosion. The thick walls of the shelter would also substantially attenuate levels of outside radiation.

Shelter building has been going on for many years, and shelters of some sort are now available for nine tenths of the population. There is, furthermore, a substantial and efficient Civil Defence organization to provide the necessary command and control, medical facilities, stockpiles (and so on) needed. The Swiss are also aware of deficiencies in the system and will certainly continue to invest heavily in Civil Defence in order to be better prepared – as they see it.

If we set aside possible criticisms – such as whether Swiss shelters would be adequate in the kind of attack set out for Moscow in the last chapter, or how survivors might fare in the longer term – there is still one very important point that must be made *even* in regard to the Swiss system. Some warning time is needed to get the people into the shelters – therefore the availability of that warning is assumed. As a recent Swiss official review stated:

. . . Our CD conception proceeds from the assumption that the first employment of means of mass destruction will be preceded by increased political or military activities abroad, rendering an early warning of days or weeks.

Should that assumption be violated, or the period of tension be prolonged and complex, would the people be in their shelters when the attack came?

SOVIET CIVIL DEFENCE

Civil Defence in the Soviet Union, like that of Switzerland, is a substantial long-term programme; but it is based on a different policy for the majority of the urban population. This policy is mass urban evacuation (or relocation) and then protection against fall-out in the new location.

It has to be clearly stated, again, that the Soviet Civil Defence system is integrated into the overall security policy. It is said to be both a humanitarian effort and a means of helping to convince possible adversaries that the Soviet Union cannot be defeated. About 100,000 full-time personnel are thought to run the system, and the general population are supposed to be highly involved. There are, however, doubts about the effectiveness of implementation of Civil Defence policies in different parts of the country.

Some blast sheltering is provided for the leadership, and at key economic installations. There is also some blast sheltering for the urban population. There is no doubt, however, that the major policy for the urban population is evacuation. This presents enormous difficulties. For example, would it be possible to actually carry out a major mass urban evacuation? Could expedient shelters be built in mid-winter? What would be the response of adversaries if they detected an evacuation? Would they think it a prelude to an attack on them?

Nevertheless, it is surely true that if the missiles fell on the cities and the population was in good fall-out shelters elsewhere, immediate casualties would be reduced. Yet, reservations must remain. First, there really is little that can be done to protect industry, so the economic basis of the society (and therefore its longer-term prospects) would be severely damaged. Second, in an age of overkill a malevolent opponent could surely target the relocated population as well.

As a United States Central Intelligence Agency report stated in 1978, '. . . They cannot have confidence . . . in the degree of protection their civil defences would afford them, given the many uncertainties attendant to a nuclear exchange.' Thus, even in a large country, fall-out sheltering is not necessarily a satisfactory Civil Defence policy.

CIVIL DEFENCE IN THE UNITED STATES

The Civil Defence programme in the United States has undergone numerous changes in organization and policy since 1946. It has also been subject to frequent examination in Congressional studies and hearings. The story is too complex to be recounted in detail here; but it is, essentially, a tale of Civil Defence enthusiasts being restricted by an unbelieving Congress which just would not vote adequate money for the policies envisaged.

From our point of view it is important to understand that from the early 1960s through the 1970s the programme was dominated by President Kennedy's 'insurance policy' concept. This held that Civil Defence, '. . . cannot be obtained cheaply, . . . cannot give assurance of blast protection . . . cannot deter a nuclear attack.' Yet as deterrence assumed rational acts by rational men and accidents could occur, '. . . civil defence can be readily justifiable – as insurance for the civilian population in case of an enemy miscalculation.'

As we shall see later, in regard to British Civil Defence, what the insurance policy rationale does not do is to specify how much insurance is to be paid, and for what. In fact the author of a major study of American Civil Defence policies between 1945 and 1975 was forced to conclude that at the end of his period of study, the United States still '. . . had only a rudimentary civil defence system . . .'. In the mid-1970s, however, a renewed public debate broke out in the United States on Civil Defence. This was precipitated by a number of factors such as the supposed efficiency of the Soviet Civil Defence system, and the rethinking of the United States' defence policy. A long series of new Congressional hearings was held in which advocates and critics of Civil Defence for nuclear war put their cases in detail. Eventually, President Carter issued Presidential Directive 41, which changed the old insurance policy concept by linking Civil Defence to the strategic balance and by making large-scale urban evacuation a major new element of American Civil Defence.

Subsequently the newly organized American Federal Emergency Management Agency has argued that an investment of about $2640 million over seven years on crisis relocation planning and support capabilities would save 80 per cent of the United States population in a major Soviet attack in the mid-1980s. Naturally, opponents of such ideas point to the same problems for American evacuation plans as they had suggested for Soviet evacuation plans. And though the situation may change as President Reagan's appointees press their policies, it is fair to say that Congress has, to date, still not been convinced of the utility of massive Civil Defence expenditure.

A good example of the tough opposition that the Civil Defence lobby faces in the United States can be found in Kaplan's work. Referring to a major study which suggested that the Soviet Civil Defence system was effective, Kaplan said,

. . . the basic analysis, common to virtually all studies expressing concern over Soviet civil defence . . . suffers from unrealistic assumptions, leaps of faith, violations of logic and a superficial understanding of the dynamics of a national economy . . .

He continued later, in regard to assumptions that what was in the Soviet literature actually happened on the ground,

Several Soviet sources stress . . . the installing of 'deep faith' in the effectiveness of civil defence measures, . . . Yet this seems to have failed. A standard Russian joke goes: What do you do when you hear the alert? Put on a sheet and crawl to the cemetery –slowly. Why slowly? So you don't spread panic! . . .'

BRITISH CIVIL DEFENCE

That brief survey of three other Civil Defence systems was intended to outline something of the range of policies which might be chosen, and some of the ways in which they might be pursued. How does British Civil Defence fit into that overall picture?

It is necessary, first, to understand a little history. Peter Laurie, who is far from unsympathetic towards Civil Defence, put the crucial facts thus:

. . . as the realisation of the very heavy pre-emptive strikes that would be sent against Britain as the island base of the NATO alliance bit into the official and the public mind, so the usefulness of the Civil Defence Corps . . . became difficult to accept . . .

So in 1968 Mr Callaghan, the Home Secretary, abolished the Corps and put Civil Defence on a 'care and maintenance' basis. Significantly, he used the 'insurance policy' rationale to justify his action. This basic rationale appears to have remained through the reorganization of the early 1970s and the recent modest increase in finance for Civil Defence.

Minimal study of *Protect and Survive* will show that British Civil Defence policy for the general public is based on the concept of *in-place fall-out sheltering*. The public are to stay at home and build fall-out shelters if an attack is threatened. Such shelters will not protect against the blast effect of nuclear weapons, but if undamaged by blast or fire they can give some protection against radiation. The idea, simply, is that the material of the shelter will attenuate the outside radiation. Thus, if the outside radiation is 30 rem per hour, a shelter with a protective factor of 15 would cut that to 2 rem per hour. If people stay inside their shelters until radiation levels drop it is hoped that casualties will be substantially reduced.

As building blast shelters for everyone is very expensive and evacuation is of uncertain value (particularly in a small, heavily targeted country) this might seem a reasonable policy choice. Many reservations are, however, in order. It has to be said, for example, that the policy involves *accepting massive urban casualties if people stay put in cities, and chaos (and massive casualties) if they choose not to do so.*

The British Civil Defence back-up organization also leaves a great deal to be desired. The command-and-control system, for example, is based on twenty-four sub-regional headquarters. These headquarters then link down to county and on down to district headquarters. The lower levels will be manned by local authority officials. As a recent Conservative party pamphlet remarked scathingly,

Most districts appear to have nominated people who fill key roles, e.g. food officer, information officer, billeting officer. However, these appear to be only nominations . . .

Most districts have selected a wartime headquarters. However, many of them are above ground, many have no communications equipment installed, and at least one, situated underground, floods when it rains . . .

The pamphlet goes on to criticize the system, for example, for lack of proper radiation monitoring equipment, for lack of coordination and commitment at the centre, for an obsession with secrecy – in fact it has little that is good to say.

No doubt the recent increase in funding will go some way to remedy some of the defects. Yet, at the same time it has to be acknowledged that many local councils have been taken over recently by Labour councillors who will, no doubt, comply with their statutory responsibilities for Civil Defence, but who will also ensure that no more than the minimum is done – because they are not convinced of the value of Civil Defence in Britain.

Furthermore, it has to be said that closer study of the way the system is supposed to operate does not increase *our* confidence either. The standard publicly available Home Office text *Nuclear Weapons* suggests, for example, that,

On the explosion of a nuclear weapon, information relating to the power, location and height of burst would be reported from monitoring posts to group controls. . . . When the radiac instruments at the monitoring posts begin to record the presence of fallout, the times of arrival and, at short intervals, the dose-rates would be reported. . . . Previous predictions would be amended and further warnings would be issued to the public. . . . Detailed information about the fallout situation would be passed on to local and central government wartime headquarters . . .

Whilst it is true that one of the few parts of the British Civil Defence system to be in reasonable shape is the 10,000-strong volunteer UK Warning and Monitoring organization, that statement does not seem to take account of the probable post-attack conditions. For example, would there be only one bomb? Would the monitoring posts be intact? Would the communications actually work that smoothly? Would it be possible to produce sufficiently accurate fall-out predictions in some kinds of British weather conditions? Would the public actually be in a state to act rationally on information given to them? In short, have the authors of this piece of planning in wonderland actually taken into account what happened when the two tactical (by modern standards) bombs fell on Hiroshima and Nagasaki – let alone thought through the possible effects of a multi-megaton attack? Or have these planners fallen into the standard trap of assuming that the conditions required for their system to work will be the conditions that actually will occur?

It would be possible to write a whole chapter of such criticisms and worries about British Civil Defence, and though we shall have more to say on the assumptions regarding radiation in the next chapter, it is unnecessary to pursue the matter further here. The plain fact is that we too have a 'rudimentary' Civil Defence system, and that should not surprise us because it is exactly what we paid for. During the late 1970s expenditure was about £25 million per year and it has now been increased to about £45 million. That kind of money goes nowhere nationally.

That is what *has* been done. What *could* usefully be done? If you personally have the money you might build a blast shelter and hope that you are not cheated by the salesman, designer or builder, that no missiles fall too close, and that you would somehow survive the longer-term problems when you emerge. Most of us do not have that option, so we have to ask what else the Government might be prepared to do.

In our opinion the Government will do very little more than it is doing at present. Our first reason for believing this is financial. We believe that there are, and will continue to be, many other possibilities for Government expenditure which will be given greater priority than Civil Defence in difficult financial circumstances (not the least of these, of course, will be expenditure on armaments). Second, we believe that the Government will always be reluctant to spend a great deal more on Civil Defence because, as Peter Goodwin has argued so cogently in *Nuclear War: The Facts on Our Survival*, to do so is to call present defence policy into question. If you greatly increase the premiums doesn't it suggest that you are worried over the insurance risk? More than that, however, we believe that our Government has made very careful study of the likely immediate effects on Britain of a nuclear war and is therefore quite convinced that greatly increased Civil Defence expenditure would be a waste of national resources.

THE OFFICIAL VIEW OF THE REALITY OF NUCLEAR WAR

Some readers will have heard of plans to empty hospitals in the pre-attack period, or not to waste the fire service in the immediate aftermath of attack, or not to let doctors treat the injured. These stories derive from a set of circulars sent by the Home Office to local authorities over the last decade. The circulars instruct officials on what to expect in a nuclear attack on Britain, and how to plan for such an event. These circulars have recently become more openly available to the public and have been mentioned here and there in the press. It is instructive to attempt to see the set of circulars as a whole. We have therefore reordered the series in an attempt to picture what the government believes is likely to happen during the attack period. The titles used are exactly as in the circulars, and all quotes are direct.

We must note at the outset that the Home Office is aware of the changing strategic context that we dealt with in Part 1 of this book. Circular ES 1/1981 dated 20 March 1981 states,

. . . Changes in strategic thinking mean that we must be prepared . . . for the possibility of hostilities occurring at short notice. In future, emergency plans will have to be maintained at a higher state of readiness and be capable of dealing with a variety of forms of attack, ranging . . . to the devastating consequences of strategic nuclear attack . . . the basic essentials of plans should be capable of implementation within 48 hours.

The Home Office might perhaps accept our Part 1 sub-title 'Ready for War'!

Before we proceed to examine the details of life in post-strike Britain, readers should grasp the implication of the structure of the Civil Defence command and control system. The circular on *Machinery of Government in War* (ES 7/1973) states that,

In any future war involving the widespread use of nuclear weapons, it would be impossible to rely on the exercise of powers of government from the capital. The basis of the wartime machinery of internal government is therefore the decentralisation and concentration of all functions within 10 home defence regions. . . . Wartime regional government would be headed by Commissioners having full authority to govern . . .

Until such time as regional government could be established . . . the sub-regional headquarters would be the highest effective level of internal government . . .

As we shall see, much of 'government' decision-making would have to be far below the sub-regional level in the post-attack period. It has to be acknowledged however, that ES 7/1973 gives a reasonable description of the kind of decision-making environment many officials will have to face:

Post-attack decisions . . . should not be compared with the more deliberate and often prolonged, peacetime planning and decision-taking process of government. Inevitably post-attack plans would be crude and simple. The urgent decisions of the County Controller would be arbitrary and, to some people, would appear harsh and inequitable . . .

With that setting we can turn to the attack and its effects.

Circular ES 3/1973 sets out the *Home Defence Planning Assumptions*. It states,

. . . the scale and pattern of attack cannot be determined with precision but, whatever the scale, an attack by thermo-nuclear weapons directed against civil and military installations and against centres of population, with the attendant threat of widespread radioactive fall-out, would result in enormous casualties and extensive damage . . . solely for the purpose of survival planning, it can be assumed that the population survival rate would range from 60% in the worse affected areas to 95% in the least affected areas. On the other hand loss of essential services and productive capacity due to installation damage, loss of power supplies and lack of raw materials could be as high as 80% . . .

Few, if any, parts of the country would expect to be completely unaffected. Those parts which escaped the direct effect of explosions and subsequent radioactive fall-out would be affected in varying degrees by widespread disruption of communications and essential services . . .

ES 10/1974 *Public Survival under Fall-out Conditions* fills in the details on fall-out:

It is predicted from various possible patterns of nuclear attack on the United Kingdom that there would be extensive and overlapping areas of heavy fall-out in which the early radiation intensity (measured as the dose-rate in air) might be in the order of thousands rather than hundreds of roentgens per hour. . . . Whereas it used to be considered that the areas of high intensity would be relatively small and surrounded by large tracts of comparatively unaffected territory, the present assumption is that over a large part of the country there would be no such areas readily accessible to those who found themselves in the worst affected places . . .

Thus, we are seeing here that the Home Office is expecting attacks at the major strategic level discussed in the *later* parts of the last chapter.

It is important also to understand that you will *not* be getting any help if you are in a badly affected area. ES 5/1974 *War Emergency Planning for the Fire Service* makes it clear that the Fire Brigade will *not* be coming:

It is envisaged that, in the period immediately following nuclear attack, fire fighting would be undertaken only when the return was judged to be worthwhile and where the survival of organised fire service resources would not be prejudiced. Planning should therefore be directed towards the preservation of the fire service for its role in the longer survival period.

The hospitals would, of course, already have been cleared to a large extent. ES 1/1977 *The Preparation and Organisation of the Health Service for War* gives an indication of the changing criteria of care:

During a period of crisis and when so directed, Health Authorities should arrange for all patients in hospitals, nursing and convalescent homes, whose retention was not medically essential, to be sent home . . .

. . . Discharge should not . . . be held up merely because home conditions were not ideal or could not be checked and it must be accepted that the crisis would entail hardship. Criteria for selecting patients for discharge should be based on those which would have to be adopted, following an attack with many casualties . . .

This circular also confirms that the Health Service will *not* be coming looking for the injured:

. . . After a nuclear attack, radioactive fall-out, either in the area or drifting towards it, might be at lethal or near lethal levels. It would be essential that staff, vital to the long-term recovery of the country, should not be wasted by allowing them to enter areas of high radioactivity and no staff should leave shelter until authorised to do so . . .

Even if you managed to get an injured person to a hospital you should *not* assume that treatment would be available:

. . . In general, hospitals should, initially, accept only those casualties who, after limited surgical procedures, would be likely to be alive after seven days, with a fair chance of eventual recovery. The more complete the recovery that could be expected, the higher the priority for admission . . .

It would appear, then, that the Health Service is under no illusions. In fact, it is ready to *reverse* its normal mode of operation in post-attack Britain!

It will be simpler to leave comments on shelters and radioactive protection arrangements until the next chapter when we take a closer look at the incidence of illness in the longer term. So let us assume that you have no problems on that count.

ES 6/1976 *Water Services in War* shows that there will be very difficult problems in obtaining your prime requirement for survival:

. . . It can be said with absolute assurance that any widespread nuclear attack would quickly disrupt the distribution system for domestic and industrial water. . . Outside the areas of total destruction close to the burst of the weapon, particularly vulnerable elements of many systems are water towers, surface reservoirs and pumping stations whether dependent on mains electricity or regular deliveries of fuel . . .

. . . for planning purposes it should be assumed that in all areas there would be prolonged disruption of piped drinking water supplies . . .

The survivors will have to face up to the consequences of this disruption:

. . . Human survivors should, for planning purposes, be deemed to have access to sufficient water to keep them alive for at least 14 days after attack . . .

. . . immediate post-attack domestic consumption might be based on a litre per person per day, it would be important to raise the public allocation to ten litres per person per day . . .

A litre is about one and three quarter pints!

Food would also be scarce, ES 1/1979 *Food and Agriculture Controls in War* paints the gloomy overall picture:

. . . After nuclear attack food would be scarce, lacking in variety and unevenly distributed throughout the country. It would be prudent to plan on the assumption that no significant food imports would be received for some time, that peacetime systems of food processing and distribution would cease to function and all areas, even where no physical damage had been suffered, would have to rely on emergency feeding arrangements. It should be assumed that in general any more sophisticated system for feeding the population would be impractical for some time.

The emergency feeding arrangements would be communal:

. . . Having regard to the likely consequences of nuclear attack it is probable that for a considerable time food distribution would have to be confined to maintaining supplies to emergency feeding centres for the provision, initially, of simple meals. As time went on and as supplies, organisation and facilities improved it should be possible to introduce at the centres a variety of cooked food and supplements to take home.

The reader may now be beginning to imagine some of the longer-term consequences of a nuclear attack. ES 1/1979 indicates the depth of the post-attack crisis and the measures that would have to be taken:

. . . the second aim (for agriculture) would entail a re-orientation towards subsistence agriculture growing more food crops, particularly cereals.

Plans for the control of agriculture are based on groupings of agricultural holdings. As a national average, each group would comprise about 800 agricultural holdings . . .

Agricultural radioactivity officers would be deployed in each region to divisional office level . . .

But, we are jumping ahead too fast. There will be more immediate issues than land tenure and civil liberties.

Circular ES 8/1976 deals with *Environmental Health in War*. This spells out clearly the effects of a nuclear attack on the things we take for granted in a modern society:

. . . if nuclear weapons are used to any significant extent, the breakdown of these services, on which most of the public unquestionably rely, would be inevitable over much of the country. Water would not flow from the tap or into the sewerage system. Electricity would be cut off. Refuse collection would cease. Large numbers of casualties would lie where they died. In such conditions, certain diseases could spread rapidly . . .

The drainage of urine and the burying of faeces into the ground, provided these do not lead to an immediate contamination of drinking water, would be infinitely preferable to allowing random distribution over the surface of the ground. . . . Some communal facilities would be essential in all areas, for living conditions would not be conducive to bowel control and regular habits . . .

And then there will be the many corpses. ES 8/1976 does not mince words on this matter:

The whole subject of the burial of the dead is surrounded by a reluctance to discuss the matter, overlain with different religious susceptibilities. The unpalatable fact of a nuclear war involving large numbers of civilian casualties is that the religious rites and personal wishes, previously expressed by the deceased or now by the next-of-kin, would have to be ignored. Many of the bodies could not be identified, even with scientific assistance, from the remains. It would not be practicable to devote scarce resources to the separate registration and burial of those who could be identified.

If you do not believe that this could happen see David Irving's harrowing account of the aftermath of the RAF raid on Dresden.

In a modern society many families have members living in different parts of the country. In such families there would naturally be great anxiety (amongst survivors) over the fate of members in other areas. There would be little chance that they could discover what had happened. ES 2/1977 *Inland Transport in War* states,

Extensive damage to roads, bridges, railway tracks, rolling stock, signalling systems, aircraft, runways, canals and locks would bring inland transport to a halt in some areas. In other areas, parts of the system would survive undamaged or could be repaired . . .

But even if the means of transport were not destroyed ES 5/1976 *Energy Supplies in War* shows that the general public would not be able to travel:

It may be assumed that no petrol or other fuel rationing scheme of the type operated in World War II could be introduced. . . . There could be no equitable distribution of available supplies to individual consumers. . . . Generally speaking, only official transport would be allowed on the roads . . .

Additionally, information services would be quite primitive. ES 2/1975 *Information Services in War* states,

In the aftermath of a nuclear attack, in order to conserve transmitting and battery receiving power, broadcasting would be confined strictly to the dissemination of essential information at certain set times. It must be assumed that, of the mass information media, only sound broadcasting could continue. There would be no television, and the national and local newspapers would not be produced . . .

This circular also specifically addresses the problem of missing family members:

For some time after an attack the district service would find it impossible to deal with specific inquiries about the fate of individuals in the seriously affected areas . . . local nominal rolls of survivors could be prepared and built up into local registers although, for as long as the death toll from injuries and radiation effects continued at a high level, the effort involved in compiling nominal rolls would not be justified. Until national postal services were restored, there would be no way, except on a very limited territorial basis, of helping to allay grave public anxiety as to the fate of relatives.

The individual person, then, will have to wait for the national economy to recover. But what state will that be in?

ES 5/1976 *Energy Supplies in War* is, perhaps, the crucial document for estimating the potential for economic recovery in the short term. Its message is as bleak as everything else quoted in this section:

Many of the energy forms on which modern society has come to depend are relatively recent innovations and are not essential. . . . For example, electricity and gas were unknown in many rural parts 40 years ago and water came from a well, not from a tap at the end of public supply . . .

. . . after a significant nuclear attack and the attendant problem of radioactive fallout, energy production everywhere would be considerably reduced and may be brought to a halt.

Specifically the circular states,

Electricity: there would be widespread damage to the national grid and area board distribution systems most of which are above ground and therefore vulnerable to damage by blast. . . . Many generating stations could be destroyed or inoperable . . . overhead power lines would be sensitive to the effects of electromagnetic pulse (EMP). . . . Induced voltages could produce electrical damage to sub-stations, control equipment, switching centres and communication systems . . .

Gas: . . . Surface installations, communications, telemetering, computerised and other control systems would suffer not only blast and fire damage but also the added effects of EMP and the loss of electricity mentioned in the previous paragraph . . .

Coal: Some pit installations might be destroyed and many, if not all, others would be immobilised through lack of power to operate winding gear, lighting, pumping. . . . Pits, particularly those which are liable to flooding, which are left unworked and

The nuclear family

without adequate maintenance soon deteriorate to a point where working faces collapse and equipment is lost . . .

Oil: Quite apart from the possible cessation of deliveries of crude oil to refineries and even the destruction of some refineries, there would be losses of crude and particularly refined products in tanks at refineries and, in the case of products, at other storage and distribution depots. The destruction of the pipeline terminals from the North Sea oil fields and the off-shore installations themselves would result in the almost total loss of domestic production . . .

Not surprisingly the circular concludes,

General: . . . For planning purposes it may be assumed that, after a nuclear attack, all energy production and supply would soon cease and it could be several weeks and certainly longer in the case of oil before even the most irregular and intermittent supply could be started.

There can be no conclusion from this data other than that Britain would cease to be a modern economy.

Naturally the realists in the Home Office do not suppose that law and order will be maintained in such circumstances. ES 11/1974 *Armed Forces in War* states,

. . . it may be assumed that units of the armed forces would be deployed on those tasks for which their discipline, skill and training have befitted them. . . . Examples which spring to mind include armed guards for food depots, ports, warehouses, factories and armed escorts for convoys of essential supplies.

Our normal legal traditions are also thought to be out of place. The famous ES 3/1976 *Briefing Material for Wartime Controllers* states,

In conditions in which death, destruction and injury were commonplace, such penalties as probation, fines or sentences of imprisonment would no longer be effective . . . in the case of flagrantly anti-social behaviour there might be a need for harsher penalties than would be generally acceptable in peacetime . . .

. . . It would . . . be possible to hold an emergency court anywhere in a region, where radiological conditions permitted movement. . . . In capital cases, where practicable, there would be a jury of not more than five, empowered summarily, or a court consisting of not less than three commissioners. In other cases, commissioners would sit with or without a jury as they saw fit . . .

Threats to established rights would, as in the agricultural example given previously, be present even if you were law-abiding. Circular ES 7/1976 *Homelessness in War* contains the remark that,

. . . Some householders may be willing to take in homeless people, others may have to be persuaded by a representative of the controller or by those needing shelter . . .

ES 4/1975 *Construction Work and Building Materials in War* states,

As regards work, these powers would enable the various Ministers or Commissioners to recruit and direct labour, to control all building and civil engineering undertakings and operations and to bring them under a single Emergency Works Organisation . . .

Many other examples could be given.

Finally then, what about society and culture in post-attack Britain? ES 2/1976 contains some frightening possibilities on *Community Organisation in War*:

'Community' is a term with many meanings; in this memorandum it describes a group of people of no predetermined number, who live (or possibly work) in a particular locality and share a recognised identity and common interests . . .

. . . Some local authorities, in response to local demands, have nominated and briefed wartime community leaders or advisers for this purpose (community organisation) in normal peacetime, and in some cases have vested in them some semblance of wartime authority . . .

. . . Such leaders should not act in war independently of the district controller. Only in the absence of any evidence that the district controller and his key staff had survived the attack should these leaders . . . act as if they held a district controller's powers . . .

Perhaps it is all intended for the best, but is it what we would normally regard as British society? And for culture, ES 7/1973 *Machinery of Government in War* puts it clearly enough:

A number of local government peacetime services would not be regarded as essential in the post-attack period and some redeployment of staff would be possible. For example, schools, libraries and parks would not be operating as in normal times. County and district plans should provide for the mobilisation and redeployment of local government staff . . .

In other words, the schools and libraries will be shut!

You have probably found this section very depressing to read. Used as we are to the discussion of nuclear war, it has been terribly depressing for us to write. The reason is partly, of course, the detail in the Home Office circulars. More than that, however, is the clear impression of *very detailed and realistic studies going on quietly in the Home Office over the last decade – with very few of the results being intended to reach the general public.*

The Ministry of Disinformation: various positions adopted by British government on the issue of nuclear war.

We have already expressed our scepticism of the view that Britain might suffer just a 200 megaton attack, but even if that were all, it is apparent from the knowledge of the effects of nuclear weapons that this would be truly catastrophic. We find it most worrying that the government is willing to publish pamphlets like *Protect and Survive* which are, frankly, deliberately reassuring and largely unrelated to any sizeable attack, while at the same time undertaking more realistic and detailed studies of the effects of nuclear war which are *not* circulated to the general public.

CONCLUSIONS: WHAT SHOULD WE THINK ABOUT BRITISH CIVIL DEFENCE?

Quite clearly, we have to conclude that Britain has a rudimentary Civil Defence system which will, at best, be of marginal significance in the kind of attack that Britain would suffer in a nuclear war. Moreover, this chapter has only dealt with the immediate post-attack period. As we shall see in the next chapter, even if a quite extraordinarily massive investment was now made in Civil Defence and this succeeded in dealing to some extent with the short-term effects, it could just mean that more people would die in the appalling few years that would follow.

Why then do advocates of Civil Defence argue so strongly for it? First, one suspects, that they too may have difficulties in grasping the change of scale of destruction that nuclear weapons have brought about. Second, we must also recognize the tremendous psychological pressures that there must be for people charged with trying to look after our society in such terrible circumstances. (To question assumptions could be very disturbing.) Third, and importantly, we must recognize their humanitarian motives. When a county planning officer says that there will be some survivors and he must look to *their* welfare, we must accept that he probably does feel this strongly, for Civil Defence would save some lives.

Yet, if the advocates of Civil Defence wish us to give full weight to their humanitarian motives they must do all they can to eliminate suspicion of their motives. *They must speak and write truthfully and openly*. Only in that way will we be able to see that they are not trying to deceive us.

More than that, Governmental advocates of Civil Defence must distinguish clearly *for the public* the humanitarian and defence policy reasons for their support of Civil Defence. If Civil Defence is part of our system of deterrence by virtue of showing that we will use our nuclear weapons if we have to, it is also part of deterrence in the sense that it is integral to the process which may lead to the use of those weapons. At least people who believe in Civil Defence, if they wish to convince us that they are not trying to make nuclear war *thinkable* and thus *acceptable* to the public, will have to *begin* by stressing the real truth of nuclear war.

What most of this means, and it saddens us to write it, is that there have to be further major changes in the performance of the Home Office in regard to Civil Defence information to the public. Somehow it has to show that it believes that it is part of a democratic society and that the public are intelligent adults – otherwise what else can it expect than that we will believe it has something to hide?

REFERENCES

Arms Control and Disarmament Agency (1978). *An Analysis of Civil Defence in Nuclear War*. State Department, Washington D.C.

Assembly of Western European Union (1980). *Nuclear, Biological and Chemical Protection*. (Mr Banks, Rapporteur) Document 838, Assembly of Western European Union.

Blanchard, W. (1980). *American Civil Defence 1945–75: The Evolution of Programs and Policies*. Ph.D. thesis, University of Virginia, USA.

Committee on Banking, Housing and Urban Affairs. United States Senate (W. Proxmire, Chairman) (1979). Hearing on *Civil Defence*. US Government Printing Office, Washington D.C.

Director of Central Intelligence (1978). *Soviet Civil Defence*. NI 78–10003, CIA, Washington D.C.

Federal Office of Civil Defence (1980). *The Swiss Civil Defence*. Federal Office of Civil Defence, Berne.

Goodwin, P. (1981). *Nuclear War: The Facts on Our Survival*. Ash & Grant, London.

Hodgson, R. and Banks, R. (1979). *Britain's Home Defence Gamble*. Conservative Political Centre, London.

Home Office (1980). *Protect and Survive*. HMSO, London.

Home Office (1981). *Domestic Nuclear Shelters*. HMSO, London.

Irving, D. (1963). *The Destruction of Dresden*. Kimber, London.

Kaplan, F. M. (1978). *The Soviet Civil Defence Myth*. Bulletin of the Atomic Scientists, March, pp. 15–20, April, pp. 41–51.

Kincaid, W. (1978). *Repeating History: The Civil Defence Debate Renewed*. International Security, Winter 1978, pp. 99–120.

Laurie, P. (1979). *Beneath the City Streets*, (Revised Edition). Granada, London.

Swiss Federal Council (1979). *Interim Report of the Federal Council to the Federal Assembly on the Security Policy of Switzerland*. Copy from Arms Control and Disarmament Information Unit, University of Sussex.

8
Long-term Effects of Nuclear Attack

In the first three chapters of this section on the effects of nuclear war we have concentrated on the physical effects of the use of nuclear weapons and on the immediate post-attack period. It is understandable that most of our thinking stops there – the physical effects and immediate chaos are dramatic and horrible enough. However, to stop there is to omit a great deal more that needs to be thought about by anyone concerned with the possibility of nuclear war. As, for example, de Kadt and Stonier pointed out in the early 1960s, there are a large number of equally horrible possibilities in the longer term. These include the destruction of the economy, famines, epidemics, social and political disintegration, cancer, genetic damage, and irreversible damage to the environment.

NATURAL DISASTERS

We can gain an initial idea of the nature of the consequences of nuclear war by looking briefly at the more familiar example of a natural disaster. If an earthquake strikes a populous region, the first problem is rescue (many readers will recall the difficult operations in winter weather during the immediate aftermath of the Italian earthquake near Naples in 1980). Eventually, however, the television cameras go away and the survivors have to turn from rescue to rebuilding. Even with outside help this is difficult. At the simplest level, it just takes time and resources to rebuild houses and factories. Additionally, modern economies are complex and not easily restarted after massive disruption. Suppliers of materials may have gone out of business; markets may have been taken over by other firms. Roads and railways may no longer be adequate.

There are other, less obvious, consequences which may be easily missed. People who have experienced a major disaster like an earthquake may have great anxiety over a possible recurrence, but have little chance to move elsewhere. Some survivors will have lost close relatives in dreadful circumstances, and this will add to their psychological burden. Such losses will also have effects in terms of the society and economy. Families which lose the father or mother (or both) will face severe difficulties for many years. Losses of large numbers of children will have social and economic effects at a later stage.

It must also be recognized that the quality of the outside support given will be important not only for its immediate direct effect, but also for the survivors' view of the legitimacy of their local and national government. The immediate response will inevitably be *ad hoc*, but should disorganization and ineffective action persist, the survivors will begin to question the authorities' competence – and soon the possibility of withdrawal of support for the authorities will arise.

Finally, of course, the natural disaster could be so severe as to effectively destroy the society or even the natural system on which it is based. A disaster could produce so many casualties and so much social and economic disruption that the society could never recover.

In short then, a natural disaster has clear-cut, direct, physical effects. In an earthquake, buildings fall down and people are killed and injured. The disaster can have *no less important* long-term consequences. Families can be broken up, economic systems can be disrupted, faith in social systems can be eroded, and the natural basis of the population's existence can disappear. With that broad sketch in mind, let us now turn back to the consequences of nuclear war.

NUCLEAR WAR: THE LONG-TERM

There are two key differences which need to be understood when comparing the long-term effects of natural disasters and a nuclear war. There is the far greater scale of nuclear war. Natural disasters can certainly produce enormously widespread effects, but a large-scale nuclear war could spread major damage across *all* continents. Then there is the question of *intentionality*. Few of us now believe that natural disasters are 'directed' by some intelligence similar to our own. Nuclear attacks *are* directed by intelligent enemies.

When the uninitiated (like ourselves) think about a nuclear war we tend to think of a crisis or accident which happens *now*, and, as we have suggested previously, we tend to consider the *very* immediate consequences. Military strategists have other ideas in mind as well as these. The Chairman of the United States Joint Chiefs of Staff is reported to have said in 1976 that,

We do not target population *per se* any longer. We used to. What we are doing now is targeting a war recovery capability.

The meaning of that change was detailed in the 1977 United States Department of Defense Annual Report which reportedly stated that,

. . . an important objective of the assured retaliation mission should be to retard significantly the ability of the USSR to recover from a nuclear exchange and regain the status of a 20th century military and industrial power more rapidly than the United States.

There is no reason to believe that the Soviet Union has not also got such considerations in mind.

The reader may have some difficulty in grasping this

change of focus – we certainly did. We will, therefore, pursue the matter a little further. In 1979 the United States Senate Committee on Banking, Housing and Urban Affairs published a study by Dr A. Katz on *Economic and Social Consequences of Nuclear Attacks on the United States*. In an attempt to properly set the scene for the study it was emphasized that,

. . . A nuclear exchange of the magnitude addressed in this study implies serious damage in the Soviet Union, the United States and probably Europe. Major political upheavals and contests for hegemony in various regions of the world are possible consequences . . . and may significantly affect responses to requests for immediate or long-term recovery assistance . . .

War does *not* stop when the bombs fall. The struggle apparently goes on! This may not be the case in fact, but it is sufficient that people believe it for them to act on that assumption.

Katz is quite explicit as to what may happen to the superpowers:

An extreme form of changed status for either the United States or the Soviet Union would be that of a client state, implying that foreign policy and/or internal institutions are controlled to some degree by other nations . . .

The game, then, is somewhat expanded from the public's normal understanding. Our leaders are not just thinking about counterforce or population attacks and then stopping. They are considering how to attack other *societies* in ways that will be so devastating that it will take them many years to recover – if indeed they ever recover. It is in this context, as we have seen, that the position of neutral countries becomes problematic. It is not difficult to imagine the military strategists of a superpower – which may be reduced to rubble – asking whether it is better that the neutrals be left alone in the war or attacked. The former course leaves some hope of organized help, the latter reduces the risk of domination!

This is clearly a mad world which most of us can only look at from afar – and hope that it will all go away. But it is most important that we do understand what is afoot because it is our future they are discussing!

STUDIES OF CONSEQUENCES

Before we proceed to examine some of the possibilities it is necessary to say a little about the available data. We have two sources of relatively hard 'objective' data. We do know a good deal about the effects of natural disasters (as we briefly sketched earlier). We also know a good deal about the specific issue of radiation and its effects from studies of the survivors of Hiroshima and Nagasaki and from studies of fall-out from bomb tests. In both instances there is also a major literature of related scientific work which supports and extends the data of most interest to us.

As readers will recall from Chapter 6 there is also massive uncertainty about the indirect effects of the use of nuclear weapons, and these uncertainties increase as the discussion moves to less tangible and longer-term possibilities. A typical study will therefore postulate an attack and state the direct effects. It will then draw on relatively firm data to spell out some of the indirect consequences – and then move on to more and more speculative areas of enquiry. Naturally, there will be a possibility that the (perhaps unconscious) preferences of the author of the study will colour the findings more as things become less definite. Readers must therefore be cautious in accepting conclusions too easily.

We do not have space here to look in detail at the large number of, mainly American, studies that have been carried out and published in the open literature over the last few decades. It is more useful for our purposes to concentrate instead on one study of the economic consequences, as this is clearly of central importance, and is a subject that every reader knows something about. Before we do that, however, there is one other important issue.

A QUESTION OF TIME

In order to convey something of the reality of a nuclear attack the Office of Technology Assessments study of *The Effects of Nuclear War* contains a fictional account of a largely undamaged town after an attack on the United States. Nan Randall, the author of this part of the study, seems to have read many of the post-attack studies very carefully and gives a convincing account of what it might be like in the year following the attack. She then turns to the longer-term consequences.

In a nice sideswipe at the defence analysts the story ends with a conference *one year after the attack* in which experts attempt to assess what to do. There are obviously major difficulties with the economy:

'We are in the classic race,' remarked one of the participants who had written a major study of post attack recovery some years before. 'We have to be able to produce new goods and materials before we exhaust our stored supplies. . . . Right now we are a long way from that capability . . .'

There are some optimists who cite the post-World War II recovery of Germany and Japan, but this is dismissed by others who point out that conditions are entirely different – for example, there is no large economy (equivalent to the United States in 1945) to pump in the required aid.

Some pessimists believe that it might be possible to achieve the status of a third world country (before the war). This would have a small technologically advanced segment but the rest of the people would be agrarian or unskilled. One participant, however, puts the 'real' pessimist's view:

'. . . After a while, in a few generations, no one remembers how the machines worked at all. They remember the important things: how to plant crops, how to train draft horses and oxen, how to make a simple pump. We will have survived biologically, but our way of life is going to be unrecognisable. In several generations, the United States is going to resemble a late medieval society . . .

The point in retelling this story is not to say that we agree or disagree with it. For our purposes what the ending of Randall's story does is to highlight the *time span* of the consequences that we must consider. We are dealing with events that could blight people's lives for generations.

ECONOMIC AND SOCIAL CONSEQUENCES OF NUCLEAR ATTACKS

The depression in the western economies in recent years has shown how fundamentally dependent our societies are on our economies. The Congressional study by Katz seeks to discover what damage would result from nuclear attacks directed at the economic foundation of a modern society and what further consequences would follow.

An earlier study by the Stanford Research Institute had identified thirty-four major categories of industry, and then established the geographical distribution of the capacity in these industries (recall the oil refinery example given in Chapter 6). From this information seventy-one 'Standard Metropolitan Statistical Areas' were identified where there were the largest concentrations of these industries. The list is not surprising: New York, Los Angeles, Chicago, Philadelphia, Detroit and so on.

The Stanford study assumed that plant would be effectively destroyed if it was in the 9 lbs per square inch blast overpressure area produced by a nuclear weapon. Then, by comparing 9 psi blast areas and the areas of the cities, it was possible to show what weight of attack was required to neutralize the major industries. The Stanford study concluded that,

. . . approximately 500 one-megaton nuclear weapons would accomplish the objective of neutralising the productive capacity of the 71 US standard metropolitan statistical areas chosen by SRI. In addition, the study calculated that 200 or 300 *more* weapons with smaller yields of one-hundred kilotons apiece would reduce eight selected manufacturing sectors to two or three per cent of their former capacity . . .

Katz began by arguing that it was rather more reasonable to take the 5 psi overpressure area as an indicator of effective destruction (readers should check back to the example attack on Detroit in Chapter 6 to see if they agree). On this criterion it was not difficult to show that 400, 300, 200, and 100 megaton attacks would have very damaging effects on industrial capacity, particularly if supplemented by the attacks with smaller weapons.

The implications for the much smaller British economy are clear. Katz stresses how much his result is dependent on the urban concentration in the United States, where he states that 60 per cent of the people live on only 1 per cent of the total land area. It is in that context that we should read the statement (in *Domestic Nuclear Shelters*) that,

. . . Estimates suggest that about 5 per cent of the land area of the UK might suffer seriously from the effects of blast . . . about 80 per cent of the land area might suffer no blast effects at all . . .

Ask yourself where that 5 per cent is likely to be!

The attacks would have many other direct effects. For example, most institutions of higher education are in urban areas. If most medical schools and teaching hospitals are destroyed, government has to invest scarce resources over a long time in order to replace the doctors – who also live in greater proportion in urban areas and thus are likely to be killed at higher than the average rate.

The study goes on to look at the more indirect psychological, social and political consequences of the attacks. Katz's conclusions are every bit as gloomy as those of the Home Office circulars reviewed in the last chapter. For example:

The experience of nuclear war is likely to have devastating psychological effects . . .

Families will be particularly vulnerable to the effects of widespread nuclear attacks; they will be broken up by death, severe injury or disease, evacuation, or military and labour conscription . . .

. . . Decentralisation of political power and more authoritarian methods of political, social and economic control are likely responses to post-attack conditions. Widespread disaffection may ensue . . .

There are many other studies of the possibility of economic viability after nuclear attack and it would be fair to say that some of these are more optimistic than Katz. Yet, it can surely not be in doubt that in the kind of attack *we* are likely to suffer there would be *severe* long-term economic and social consequences.

The reality is that a relatively small nuclear attack would reduce American economic activity to a small proportion of current levels. Apply that to Britain and you can appreciate that the remains of the country would be a ruin. This is, of course, leaving out all the many other effects of the attack.

MEDICAL CONSEQUENCES OF THE RADIATION AT HIROSHIMA AND NAGASAKI

It must be remembered in the following discussion that the bombs dropped in 1945 on Hiroshima and Nagasaki were air-burst and small (tactical) weapons by present-day standards. The radiation released was therefore small in comparison to what would probably be experienced in a modern nuclear war where many megaton weapons would be ground-burst.

The 1977 International Symposium *Call from Hibakusha of Hiroshima and Nagasaki* has a series of working documents which summarize various aspects of the survivors' ('Hibakushas') experience. Working document I contains a brief review of the radiation produced by the bombs. The document states that a semi-lethal dose of 400 rads would have been received from the *initial* radiation by anyone about 1020 meters (0.6 miles) from the hypocentre (point on the ground below where the bomb exploded) at Hiroshima and 1200 meters at Nagasaki. The term *rad* should be noted here. The doses given were obtained by simply adding the gamma radiation and neutron estimates. These have different effects on tissue and therefore the doses in *rems* would be somewhat different. This is important because the Hiroshima bomb produced more neutrons than the Nagasaki bomb. Both gamma rays and neutrons attenuate quite quickly in air and at a range of 2500 meters (1.6 miles) the dose from the initial radiation was 0.2 rad at Hiroshima and 2.9 rad at Nagasaki – in both cases from gamma radiation only, the neutrons being completely attenuated at this range.

Anyone entering near the hypocentre within about 100 hours of the explosion would also have received gamma radiation from material which had become radioactive as a result of the effect of the initial radiation. The maximum dose that could have been received from such *induced* radiation was estimated to be about 130 rad in Hiroshima and 50 rad in Nagasaki. Finally, radiation could have been received from the material brought down in the 'black rain'. The working document states that maximum doses from this source would have been about 40 rads in Hiroshima and about 150 rads in Nagasaki.

All this may sound very confusing. The essential point to be grasped is that although some survivors received doses of 100 rads (or more), most received low doses. Professor Edward P. Radford emphasized this point in his personal statement in the National Academy of Sciences report *The Effects on Populations of Exposure to Low Levels of Ionising Radiation BEIR III* (1980). Radford stated,

. . . It is not generally recognised that the strength of the Japanese data in epidemiologic terms lies in data obtained for low doses. . . . The major part of the . . . survivors with significant exposures are in the two dose groups . . . a mean *tissue* dose of about 11 rad, and . . . a mean *tissue* dose of about 35 rad. . . .

What then were the long-term consequences of this radiation?

We are in a good position to answer this question because the survivors have been subject to intensive long-term medical research. In particular, a 109,000 person sample of the 285,000 survivors who were in the cities for the 1950 census has been studied in the Life Span Study established by the Atomic Bomb Casualty Commission. The Life Span Study investigated the *mortality patterns* of these survivors. Additionally, 20,000 people from the Life Span Study sample have taken part in the Adult Health Survey. This is a systematic programme of medical examinations at two-year intervals. A short summary of the medical research findings is given in working document II in the 1977 International Symposium. Major summaries are available in the *Life Span Study Reports* (the latest is No. 8, 1978) and in a special supplement of the *Journal of Radiation Research* (1975). For present purposes we will concentrate on outlining the basic findings; readers are referred to these summaries for the details of original papers.

Before looking at the effects, the reader must understand something of the basis of the medical research. It is possible to discover where survivors were at the time of the bombing and if they were shielded from the radiation. Studies by physical scientists of the radiation and shielding allow an estimated dose to be made for each person. It is not possible, however, to directly connect any person's individual radiation experience with a particular outcome for that person. What is done is to compare the rates of various medical effects for groups of people (with similar doses received) with those for the non-affected population. Over a number of years it is then possible to see if the exposed population (with a particular dose received) has a greater than normal incidence of a particular medical effect.

Scientists have been using radioactive material since about the turn of the century, so certain effects of the

radiation were expected as soon as the bombing occurred
(see Eisenbud). For example, it was known in the 1920s
that radiation could have a severe effect on children in the
womb. This effect is well established at Hiroshima and
Nagasaki. W. J. Blot's summary states,

Studies of growth and development of Hiroshima and Nagasaki
children have shown significant long-range effects associated
with exposure to the atomic bombs. Radiation to the fetus
during early pregnancy, even at relatively low doses, may
result in reduced growth, smaller head size, and mental
retardation . . .

As the body of the paper makes clear, the effect was
practically limited to fetuses exposed before the eight-
eenth week of pregnancy. Head circumference was significantly decreased at doses as low as 10 to 19 rads, but
there was an increase in frequency of the effect with
increasing dose. There are other effects such as an increase in cataracts in adults and so on.

However, we will turn now to the problem of *cancer*
which has so plagued the survivors of the bombings. The
first indication of such problems for the survivors was the
occurrence of leukemia. This began to be noticed in the
1940s and its incidence peaked in the early 1950s. M. and
T. Ichimaru reported on the incidence of leukemia in the
1975 review. Their summary stated,

. . . Leukemia appeared early and was one of the most strikingly evident somatic effects of radiation in atomic bomb survivors. Leukemogenic effects of radiation vary by quality and quantity of radiation dose, age at the time of exposure, elapsed time after exposure and type of leukemia. Although the risk of leukemia in . . . survivors is now greatly reduced . . . there is no evidence that the risk of leukemia has returned to control levels (normal) in those survivors who received a significant radiation dose . . .

So almost thirty years after the bombing, exposed survivors were still not free of the lingering threat of leukemia. Although the effects are not simple to understand it is not too difficult to interpret the findings. Most importantly, it is clear that there is a threat at low dose rates and that the threat increases with dose rate. The authors, for instance, state that,

The dose response relationship differs by type of leukemia. The risk of chronic granulocytic leukemia is significantly increased for Hiroshima survivors in the low dose region, but no such increase can be observed in the Nagasaki survivors. The risk of acute leukemia is elevated for those who received 100 rads or more in each city. . . .

Leukemia, however, is at least on the decline. Unfortunately, other cancers are still on the increase.

The 1978 *Life Span Study Report* states the essential facts:

The leukemogenic effect that dominated any consideration of late mortality effects until recently has now been exceeded by the effects of radiation on forms of cancer other than leukemia. . . . Sites of cancer that seemed especially involved in the continued increase in absolute risk . . . were the respiratory organs and the digestive organs. Incidence data suggest that breast cancer is also on the rise. . . .

Beebe and Kato deal with the subject of cancers other than leukemia in the 1975 review. They point out, that

. . . the first statistically sound evidence that another form of cancer was also involved was a dose related excess of thyroid cancer . . . reported in 1963 . . .

The authors suggest that the risk of thyroid cancer is of the same order as that for leukemia. Breast cancer was associated with bomb radiation in 1968. Beebe and Kato note carefully that,

. . . if those under 10 ATB (age at the time of the bombing) follow the course of those who were older ATB, the peak effect lies well in the future. For all age groups except those under 10 ATB, women exposed to the high doses have already experienced about as many, or even more, breast cancers as would normally be experienced in the remaining years of their lives . . . the data . . . thus far contain no evidence that breast cancer appears earlier in the lifetime . . . there is simply more of it at the ages when breast cancer normally occurs.

Lung cancer was also shown to be associated with the bomb radiation in 1968. The authors stress the consequences still to come:

Even more than in the case of breast cancer the effect of atomic radiations on lung cancer thus far visible is limited to those in the older ATB; only amongst those 35 or older ATB had there been sufficient numbers of deaths from lung cancer to permit search for a radiation effect. . . . Since only 39 per cent of the sample were 35 or older ATB, there is every reason to expect that the peak effect lies in the future . . .

Good evidence is now also available to link incidence of salivary gland and stomach cancer to the radiation.

In fact, the 1978 *Life Span Study Report* concludes that,

Reviewing the experience of ABCC (Atomic Bomb Casualty Commission) over the past 20 years, and seeing the accumulating evidence of radiation-induced cancer in an increasing number of tissues, one is compelled to recognise the likelihood that most tissues may, in time, be shown to be sensitive to the whole-body single dose of A-bomb ionizing radiation.

Scientists in the 1975 review recommended that the research on the survivors would have to go on to 1995 – fifty years on from the bombing! Given the almost certain genetic effects of radiation (see the BEIR III Report) it is clear that we are dealing here with very long-term effects indeed.

All of this research 'objectivity' should not blind us to the human consequences of these effects. Anyone who has ever felt that they *might* have cancer can perhaps imagine how almost any illness could easily increase anxiety for the survivors of the bombings. Furthermore, this anxiety for the survivor comes on top of the pronounced psychological effects which are known to have resulted from the devastating original experience of the bombing.

HOW MUCH CANCER WOULD BE CAUSED BY A NUCLEAR WAR?

The number of Japanese survivors is not large, the radiation received was often in the low dose range and the excess-incidence rates of medical problems are small proportions of the normal rates. Does this mean that long-term cancer induction will really be of little consequence after a major nuclear war? Katz's study contains an instructive calculation in regard to this issue. He points first to the rates of cancer.

The rate of increase for all cancers is about 50 to 165 cases per million persons exposed per rem over 25 or more years. This corresponds to a rate of 2.5 to 8.5 cases per year per million people exposed per rem per year after five years . . .

Katz then simply looks at the implications of a 200 rem dose for a population:

. . . if one million persons survive doses of 200 rem, then we would expect to see 500 to 1650 cases of cancer per year beginning 4 to 5 years later (2.5 to 8.5 times 200) and continuing for at least 25 years after exposure, resulting in a total of 10,000 to 33,000 (500 to 1650 times 20) deaths in excess of the current rate. . . .

The consequences are significant:

. . . This would be an increase for those 25 years of 25 to 85 per cent over the 40,000 cancer deaths per million of population (1620 per year) expected from the present cancer deaths rate.

Now for 'planning purposes' that may be something that could be disregarded in relation to the other more immediate casualties. Yet, in terms of many other criteria it is surely far from insignificant.

Katz, however, assumes a radiation dose of 200 rem, and that is important in producing his figures for death rates. How realistic is that figure? It will be recalled that in the Office of Technology Assessments Study an example of a 1 megaton ground-burst on Detroit was given. At the end of one week there was a 3000 rem accumulated dose contour about thirty miles long and seven miles wide. Inside that contour people who were unshielded would receive at least 3000 rems. The chances of survival for people in shelter would depend on the protective factor of their shelter.

All manner of statements have been made about what protective factors can and cannot be obtained by people given minimal instructions. Much of the argument appears complex. The reader is therefore referred to the instructive discussion of protective factors of British houses given by de Kadt. Interestingly de Kadt comes to about the same conclusion as the Home Office realists who state, in ES 10/1974 *Public Survival under Fall-Out Conditions*, that,

The protective factors of houses, even when increased by improvised measures, vary enormously. Obviously persons who are unable to benefit from living in accommodation with a good protective factor, even when improvements have been made to the rooms, are at greater risk. *The tables used in this memorandum are based on a protective factor of 15 . . .* [Our emphasis.]

Now if one assumes a protective factor of 15, people would receive a dose of at least 200 rem within the 3000 rem contour in a week. It would be necessary to add all kinds of qualifications to such a simple calculation, but it serves to emphasize that Katz's assumption is not wildly unreasonable. In fact, the Home Office in *Nuclear Weapons* (1980) produces a similar set of figures for cancers to those of Katz, but using 100 rem rather than 200 rem as the dose rate. It has to be added that there are many ways in which the dose rate might be increased rather than decreased – multiple ground-bursts with over-lapping fall-out, or surprise attack on an unsheltered population being two obvious possibilities. Moreover, it must be understood that the surving population after a nuclear war would face added radiation hazards. An insight into these hazards can be gained from an examination of some of the work on delayed fall-out from bomb tests.

FALL-OUT IN THE LONGER TERM

Working document V of the 1977 International Symposium takes up the problem of 'Nuclear Weapons and Radioactive Pollution of the Earth's Environment'. The authors point out that prior to the 1963 Test Ban Treaty there had been considerable pollution of the environment, mainly by the United States and the Soviet Union.

. . . the total energy released by the end of 1962 from nuclear explosions has been estimated to be 511 M. T. (megatons TNT equivalent) of which 194 M. T. (air, 139 M. T.) was from nuclear fission . . .

Since that time China and France have added to the problem.

. . . The total energy of explosions conducted by the PRC and France is estimated to be about 25 M. T. . . . which is about 5% of the total energy from explosions conducted by the USA and USSR . . .

It is known that a wide variety of fission products and neutron-induced radioactive products result from such explosions, and that after a few months of dispersal in the upper atmosphere the *delayed fall-out* begins to come back to earth. When it does arrive at the surface it does not simply go away. The authors of the working document point out, for example, that,

. . . Radioactive nuclides contaminate vegetation and grass and are absorbed in the soil surface and transferred with different concentration factors into various kinds of food and then taken up into human bodies . . .

Furthermore, the take-up of dangerous material into human bodies can be quite specific:

As is well known, strontium is a sister element of calcium, which belongs to the alkali earth-chemical family, and the accumulation of Sr-90 in human bones, consisting mainly of calcium phosphate is inevitable . . .

Thus, as a result of such fall-out these radioactive substances can become preferentially placed in the bodies of human beings where the radiation they produce can cause injury in the longer term.

It is important to understand the time scale of this problem. The authors conclude:

It should be emphasised that even now, environmental radioactivity except in the atmosphere . . . has not appreciably decreased, despite the fact that fourteen years have passed since the ratification of the limited test ban treaty in 1963 . . . the reasons for the apparent balancing of environmental radioactivity are that the residence times of the radionuclides in the earth's environment, such as Sr-90, Cs-137, Pu-239 etc. are very long. . . .

This, it must be remembered, is the result of a very small (in comparison with what might happen in a nuclear war) amount of detonated megatonnage – and most of that airburst. For comparison, it should be noted that the Office of Technology Assessment study *The Effects of Nuclear War* in its chapter on long-term effects concludes that, 'A large nuclear war could cause deaths in the low millions *outside* the combatant countries . . .' [our emphasis] but cautiously adds that things could be worse: 'These results might not apply if an attacker sets out deliberately to create very high radiation levels.'

What can be said, of course, is that all the problems associated with delayed fall-out – integration into the environmental system, preferential take-up in our bodies, long-term effects – have also to be faced for the greater concentrations of direct immediate fall-out. It really is a tragic oversimplification to imagine that fall-out problems are over once radiation levels are 'safe' enough for people to leave their shelters.

FOOTNOTE: ON ACCEPTING ASSUMPTIONS

It will be recalled that in the previous section on the medical effects of the bombings of Hiroshima and Nagasaki we quoted from a personal statement by Professor Radford in the BEIR III Report. This personal statement resulted from the considerable controversy that arose because of the difficulty the committee had in agreeing what the effects of low levels of radiation are on human beings. A major source of data in the debate was clearly that from the survivors of Hiroshima and Nagasaki and, as we have shown, that is complicated by the different types of radiation thought to have been produced by the two bombs.

Or that was the case until very recently. The doses used in the medical studies are called the T65 (tentative estimates) and these were widely accepted. They have now to be challenged strongly. The whole story can be followed in Professor Rotblat's paper 'Hazards of low-level radiation – less agreement, more confusion' and in a *Science* article, 'New A-Bomb Studies After Radiation Estimates'. The essential facts are set out by Rotblat. He states that the new studies present the following conclusions on the T65 dose estimates:

The neutron dose in Hiroshima was grossly exaggerated (by a factor of 6 to 20) so that the neutron contribution to the biological effect was very small.
:   the gamma-ray dose in Hiroshima was underestimated
:   the gamma-ray dose in Nagasaki was overestimated
The effect of the consequent changes . . . is dramatic: they completely abolish the difference between the two cities.

The radiation effects on long-term cancer rates in the survivors would therefore become much simpler to understand.

There could be other consequences. As the *Science* report puts it:

. . . It is too early to say precisely . . . because the doses must be recalculated for each radiation victim. But most of the researchers who spoke to *Science* said the new data would probably increase the risk estimates for gamma radiation.

Gamma radiation, of course, is the main threat from fall-out.

BRITISH CIVIL DEFENCE PLANNING IN A LONG-TERM CONTEXT

In Chapter 7 we indicated our unease over much of British Civil Defence planning. We also suggested that there might be a tendency for Civil Defence planners to make assumptions (perhaps unconsciously) about what might happen on the basis of what their system could cope with. Nowhere do these two points come together more clearly than in the treatment of radiation from fall-out.

The standard Home Office text *Nuclear Weapons* contains a chapter on 'Biological Effects of Nuclear Radiations'. Here it is acknowledged that radiation can have long-term consequences:

Long-term injuries include anaemia, leukaemia (a form of blood cancer developing three to six years after exposure) as well as tumours and cancers of the bones or tissues which may develop much later . . .

As we pointed out previously, figures are then given for death rates on the assumption of population exposure to 100 rems. Earlier in the chapter, however, we have been told that in wartime people may take doses of 150 rems because for Civil Defence purposes, ' . . . Long-term effects are not taken into account . . .' Lest this appears to be an aberration, it needs to be added that other instances appear, for example, in a later chapter which deals with 'Hazards to Food, Water, Crops and Livestock'. Here we learn that,

. . . A large proportion of the ingested activity would pass through the gastro-intestinal tract and be excreted. Because of the longer residence time and concentration of material in the lower large intestine, this organ would tend to be the most heavily irradiated. The evidence suggests that doses of about *50r/day* would be unlikely to produce any *short-term* effects on this organ . . . [Our emphasis]

It apparently follows therefore that contaminated food is no problem, ' . . . Assuming simple precautions are taken over food, this dose-rate is not likely to be exceeded . . .' Delayed fall-out is taken to be even less of a problem:

A longer term ingestion hazard might arise from radioactivity taken into the plant through the roots and from the superficial contamination resulting from world-wide fallout. The particle sizes and their solubility enhance the potential ingestion hazard in terms of radioactivity deposited . . . but at the same time only the longer lived nuclides would remain. This hazard should be discounted for home defence planning purposes.

What else, one begins to wonder, 'should (or has) been discounted' for home defence planning purposes? Could it be that anything beyond present capabilities is discounted?

CONCLUSIONS

In these four chapters on the effects of nuclear war we have tried to use official sources wherever possible. Be-

cause of the shortage of published material in Britain this
means reliance on American writings. It is perhaps stating
the obvious to say that a general nuclear war would be
devastating. Projections by the US National Security
Council suggest casualties running at well over 300 million
dead in the Northern Hemisphere as a direct result of the
conflict. Long-term casualties would be far higher.

Even the sober studies we have used indicate a ruined
civilization, plagued by long-term effects of radiation,
lack of medical care, shelter, food and social stability. *The
effects could last for many centuries, indeed complete
recovery might never happen.*

The position for Britain is particularly bad. It is a
heavily populated island occupying a critically important
strategic position with an abundance of targets. In a real
sense it has *a population which cannot be protected*. To
talk of providing effective blast-proof and radiation-proof

Translation *'Probably a totem for one of their primitive phallic
cults.'*

shelters for the whole population is unreal. It would cost perhaps £200,000,000,000 to achieve and could be partially countered by an attack using much larger groundburst weapons to destroy the shelters.

In any case what is the point of urban sheltering if, as suggested in the OTA study, the remains of cities would be contaminated for many years and the survivors would be scrabbling around in a kind of radioactive stone age? What, too, would be the point of attempting general evacuation? In Britain an attacker could still destroy the people by using large air-burst weapons in a patternbombing attack. There is so much 'overkill' available and Britain is such a small place that if an attacker wants to destroy the country *then no civil defence will prevent it*.

These are extreme examples, but they must be stated as a counter to the optimistic nonsense which is so often employed. Given the uncertainties no one can tell precisely what will happen. In Barnaby's study *The Nuclear Arms Race*, he concludes that in a nuclear world war the bulk of the urban population of the Northern Hemisphere would be killed by blast and fire and most of the rural population would be killed by radiation from fall-out. He also considers long-term consequences such as damage to the protective ozone-layer in the upper atmosphere. He concludes that no one knows whether human life would, in the long term, survive a nuclear war in which the existing 50,000 or so nuclear warheads were detonated.

We would certainly agree with a recent comment by Air Marshal Mavor, former Principal of the Home Defence College and now co-ordinator of Civil Defence volunteers for the Home Office. He told an *Observer* correspondent

'. . . for with the advent of atomic weapons we have come either to the last page of war, at any rate on the major international scale we have known in the past, or to the last page of history.'
B. H. Liddell Hart, 1971

(see 'Dugout Britain: Or What Happens When the Bomb Drops', *Observer* 5 July 1981) that '. . . if there is one thing that is near as dammit certain, it is that after nuclear war we will never pass this way again.' In the light of Barnaby's remarks we would add that we might not pass *any* way again.

REFERENCES

Beebe, G. W. *et al* (1978). *Life Span Study Report 8: Mortality Experience of Atomic Bomb Survivors 1950–74.* Radiation Effects Research Foundation, Japan.

Committee on the Biological Effects of Ionizing Radiations (1980). *The Effects on Populations of Exposure to Low Levels of Ionizing Radiation BEIR III.* National Academy of Sciences, Washington D.C.

Defence Civil Preparedness Agency (1979). *Research Report on Recovery from Nuclear Attack*, Information Bulletin No. 307. Federal Emergency Management Agency, Washington D.C.

Defence Civil Preparedness Agency (1979). *Civil Defence for the 1980s – Current Issues.* Federal Emergency Management Agency, Washington D.C.

Senate Committee on the Budget, *Hearings, First Concurrent Resolution on the Budget, Fiscal Year 1977.* Vol III, 94 Congress, 2nd Session. Secretary of Defense (1977).

Annual Report of Secretary of Defense Donald H. Rumsfeld to Congress, 17 January 1977.

Eisenbud, M. (1973). *Environmental Radioactivity.* Academic Press, New York.

Ferris, P. (1981). 'Dugout Britain: Or What Happens When the Bomb Drops'. *Observer*, London (5 July).

Garrison, J. (1980). *From Hiroshima to Harrisburg: The Unholy Alliance.* SCM Press, London.

Home Office (1980). *Nuclear Weapons.* HMSO, London.

Home Office (1981). *Domestic Nuclear Shelters.* HMSO, London.

Home Office (1974). Circular ES 10/1974 *Public Survival Under Fall-Out Conditions.* Home Office, London.

de Kadt, E. J. (1964). *British Defence Policy and Nuclear War.* Frank Cass, London.

Katz, A. (1979). *Economic and Social Consequences of Nuclear*

Attacks on the United States. A study prepared for the Joint Committee on Defense Production. Published by the Committee on Banking, Housing and Urban Affairs, United States Senate.

Lifton, R. J. (1968). *Death in Life: The Survivors of Hiroshima*. Weidenfeld and Nicolson, London.

News and Comment (1981). 'New A-Bomb Studies After Radiation Estimates'. *Science* 212, pp. 900–03 (May).

Office of Technology Assessment (1980). *The Effects of Nuclear War*. United States Congress, Washington D.C. (Published by Croom Helm, London.)

Rotblat, J. (1981). 'Hazards of low-level radiation – less agreement, more confusion.' *Bulletin of the Atomic Scientists*. June/July, pp. 31–6.

Stonier, T. (1964). *Nuclear Disaster*. Penguin, London.

Call from Hibakusha of Hiroshima and Nagasaki: Proceedings of the International Symposium of the Damage and After-Effects of the Atomic Bombing of Hiroshima and Nagasaki. Pergamon Press, Oxford.

Working Document 1 *Physical Destruction and Human Casualties Caused by the Atomic Bomb*.

Working Document II *Medical Effects of the Atomic Bombing*.

Working Document V *Nuclear Weapons and Radioactive Pollution of the Earth's Environment*.

Supplement (1975). *A Review of Thirty Years' Study of Hiroshima and Nagasaki Atomic Bomb Survivors*. Journal of Radiation Research, Japan.

Blot, W. J. (1975). Growth and Development Following Prenatal and Childhood Exposures to Atomic Radiation, pp. 82–8.

Ichimaru, M. and Ichimaru, T. (1975). Leukemia and Related Disorders, pp. 89–96.

Beebe, G. W. and Kato, H. (1975). Cancers other than Leukemia, pp. 97–197.

Part 3

The Failure of Disarmament

9
Attempts at Negotiation

Until the end of the last century, 'disarmament' was advocated mainly by the peace movements in various countries, whilst their governments took little interest in it. The 1899 Hague Peace Conference – held partly as a result of the constant pressure exerted by the peace movement upon governments – was a turning point. For the first time representatives from the main countries of the world met in the hope of stopping the arms race of their day. But the many wars which have followed, as well as the numerous disarmament conferences, are evidence of the manifest failure of that first, official, attempt to disarm.

Eighty years later, it is hard to believe that there was a time when disarmament was not considered sufficiently important to justify conferences. That peace is all-important, and that it will come about only if disarmament or at least arms control takes place is now proclaimed by virtually all governments. As tangible evidence of their peace policy, they can now refer to their proposals for and participation in all kinds of negotiations for disarmament and arms control. Meanwhile hardly a day goes by without at least one war being fought somewhere. Since 1945, however, and with increasing intensity in the last two decades, disarmament talks have been held. The number of participants ranges from two to virtually all the world's states, with sometimes a few representatives from each state and sometimes large delegations; the forum in which discussions are held ranges from informal contacts to the United Nations General Assembly, and the scope of the agenda ranges from specific weapons and/or aspects of their use to a consideration of all weapons.

The discussions may take place for a limited time and be concluded (whether they were successful or not), or they may take place in a semi-permanent conference. And whereas disarmament was once discussed only in one city (and for a few months only), today Geneva, New York, Helsinki and Belgrade, Vienna and Madrid, Moscow and Washington host disarmament conferences on a more or less permanent basis. Most governments now have their full-time disarmament experts, drawn mainly from the disarmament units in the foreign office and defence departments.

There is an infrastructure – i.e. people, plans, places – for disarmament which has never existed before and which is an indication of the scope of the problem and the nature of the response. It would be surprising if this constant governmental concern with disarmament had not led to any agreements. Some of these have been between two states (bilateral), some between many (multilateral); some have dealt with nuclear weapons, others with chemical and bacteriological weapons, still others with conventional military forces. Often agreements are in the nature of arms control or, alternatively, 'non-armament' rather than disarmament measures. In what follows we will present a brief survey of the most important negotiations, leaving the bilateral and highly important and complex SALT negotiations until the next chapter.

One of the most conspicuous manifestations of the nuclear age was the testing in the atmosphere of nuclear devices, a practice which in the 1950s became increasingly criticized, especially when radioactive fall-out from the United States bomb at Bikini Atoll led to the death of a number of Japanese fishermen in 1954. For almost ten years since Hiroshima and Nagasaki the issue had been virtually dormant. Now the public became aware and opinion was mobilized whilst prominent scientists and public figures such as Bertrand Russell and Albert Einstein launched their 'Pugwash' manifesto. In the United Nations the so-called 'non-aligned' nations demanded that nuclear testing be discussed as a matter of urgency. The nuclear weapons powers (then comprising the USA, USSR and UK) responded with an expert group to study the feasibility of a test ban and the detection of its possible violations; the same countries also agreed to a voluntary moratorium on nuclear-weapons testing, which lasted from 1958 until 1961 when the USSR, followed by the USA, resumed testing in the atmosphere and underground as well. In 1962 and 1963 in Geneva the UN Disarmament Committee revived the negotiations about a comprehensive test ban, forbidding all nuclear test explosions. In the summer of 1963, when such a treaty seemed in sight, the two superpowers suddenly left the multilateral negotiations in Geneva for bilateral talks in Moscow, and very soon agreed on a *partial* ban. The Partial Test Ban Treaty prohibits nuclear weapons tests in the atmosphere, in outer space and under water – but not underground; it contains a clear commitment for the signatories to work for a comprehensive test ban forbidding tests in all environments.

The greatest benefit of this Treaty was that it stopped radioactive pollution; hence its description as a public health measure. Yet in terms of halting the nuclear arms

---

'We are here to make a choice between the quick and the dead. That is our business. Behind the black portent of the new atomic age lies a hope which, seized upon with faith, can work out salvation. If we fail, then we have damned every man to be the slave of fear. Let us not deceive ourselves: we must elect world peace or world destruction.'

Bernard Baruch, Speech to UN Atomic Energy Commission 14 August 1946

race the Treaty is of little value: by allowing further testing of nuclear weapons and hence the development of new generations of nuclear warheads, no sacrifice was made by the parties who initiated the Treaty. They had learned all there was to know from atmospheric tests, and there was thus no harm in giving up the option of such tests. On the contrary, to the extent that the pollution which they caused was responsible for public anxiety, this concession was worth making, in that it placated public sentiments. Because the testing had become less visible and less dangerous the ground-swell of opposition against testing subsided – leaving the superpowers a free hand to refine and develop their nuclear arsenals further.

The extent of nuclear testing since the Treaty was concluded in 1963, provides ample evidence for the view that the superpowers were in no mood to give up testing altogether; the commitment to work for a comprehensive ban has remained a very dead letter indeed. In the thirty-five years since the first atomic explosion took place, until the end of 1979, a total of 1221 nuclear explosions have reportedly been conducted. The majority of those, 733 or 60 per cent, were carried out *after* the signing of the Partial Test Ban Treaty in 1963. On an annual basis the rate of explosions was 27 before the Treaty, and 45 after it. Although these figures refer to all tests, including those held by China and France (countries which have not adhered to the Treaty) and the Indian underground one of 1974, over 90 per cent of the tests have been carried out by the three nuclear weapons countries which are the 'original parties' to the Treaty – the USA, USSR and UK. Since 1975 French tests have been held underground only, whereas in the period 1975–9 China has conducted three underground and six atmospheric tests.

In 1974 the US and the USSR signed the Threshold Test Ban Treaty (TTBT) which limits the size of underground explosions to a threshold of 150 kilotons, and since 1976 both powers have conducted their explosion below or around this level. The significance of this treaty is again open to doubt. The level set for permissible explosions is so high that the two signatories can continue their test programmes without experiencing any effective restraints. They are foregoing solely those test explosions of extraordinary strength which from a military point of view, were becoming uninteresting anyway. As a means towards slowing the development of nuclear weapons the Treaty is of no consequence. The American Academy of Arts and Sciences called the Threshold Test Ban Treaty 'ultimate mockery', and spoke of,

an agreement that, in the guise of restraint, permits underground explosives equivalent to 150,000 tons of TNT. That is ten times larger than the bomb that obliterated Hiroshima, and larger than almost all the tests conducted by the US and the USSR in recent years.

Its credibility is so low that it has not even been ratified by the US Senate; formally the Treaty is not yet in force. Senator Edward Kennedy, introducing a resolution urging the negotiation of a comprehensive test ban treaty in the year following the signing of the Threshold Test Ban Treaty, referred to the latter as 'an agreement which is set so high that it seems to have been drafted by arms developers rather than arms controllers'. In 1973, pleading for a comprehensive test ban treaty as the only effective means of stopping the race for improvements of nuclear warheads between the two superpowers, he said: 'Since the Partial Test Ban Treaty was signed, we have been obligated to negotiate a permanent ban on all testing. Yet the record of the past ten years is one of flagrant disregard for that commitment.' The figures already quoted prove him right. It must be noted that the Threshold Test Ban Treaty does not extend to underground nuclear explosions which are conducted for peaceful (as opposed to military) purposes. In 1976, two years after the signing of the TTBT, an agreement was reached between the US and the USSR – the Peaceful Nuclear

Explosions Treaty – which also sets an upper limit of 150 kilotons as the permissible yield of underground nuclear explosions.

At the same time that the nuclear weapons powers are testing nuclear devices – and amidst indications that one other country, possibly South Africa, may have exploded a nuclear device in September 1979 (in the atmosphere) – talks on a comprehensive test ban treaty are taking place. Since 1977 a trilateral commission, consisting of representatives of the two superpowers and the UK, has been discussing the question of verifying compliance with a possible treaty.

Over the years, the impossibility of devising a verification system acceptable to all contracting parties, which would be perfect and not allow any violation of the treaty without detection, has been the apparent reason for the lack of progress in this area – and the inability to conclude such a treaty. Reference has also been made to earthquakes, and the difficulties in distinguishing natural events from man-made explosions. Many observers now believe, however, that these arguments can no longer be taken seriously, in view of the advances made in verification and inspection techniques, especially the availability of remote sensing devices and satellites. The superpowers are suspected of hiding behind these arguments in order not to have to give up the possibility of further testing. The trilateral commission now agrees that the envisaged treaty should provide for 'national technical means' of verification as well as for the possibility of on-site inspection. The insistence on the latter by the US has, in the past, often met with firm opposition from the USSR, which regarded this as unnecessary and as unwarranted interference in its internal affairs.

As a first step on the road to stopping the nuclear arms race, a comprehensive test ban treaty would be a small price to pay by the nuclear weapons countries. With such a treaty they would find it very difficult, if not impossible, to develop new designs of nuclear weapons or to improve the existing designs. This in itself would be a welcome development. But, of possibly even greater significance, such a treaty would provide the non-nuclear weapons countries, several of whom are on the threshold of joining the 'nuclear club' with the first tangible evidence that the nuclear weapons countries are actually serious about their concern, voiced so widely, over the nuclear threat. It would, in particular, give much needed support to the Non-Proliferation Treaty by demonstrating that the nuclear weapons powers are fully aware of *their* responsibilities in preventing horizontal proliferation, i.e. the spread of nuclear weapons to other countries, by curtailing their own (vertical) proliferation of these weapons. We shall now take a closer look at this potentially important treaty.

NON-PROLIFERATION TREATY

From the moment the atomic bomb was born, it was realized that the issue of its control and the prevention of its spread, was of paramount importance for the future security of the world. The dropping of the first bombs in the closing stages of the Second World War coincided with the formation of the United Nations Organization, the charter of which, signed in June, came into force in October of the same year, 1945. It was appropriate that the very first resolution passed by the General Assembly, in January 1946, unanimously established the UN Atomic Energy Commission. (To avoid possible confusion, it should be noted that at this time 'atomic energy' referred in the first instance to the concrete application which had been made of this energy, i.e. as a weapon and not so much to its possible 'peaceful' use in industry.) Its brief was to draw up plans for the control of atomic energy. At the same time the Commission was charged with planning for the elimination of atomic weapons and of all other major weapons of mass destruction. In the immediate post-war

period, disarmament negotiations were almost entirely concerned with these questions.

By the middle of the year, in June 1946, the Americans submitted their plan – the Baruch Plan; the Soviet Union submitted a counter-proposal – the Gromyko Plan. The fundamental difference between the two proposals revolved around the question of the destruction of the weapons concerned and control to prevent their production in future. Whereas in the American plan a control scheme would have to be agreed before these weapons would be prohibited and any existing ones destroyed, in the Soviet plan the sequence was reversed, i.e. any such weapons in existence had to be destroyed first, before the establishment of international control over atomic energy.

Despite later modifications to these proposals, they established from the very beginning of the nuclear age, an unfortunate and conflicting pattern in which both superpowers have since approached disarmament and arms control issues. A proposal made by one side is found to be unacceptable by the other side, its counter-proposal being similarly rejected. Whether, as has frequently been argued, such proposals are deliberately framed so that they contain elements which are totally unacceptable to the other side, and hence are calculated to lead to the failure of negotiations, is a moot point, but one for which the history of disarmament negotiations between the superpowers since 1945 seems to provide plenty of evidence.

The explanation of this particular case, viz. the monumental failure of the Atomic Energy Commission to control 'atomic energy' in the immediate post-war years, must be related to the mistrust and suspicions existing between the USA and the USSR, whose war-time alliance was very soon transformed into Cold War hostility. Some historians and political scientists have explained this failure by referring to the American monopoly of the atomic bomb and the way in which this (temporary) monopoly was exploited in the war against Japan and *vis-à-vis* the Soviet Union. By 1949 the Soviet Union had developed its atomic bomb, with Britain and France to follow in 1952 and 1960, respectively.

After many years of negotiations, the US, the USSR and the UK finally agreed on a Non-Proliferation Treaty (NPT) which was signed in 1968 and came into force in 1970. Its main purpose is to prevent an increase in the number of countries possessing nuclear weapons. The Treaty prohibits the transfer of nuclear weapons by nuclear weapons states, and the acquisition of such weapons by non-nuclear weapons states. The latter are subject to international safeguards to prevent diversion of nuclear material from peaceful uses (in industry) to weapons purposes. In order to ensure that non-nuclear weapons countries will be able to benefit from (peaceful) nuclear energy, those signing the Treaty are promised assistance in developing their nuclear energy industry – hence the need for safeguards. No such assistance would be given to countries not adhering to the Treaty. It has of course since been amply demonstrated that it is a comparatively short step to subvert nuclear energy technology into nuclear weapons technology.

Although by the end of 1979 the number of parties to the Treaty amounted to 111, the Treaty cannot be described as a success. For a start, a number of important countries – e.g. Argentina, Brazil, India, Israel, Pakistan, South Africa – as well as two nuclear weapons countries, France and China – have not signed the Treaty. It will be noted that these are precisely the countries which are very likely to have (or shortly will have) the capability to develop a nuclear weapon. At the same time several of them are involved in serious conflicts with neighbouring states, increasing the likelihood of the use of nuclear weapons in future wars as well as their further proliferation in the respective areas.

During the negotiations leading up to the Treaty it became clear why some of these countries were to abstain from voting for it when this issue finally came before the UN General Assembly in 1968. They felt that this Treaty was wholly one of superpower design, which was shown by the fact that, whereas obligations were laid on the non-nuclear weapons countries, and *only* on them, to accept international control over nuclear installations, no such obligations were laid upon the nuclear weapons countries. The Treaty, it was felt, was 'grossly discriminatory'; it seemed to assume that the responsibility for non-proliferation was solely with the non-nuclear weapons countries and entailed no obligations on members of the 'nuclear club'. In the end a promise was extracted from the latter to negotiate, in good faith, the cessation of the nuclear arms race at an early date. More than ten years after the Treaty came into force, this pledge is still unfulfilled, and there are no real signs that it will be honoured in the near future. By their negligence, the superpowers must take a major share of the responsibility for the failure of non-proliferation and for the gradual and still continuing erosion of the Treaty – which is at once a symptom as well as a cause of this failure.

Other factors have contributed to this erosion. The Treaty contained an understanding whereby the non-nuclear countries which signed the Treaty would be favoured – as against non-parties – in regard to the supply of nuclear technology and material; supplier countries were to give Non-Proliferation Treaty Parties preferential treatment over information and material aid in the (peaceful) nuclear field. But NPT parties have not been the exclusive beneficiaries of such aid and trade, and hence the nuclear powers have whittled away an important inducement to join the Treaty.

The Treaty also promised that benefits from nuclear explosions, conducted for peaceful purposes, would be made available to Treaty partners at low cost. The Treaty specifically stipulates that states should be able to obtain such benefits 'pursuant to a special international agreement . . . through an international body with adequate representation of non-nuclear weapon states.'

It further indicates that 'Negotiations on this subject

shall commence as soon as possible after the Treaty enters into force'. But nothing has come of all this: no international agreement has been reached and no such international body has been established, nor have negotiations on the subject taken place. As a result, no benefits have been made available. A good example of the lack of balance between obligations and benefits in the NPT is contained in its first two articles, concerning transfers and safeguards. Those who, at the time the NPT came into existence, were members of the 'nuclear club' are free to transfer, to each other, nuclear weapons and other nuclear explosive devices, as well as to 'assist, encourage and induce' each other to acquire and manufacture equipment for nuclear-weapons production. The non-nuclear weapons countries are not free to do any of these things.

The lack of balance is also evident in the issue of security guarantees. In order to allay the worries of the nuclear-weapon-free nations expressed during the negotiations about security, these nations were promised security guarantees against attacks or threats of attack from nuclear weapons states: the US, USSR and UK moved a resolution in the Security Council wherein they promised immediate assistance to a non-nuclear weapons nation, party to the Treaty, if it became the 'victim of an act or an object of a threat of aggression in which nuclear weapons are used'. Experts have called this resolution valueless as a protection for non-nuclear weapons countries.

Since the Treaty came into force, two review conferences have been held to assess whether its purposes and provisions are being realized. These conferences were held in Geneva in 1975 and 1980, and are in fulfilment of the provision contained in article VIII of the Treaty.

On the issue of security guarantees, especially the pledges of non-use of nuclear weapons against non-nuclear weapons countries party to the Treaty, the First Review Conference went no further than to issue an appeal to all states, to refrain from the use or threat of force in their mutual relations – a simple reiteration of the requirement of all members of the UN according to its charter, and which is irrespective of their adherence or not to the NPT. The NPT parties were unable to extract assurances from the depository governments (US, USSR, UK) that the weapons they had renounced by becoming NPT parties would not be used against them. It is ironic that amongst nuclear-weapons countries, only China, not a party to the NPT, declared that it would never, under any circumstances, be the first to use nuclear weapons against any country.

Various other grounds for dissatisfaction on the part of the non-nuclear weapons countries, described above, were voiced and discussed, but both conferences failed to solve the problems essential for the survival of the NPT. The declaration adopted in 1975 promised more favourable treatment of the parties, but contained no firm undertakings to end discriminatory supplier policies. It stressed that the responsibilities and obligations of all parties must be balanced, but did not commit the nuclear powers to fulfilling their part of the bargain by halting the nuclear arms race. In particular, an agreement on a comprehensive test ban treaty by the superpowers would be seen as a concrete indication of their sincerity regarding this promise. The only novel features were the promotion of international arrangements to ensure the physical protection of nuclear materials and a stimulus to the idea of setting up multinational nuclear fuel cycle centres. Apart from the nuclear weapons countries, most participants expressed deep disillusionment with the outcome of the conference. No significant strengthening of the NPT resulted from the Second Review Conference.

In the absence of more meaningful security guarantees which the nuclear weapons powers so far have been unwilling to grant to non-nuclear countries party to the NPT, the security of the latter can be improved by agreements amongst themselves not to introduce nuclear weapons in their respective regions. It is recognized, for example, in the Final Declaration of the First NPT Review Conference, that nuclear-weapon-free zones can contribute to the security of states and provide important support for a non-proliferation regime. This is especially true as some parties to the NPT have indicated that they might consider their adherence to the Treaty in the light of changed circumstances – especially if other countries in the region were to acquire nuclear weapons.

TREATY OF TLATELOLCO

In 1967, one year before the NPT was signed, such a regional non-proliferation treaty was signed: the Treaty of Tlatelolco, which prohibits nuclear weapons in Latin America. By this act, the countries involved thus established the first internationally recognized nuclear-weapon-free zone in a populated area of the world. Two additional protocols are attached to this Treaty. In the first one, non-Latin American states are obliged to keep their territories, which lie within the zone, free of nuclear weapons. In a second protocol, nuclear powers undertake not to use or threaten to use nuclear weapons against the countries in the region concerned. Unfortunately, the only countries in the area with any immediate nuclear weapons potential, Argentina and Brazil, are still not fully bound by the provisions of the Treaty. Under this Treaty, which was the culmination of a process initiated by the Latin American states in 1963, a regional inter-governmental agency (Agency for the Prohibition of Nuclear Weapons in Latin America, OPANAL) was established to monitor its application and, especially, to administer the control systems.

It is interesting to point out that, although of the twenty-five states which were signatories to the Treaty, twenty-two are also signatories of the NPT, three Latin American states have not signed the NPT but *have* signed the regional Treaty (Argentina, Brazil, Chile). Furthermore, the two nuclear weapons countries not parties to the NPT are parties to the additional protocols: France has signed Protocols I and II, China Protocol II. Four states have yet to join the Tlatelolco Treaty, namely, Cuba, Guyana, Dominica and Santa Lucia. Until they sign and ratify the Treaty, it will not effectively and genuinely cover the whole of Latin America. Even so, what has been accomplished so far is one of the very few successes in the disarmament – or more precisely – non-armament field.

The Treaty of Tlatelolco followed in the wake of general ideas for agreements of this kind which were first proposed in the 1950s in a European context. Of these the Rapacki plan for the creation of a nuclear-weapon-free zone in Central Europe (comprising Poland, Czechoslovakia, East and West Germany), proposed by the Polish Foreign Minister to the UN General Assembly in 1957, is undoubtedly the best known. This plan did not have the approval of the Western powers and could not be realized. There are other long-standing efforts to establish similar zones, e.g. in Africa, the Middle East, South Asia, the South Pacific. Apart from Latin America, other nuclear-weapon-free zones do exist, but these are not in inhabited areas, thus reducing somewhat their significance.

OTHER TREATIES

In 1959 the Antarctic Treaty was signed; it declared that Antarctica shall be used exclusively for peaceful purposes. An Outer Space Treaty was signed in 1967. It prohibits the *placing* of nuclear or other weapons of mass destruction in orbit around the earth; it also established that celestial bodies are to be used exclusively for peaceful purposes. As the phrasing indicates, outer space has remained open for the *passage* of ballistic missiles carrying nuclear weapons, whereas the deployment in outer space of weapons not capable of mass destruction is allowed. The same distinctions also considerably weaken the significance of the Sea-Bed Treaty of 1971, which prohibits the *emplacement* of nuclear weapons on the sea bed beyond a twelve-mile zone. The treaty permits, however, the use of the sea bed for facilities that service free-moving nuclear weapons systems and, in particular, presents no obstacle to a nuclear arms race under water. It is not surprising that Alva Myrdal has called this an 'Ocean Treaty Truncated'. With the exception of the Strategic Arms Limitation Treaty talks between the two superpowers (which will be discussed in the following chapter), the agreements and treaties mentioned above are the major ones in the field of nuclear weapons. Since these weapons constitute the foremost threat to the security of the world, their control and ultimate elimination is of the highest priority. The issue of security, however, is an undivided one, i.e. peace and security are also at risk because of the existence of conventional (non-nuclear) weapons and military forces. In the East-West context, as elsewhere, the existence of military force is related to political motives and intentions, and such factors as hostility, fear, and misperception play an important role in the processes leading to the further build-up of armaments, and account for the difficulty in bringing about disarmament.

The connection between nuclear and conventional weapons must be made not only because the factors underlying their existence and growth are common to both kinds of weapons, but also because military doctrines and logic suggest that in any future superpower confrontation it will be very difficult to prevent 'conventional' war from escalating into a nuclear one. Hence, the need for such disarmament negotiations as those on Mutual Reductions of Forces and Armaments in Central Europe (MBFR) which started in 1973 but have not yet reached a conclusion, or for measures which might facilitate this process, such as those contained in the Document on Confidence-Building Measures, which is a result of the Conference on Security and Co-operation in Europe

(CSCE) held in Helsinki in 1972, followed by review conferences in Belgrade (1977–8) and Madrid (1980–1).

Finally, we can only mention the existence of various other disarmament or non-armament agreements, such as the Convention of the Prohibition of Biological Weapons (signed in 1972), the 1925 Geneva Protocol for the prohibition of chemical and bacteriological warfare, the Environmental Modification Convention (signed in 1977), which prohibits the use of the environment (e.g. stimulation of earthquakes or landslides, control of lightning, climate modification, river diversion) as means of warfare.

Because the arms race between the superpowers threatens the entire world, it is not surprising that the lack of progress in the various disarmament negotiations between them has cast doubts on the genuineness of their many pledges to bring pressure from the whole world community to bear on their disarmament efforts. As indicated already, the Partial Test Ban Treaty would probably not have come about without the persistent efforts of a number of non-aligned countries. The United Nations and its various disarmament bodies present the ideal forum for such global discussions; in 1978 the General Assembly held a special session on disarmament (23 May – 1 July), the results of which are contained in the Final Document. The two substantive sections deal with a programme of action and a discussion of the machinery for disarmament negotiations; a follow-up conference is scheduled to take place in 1982.

REFERENCES

Stockholm International Peace Research Institute. *World Armaments and Disarmament, SIPRI Year Book 1980.* Taylor & Francis, London. The findings of this book are summarized in: *Armaments or Disarmament? SIPRI Brochure 1980*, Stockholm.

Armaments and Disarmament in the Nuclear Age. A Handbook. SIPRI, MIT Press, 1976.

Arms Control: A Survey; and Appraisal of Multilateral Agreements. SIPRI, Taylor & Francis, London, 1978.

United Nations – General Assembly. General and Complete Disarmament. *Comprehensive Study on Nuclear Weapons. Report of the Secretary-General.* UN, New York, 1980.

Disarmament. A periodic review by the United Nations. Vol III, No.2, July 1980 (Second Review Conference of the Parties to the Treaty on the Non-Proliferation of Nuclear Weapons).

United Nations. Office of Public Information. *Final Document of Assembly Session on Disarmament* (23 May – 1 July 1978).

United Nations General Assembly. A Guide to the Final Document of the *Special Session on Disarmament.* 23 May – 1 July 1978.

Myrdal, A. (1977). *The Game of Disarmament.* How the United States and Russia Run the Arms Race. Manchester University Press.

10
The SALT Talks

The evolution of interest in and general status of arms control and disarmament which was briefly reviewed at the beginning of the previous chapter has reached its climax in the Strategic Arms Limitation Treaty (SALT) negotiations which the United States and the Soviet Union have been conducting over the past decade. So much interest has been expressed in them, and so much coverage has been given to their progress (or lack of it) in the media, that the 1970s can rightly be called the SALT-decade, not merely as a description of the disarmament 'scene' of those years but, over and beyond this, as an expression of the most important item on the political agenda of the superpowers, and thus of the world as a whole.

More than ever before, disarmament, in the shape of SALT, has been the single most important issue for both politicians and policy-makers as well as a wider public. Developments between the two superpowers were immediately translated into their bearings on SALT, whereas progress or failure in SALT was itself regarded as a sensitive barometer of the evolution of Soviet-American relations.

This general interest in the SALT negotiations is to be welcomed even though they represent a belated attempt, at least ten years overdue, to deal with the problems which resulted from the development of intercontinental ballistic missiles. Although both superpowers were in possession of such missiles by the end of the 1950s, it was another decade before this technological advance found its place on their disarmament agenda. The agreements which subsequently became known as SALT I were signed in May 1972 in Moscow. The fact that on this occasion (as well as on further occasions in the SALT process) both heads of state, Nixon and Brezhnev, were present at the ceremony of signing, is a symbolic indication of the importance, mentioned already, which both countries attached to these negotiations. On this occasion a number of agreements were signed, those specifically to do with arms limitation consisting of a Treaty on the Limitation of Antiballistic Missiles (ABM Treaty) and the 'Interim Agreement on Certain Measures with Respect to the Limitation of Strategic Offensive Arms'.

SALT I: ANTI-BALLISTIC MISSILE TREATY

By limiting the deployment of anti-ballistic defence systems, the ABM Treaty guaranteed the continuation of the 'balance of terror' and the deterrence system and thus, so it is conventionally argued, of the precarious peace between the superpowers upon which it is based. As long as no effective defence against nuclear missiles existed, the doctrine of 'Mutually Assured Destruction' (MAD) would prevail. Once technological developments brought the possibility of such a defence system nearer to fruition, an agreement not to exploit these developments and thus acquire an invulnerability which would destabilize the deterrent system became necessary.

The successful conclusion of the ABM Treaty has, however, been explained by invoking more pragmatic and/or cynical arguments, such as the technical impossibility (at least at the time) or the sheer economic cost of constructing an effective ABM system; in this perspective the agreement was nothing more than a bowing to the inevitable. Being cast in the shape of an arms control agreement, it provided cause for self-congratulation and an advertisement of the earnest strivings and intentions of both superpowers *vis-à-vis* the rest of the world.

It has recently been estimated that the efficiency of the Soviet ABM system deployed around Moscow in shooting down ballistic missiles 'would probably be less than 20 per cent'. According to the same source, this system 'was at best a political gimmick to impress upon the citizens of Moscow that the Politburo was doing all in its power to protect them from the devastation likely to follow a nuclear ballistic missile attack' (Air Vice-Marshal S. W. B. Menaul, Letter to *The Times*, 6th July 1981).

The Treaty allowed each superpower to deploy a maximum of two ABM systems. One was meant to protect each nation's capital from the other's missiles. The other one was to protect an intercontinental ballistic missile launching site. In this way, the limited ABM defence system was held to be a reinforcement of the strategic deterrent system: the most precious civilian target (the nation's capital) as well as its most valuable military asset (a prominent missile site) would remain invulnerable in any nuclear attack. Each of these two systems was permitted 100 launchers and an equal number of interceptor missiles.

It is worth pointing out that at this time the United States had no ABM system, although it was beginning to build two sites. The Soviet Union had one system, Galosh, deployed around Moscow, consisting of four complexes, each comprising sixteen launchers (with associated radar and interceptor missiles), or sixty-four launchers in all. Far from being a disarmament measure, it can be seen that the ABM Treaty even has difficulties qualifying as a non-armament measure, and that when describing it as an 'arms control' agreement, not only purists of the English language might query the use which is made of the latter part of this reassuring expression!

At the summit meeting in 1974, Nixon and Brezhnev agreed to reduce the ABM installations to one site each;

whereas the Soviet Union chose to retain its Moscow site, the United States selected an ICBM site (ABM protocol of July 1974). Approaching its tenth anniversary, the ABM Treaty is in urgent need of revision and updating if it is to have any future relevance at all. The 1972 Treaty limited ABMs only in the form in which they existed at the time and thus, by omission, allowed the development and deployment of systems based on physical principles different from those envisaged in the 1972 Treaty (such as laser beams). A treaty banning the use of anti-satellite weapons is equally urgently needed.

SALT I: OFFENSIVE MISSILE NEGOTIATIONS

Whereas the first part of SALT I (the ABM Treaty) was concerned with the limitation of defensive missile systems, the second part ('Interim Agreement') was an attempt to limit offensive missile systems. This agreement introduced a temporary freeze, covering a five-year period, 1972–7, on the number of strategic ballistic missile launchers then operational or under construction, i.e. land-based (ICBM) and submarine-based (SLBM) intercontinental ballistic missile launchers capable of firing missiles to reach the territory of the other superpower (hence 'strategic'). Unlike SALT II, exact numbers of these launchers belonging to each side were not given but were subject to an understanding. The quantitative ceilings discussed were, however, so high that no real sacrifice was made in this agreement. Quantitative and qualitative loopholes in it enabled both superpowers to increase considerably their nuclear arsenals.

No limit was set on the number of warheads with which missiles could be fitted by equipping them with multiple re-entry vehicles. The increase in lethality thus obtained per missile made the numerical limitations on the missiles themselves rather irrelevant. Neither did the agreement prohibit developments affecting the quality of both missiles and warheads, such as would lead to greater targeting accuracy or more powerful warheads, developments which again made for greater lethality, and which reduced the usefulness of the quantitative restrictions introduced.

SALT II

When the Interim Agreement formally expired on 3 October 1977, negotiations for a new, more permanent agreement were well advanced, and the two parties decided to abide by the terms of the Interim Agreement pending the conclusion of its successor. Some of its essential elements were agreed on several years before, at a summit meeting between Ford and Brezhnev, held in Vladivostok in November 1974.

The framework then adopted established the principle of equal ceilings on strategic nuclear delivery vehicles, comprising the three categories of intercontinental ballistic missile launchers, submarine-based ballistic missile launchers and heavy bombers. Each side was permitted a maximum of 2400 such vehicles. Within this overall limit, a sub-limit was set on the number of ICBM and SLBM launchers which could be equipped with multiple independently targetable re-entry vehicles (MIRVs). Not more than 1320 launchers were to be so equipped, the remainder of the ICBM and SLBM missiles each carrying a single warhead only.

In Geneva in May 1977, the USA and the USSR agreed on a general framework for SALT II having three components: (a) a treaty lasting until 1985; (b) a short-term protocol dealing with the problems for which long-term solutions had yet to be found and (c) a joint statement of principles for a future SALT III. This 'three-tier' arrangement became the structure of the SALT II agreement reached two years later, and signed by Carter and Brezhnev in June 1979 in Vienna. Before some comments are made on their value, an outline of the agreements for the limitation of strategic nuclear arms will be given.

The aggregate ceiling of 2400 vehicles agreed at Vladivostok applied to the end of 1980 when this ceiling was to be lowered to 2250. By the end of 1981 any strategic nuclear systems in excess of this figure must have been dismantled. To comply with this limit, a certain amount of disarmament has to take place; it is estimated that the USA, which will have to dismantle 33 vehicles, will choose for this purpose some moth-balled bombers and/ or outdated ballistic missile launchers. The USSR will have to reduce its relevant vehicles by 254, and is equally expected to choose obsolete weapons to implement this reduction. These reductions, required to stay within the 2250 ceiling of vehicles permitted, amount to 1.5 per cent for the USA and ten per cent for the USSR. It is however, not only – or even primarily – because these cuts will be made by removing obsolete weapons systems that this part of the SALT II agreement can at best be regarded as a merely 'formal' disarmament measure – when looked at in the overall context of SALT, their irrelevance will be apparent. In particular, the sub-limits on systems able to deliver more than one warhead (MIRVs) are very high. Far from freezing the situation, let alone causing a reduction, they allow an increase in the number of missiles equipped with multiple warheads, each one of which will be capable of being aimed at a separate target. The sub-limit of 1200 on launchers of MIRVed ballistic missiles for each side will enable the USA to increase its possession of these missiles by 15 per cent whereas for the USSR this sub-limit offers the opportunity to increase its relevant arsenals by 60 per cent.

Furthermore, another sub-limit in this category of MIRVed vehicles allows a maximum of 820 ICBMs to be MIRVed. This represents an increase for the USA of 50 per cent and for the USSR of 35 per cent in this most threatening element of their strategic nuclear forces. A sub-limit of 1320 applies to the total number of MIRVed missiles (both ICBMs and SLBMs) and heavy bombers equipped with long-range cruise missiles (air-launched cruise missiles, ALCMs), i.e. those having a range of over 600 kilometres. All these 1320 vehicles are conveniently referred to as MIRVed systems. The following table provides the actual number of the different weapons systems (which are the object of SALT) for both super-powers at the time of signing as well as, in the last column, the limits and sub-limits agreed.

Salt II limits and US and Soviet strategic forces as of 18th June 1979

	Launcher	USA	USSR	SALT II limit
ICBM	MIRVed	550	608	⎰ 820
	Non-MIRVed	504	790	⎱ 1,200
	Total	1,054	1398	
SLBM	MIRVed	496	144	
	Non-MIRVed	160	806	
	Total	656	950	
Bombers	With ALCM	3	0	
	Without ALCM	570	156	
	Total	573	156	
Total MIRV vehicles (including 3 ALCM-equipped bombers)		1,049	752	1,320
Total weapons systems		2,283	2,504	2,250

To make these figures somewhat more real, we shall briefly, for the American side only, indicate what they represent. The 1054 ICBMs consist of 550 MIRVed Minutemen III missiles and 450 Minuteman II and 54 Titan II non-MIRVed missiles.

As regards SLBMs, 496 MIRVed SLBMs are carried on 31 Poseidon nuclear submarines, each submarine being equipped with 16 missiles. By 1985, with or without

SALT, it is expected that another 144 MIRVed SLBMs will be available on six Trident nuclear submarines, each submarine carrying 24 missiles. These 640 missiles on Poseidon and Trident nuclear submarines will carry an average of ten warheads each, making for a total of 6400 individually targetable nuclear warheads based on submarines. This will bring the American total of MIRVed ICBMs and SLBMs to 1190 (i.e. 550 ICBMs plus 496 and another 144 SLBMs), *still below the 1200 ceiling*! In case the seventh Trident submarine is deployed, its 24 MIRVed missiles will bring the total of US launchers in this category to 1214, which can only be done – without breaching SALT – by a reduction in the number of its Poseidon or Minuteman III launchers. Similar developments, not always as easy to document as in the case of the USA owing to the great secrecy surrounding these issues, are under way in the USSR.

As we have seen, the USA also plans to strengthen the bomber component of its strategic forces by equipping its B-52 bombers with long-range ALCMs. In case the sublimit of 1200 launchers of MIRVed ballistic missiles was reached, and in order to stay within the 1320 sub-limit which also includes bombers with ALCMs, not more than 120 of such bombers could be deployed. It is expected that these bombers will carry an average of 20 cruise missiles. This will still leave a large fleet of bombers carrying a great number of free-fall bombs and short-range attack missiles probably representing more than half of the total of

---

'The greying, heavy-set man with military medals glittering on his suit jacket and a hearing aid poking out behind his left ear turned slowly and cautiously toward his visitor and spoke of atomic weapons. "*The first time one of those things is fired in anger,*" he said, "*everything is* lost. *The warring nations would never be able to put matters back together.*"'

Leonid Brezhnev at the SALT talks, 23 October 1978, described by Don Oberdorfer in the *Washington Post*.

American strategic nuclear megatonnage.

As a result of the further expansion of strategic nuclear arms allowed under the terms of the SALT agreement – especially the high number of warheads permitted on ballistic missiles as well as the number of cruise missiles permitted on heavy bombers – the total number of deliverable warheads in the US and Soviet strategic nuclear arsenals is expected to rise by between 50 to 70 per cent between 1979 (signing of SALT II) and 1985, the year of the expiration of the treaty. *SALT II is thus not making the slightest difference to the total quantity of destructive power which is now contained in the superpowers' strategic nuclear arsenals or, more importantly still, to their further increase.*

Although these criticisms of SALT II are, by themselves, serious enough to characterize the treaty as a very inadequate one, allowing developments to continue with virtually no inhibitions or restrictions materially affecting this process, possibly even graver shortcomings have to be mentioned. Not only are the purely quantitative limitations on the various weapons systems wholly inadequate, they are such that they favour the more sophisticated and threatening systems. This latter fact, that SALT completely fails to come to grips with curtailing the qualitative aspects of the strategic nuclear arms race between the superpowers – and thus fails to ensure the future stability of deterrence – is its most fundamental weakness. The overriding rationale behind the SALT process is the need to place constraints on the nuclear arms competition between the USA and USSR in the conviction that such constraints will reduce the likelihood of nuclear war by securing strategic stability. Judged by this criterion, the failure is almost total, as will be briefly indicated.

STRATEGIC STABILITY

Strategic stability implies the prevention of technological developments and breakthroughs which would enable

one side in the nuclear arms race to undertake a pre-
emptive strike against the other side's strategic nuclear
forces, destroying them to such an extent that any retaliation and destruction they will wreak on the aggressor
will be minimal, or at any rate not sufficient to restrain the
latter from launching such an attack. Not only would the
effective and actual possession of such a capability undermine stability; the mere belief on the part of one of the
superpowers that this is the case will lead it to perceive the
situation as unstable and thus fraught with dangers and
uncertainties.

As we saw in Chapter 4, the danger in such a situation
arises not only because of the possibility or probability of
an impending attack by the side in the lead; in order to
prevent a greater gap from opening up between them, the
side which feels threatened may well decide on an attack
itself, believing that a suprise attack now may leave it in a
better military-strategic and political position than certain
defeat later. To what extent does SALT inhibit developments which might, if left unchecked, lead to instability?

Of the three types of strategic nuclear 'delivery' vehicles – ICBMs, SLBMs, bombers – the latter two are
mobile, whereas ICBMs are fixed. Their location is
known, and their only protection is the hardened silos.
Their continued invulnerability is dependent on the
impossibility or unlikelihood of attacking missiles and
warheads scoring direct hits. Virtually no amount of
reinforcement will be able to withstand the impact of a
nuclear warhead detonating directly on the target or very
close to it. Although SALT II does attempt to limit the
development of new types of ICBMs, as well as the
modernization of existing types, it does not prevent both
superpowers from making their existing ICBMs more
accurate, more explosive and more reliable. This is being
done through the improvement and replacement of re-
entry vehicles, guidance systems, warheads and other
components. We have already seen that both the United
States and the Soviet Union are engaged in intensive

efforts to do just this, a major factor in the slide to nuclear war.

Instead of focussing on these developments and trying to halt them, SALT allows the superpowers to 'counter' them by the deployment of one new type of ICBM. This is a very roundabout way of 'limiting' arms! The new ICBM type the Americans are planning is the M-X (Missile-Experimental). It is supposed to remedy the perceived vulnerability of the ICBMs by making them mobile. In one plan it is envisaged that there will be 200 missiles, for each one of which there will be 23 hardened horizontal shelters. These shelters will be placed at regular intervals of about 2 kilometres in a huge system of 200 road loops. Each loop will contain one missile, carried on a vehicle; both will be shielded by another vehicle when the missile is being moved from one shelter to another thus preventing detection of the exact location of the missile. Each M-X will probably be fitted with ten MRVs, the maximum number allowed on a new type of ICBM. The individual warheads will have an explosive yield of 335 to 500 kilotons, and are likely to be carried to their targets by manoeuvrable re-entry vehicles which use terminal guidance capable of very accurate targeting. It is likely that this planned new American system will stimulate the construction of a similar mobile ICBM system in the Soviet Union. Alternatively, it might decide to deploy a greater number of warheads on existing ICBMs and/or a greater number of MIRVed ICBMs, in order to be able to hit all 4600 M-X shelters (with terribly high fall-out effects) to ensure the 200 missiles will be made vulnerable. These options might necessitate the discontinuation of certain limitations agreed in SALT when the Treaty expires in 1985.

The outcome of these developments is predictable and familiar – they require great expenditures (in the case of M-X also a massive land area), and, by amassing more and more sophisticated and threatening weapons systems, they decrease rather than increase security. What is seen as a purely defensive reaction by one power in response to new developments and threats to security – the M-X system – is, from the other side, looked upon as itself a destabilizing factor, which in turn needs counter measures.

From this discussion it will be clear that the SALT agreement does *not* contribute to the maintenance and strengthening of strategic stability as regards the ICBM force, because too many qualitative developments are allowed – particularly those concerned with providing war-fighting rather than war-deterring characteristics.

The situation is not much different when one looks at the second component of the superpowers' strategic nuclear arsenals, the SLBMs. The SLBMs are regarded as the most stabilizing part of the strategic nuclear forces because of two main characteristics, one positive, one negative. The first feature of the submarine-based nuclear forces is their mobility which prevents, or at any rate makes difficult their detection, and thus makes them far less vulnerable to attack than the fixed, land-based ICBMs. Even if the latter could be destroyed in a pre-emptive stroke, the availability of the SLBMs to strike back is supposed to guarantee the continuation of the doctrine of Mutual Assured Destruction and, thus, deterrence. The SLBMs also contribute to strategic stability because of their inability, at present, to destroy hard targets, i.e. land-based ICBMs. At present, SLBMs and their warheads are neither accurate enough nor sufficiently powerful to constitute a first-strike weapon, able to destroy all the opponent's ICBMs in one strike. Moreover, SLBM flight times from probable launch areas are such that they provide the third component in the strategic nuclear triad, the heavy bombers, with sufficient warning time to leave their bases so that the nuclear weapons they carry will still be available for possible retaliation.

The improvements permitted under SALT affecting SLBMs will undermine the characteristics which, so far, have made for some stability in this particular weapons category. First of all, unlike its predecessor, SALT II does not contain a specific ceiling for the numbers of missile-launching submarines or their missiles. (Numbers have to be such, however, that they are in line with the overall ceiling on strategic nuclear delivery vehicles and the sub-limit on MIRVed ballistic missile launchers.) Thus, not only did President Carter approve the M-X missile (expressly allowed under SALT II) one week before signing the Treaty, but shortly before, a new type of submarine was commissioned as well, the *USS Ohio*, the first US Trident submarine. It is expected that six or seven Trident submarines will be in use by 1985. As mentioned in Chapter 1, each will be equipped with 24 SLBM launchers, each Trident I missile having a maximum range of 4600 miles. Although up to 14 re-entry vehicles and thus individually targetable warheads are permitted to be deployed on a SLBM (by both powers), it is expected that each Trident I missile will carry eight warheads only, each of about 100 kilotons. The greater range of the Trident missile will enable the submarine to move in an ocean area almost five times as large as that which has been customary up to now. This means that the new submarine, which will also be able to operate and launch missiles from greater depths than hitherto, will be more difficult to locate by the anti-submarine warfare (ASW) forces of the opponent.

The greater SLBM range also allows the Trident submarine to stay closer to home waters than before, thus reducing even further the chances of a successful enemy ASW operation. Mainly because of improvements in accuracy, the Trident I warhead could have nearly twice the hard-target destruction capability of a Poseidon warhead; even so, this capability is small in comparison with the anti-silo capabilities of ICBM warheads on both sides. Whilst this development, if further continued, may confer pre-emptive strike capability on the SLBMs as regards the opponent's ICBM force, another development is working in the same direction. The SALT agreement does not include a ban on the testing of SLBMs along so-called 'depressed trajectories', i.e. the firing of missiles along trajectories which shorten the ballistic flight path. This procedure has the effect of reducing flight time and thus warning time. The vulnerability of land-based bomber forces and, increasingly, of ICBM silos too, will be adversely affected. More powerful warheads, as well as more sophisticated precision guidance mechanisms, will be used on the Trident II SLBM, which is currently in development.

At least one of the attributes of SLBMs which make for stability, their relatively modest capabilities to destroy hard targets, is thus continuously being eroded. *SALT has not put any brakes on this process*. The other feature of SLBMs, which contributes to their being regarded as a stable deterrent, their mobility and survivability, has to be evaluated cautiously in view of developments under way and, again, the failure of SALT to prohibit these. The greater mobility and survivability are being countered by advances in anti-submarine warfare techniques. Further developments in ASW techniques could lead to the acquisition of a first-strike capability on the part of one or both superpowers against the other's SLBMs. A SALT agreement which would have included restrictions on ASW development as well as restrictions on new types of SLBMs (thus preventing increases in their accuracy and lethality) together with a ban on the testing of SLBMs along depressed trajectories would have made a considerable contribution to ensuring that at least one crucial component in the strategic nuclear arsenals of the superpowers would have been safeguarded from a threatening, destabilizing competition.

Finally, the SALT agreement does little to 'limit' the development and deployment of heavy bombers and air-launched cruise missiles (sea-launched and ground-launched cruise missiles are dealt with in the short-term protocol, appended to SALT II). The USA plans to equip, and is entitled to do so, all its 151 operational B52G bombers with 20 air-launched cruise missiles each. Another 200 operational B-52s will not be converted into ALCM carriers, but will continue to function as strategic nuclear delivery vehicles. A similar number of heavy bombers are considered to be non-operational, but are still included in the overall aggregate number. American technology is much further advanced than the Soviet Union's regarding the cruise missile; the SALT negotiations concerning this weapon contain stipulations which were largely aimed at restraining further American progress.

It must also be noted that American nuclear bombers capable of reaching the Soviet Union from bases in Europe or aircraft carriers are not covered in SALT II. At the Vladivostok summit meeting it was agreed to exclude from the SALT negotiations these so-called 'forward-based' systems. Also excluded from the Treaty is the Soviet Backfire bomber. This is regarded by the Soviet Union as a medium-range bomber, which it has solemnly promised not to modify in any way which might turn it into a 'strategic' weapon. The issue of the cruise missile and the Backfire bomber – particularly their status as strategic nuclear delivery systems – slowed down the SALT negotiations on several occasions. Eventually in these respects as well as some others, difficulties were overcome by supplementing the SALT II Treaty with a protocol, which contains certain limitations until the end of 1981 (e.g. a ban on the deployment of ground- and sea-launched long-range cruise missiles and a ban on the deployment of mobile ICBM launchers). It was expected that long-term solutions would meanwhile be worked out for these problems.

Apart from the SALT II Treaty and the protocol, a joint statement of principles and basic guidelines was agreed upon concerning future negotiations on the limitation of strategic nuclear arms (SALT III). It is indicative of the lack of progress made in SALT II that for many, the promise of a further SALT agreement with, hopefully, more substantial arms limitation successes than have been achieved so far, is SALT II's greatest significance. SALT has brought about more openness and a wider dissemination of information, including basic data, regarding the various nuclear weapons in the arsenals of the superpowers.

This is a small but welcome advance in an area which is normally rife with suspicion and secrecy, factors which themselves contribute to fuelling the arms race. Finally, the fact that the nuclear arms competition will continue, but will now be more predictable as a result of the (often nominal) limitations imposed, is seen as another gain. These positive aspects of SALT pale into insignificance, however, when confronted with the failure to limit nuclear armaments, to say nothing of disarmament. This failure is all the more tragic as it amounts to a breach of the promise contained in the Non-Proliferation Treaty, thereby virtually ensuring future world-wide proliferation of nuclear arms.

In the period leading up to the signing of SALT II, powerful sections of public opinion in the USA criticized the Treaty and the positions taken by the American negotiators for having jeopardized American security – it was felt that the Treaty was highly unbalanced, favouring the Soviet Union. Its acceptance and ratification by the Senate was therefore always uncertain, or to be gained only after measures of compensation – for example an increase in the overall level of military expenditures, or strengthening forces not directly to do with SALT – had been agreed to by the American Government. It was therefore hardly surprising that the Soviet invasion of Afghanistan dealt a mortal blow to any hopes of ratification; the change of government in the USA completed the process. SALT II does not have the approval of the present Reagan administration. Later in 1981 'preliminary' talks with the Soviet Union have been promised with a view to bringing about a more meaningful agreement.

REFERENCES

The analysis of the SALT II Treaty in this chapter closely follows that made by the Stockholm International Peace Research Institute (SIPRI) in *World Armaments and Disarmament*: *SIPRI Yearbook 1980*. Taylor & Francis, London, 1980.

See especially:

Chapter 6. SALT II: an analysis of the agreements, pp. 209–24.

Chapter 7. Verification of the SALT II Treaty, pp. 285–315.

Chapter 6 also contains, in appendix, the texts of the Treaty and the Protocol, as well as the several statements and understandings; pp. 245–74.

There is also a useful 'Index to the SALT II Treaty', pp. 275–83.

11
Why the Failure?

In trying to explain the failure of disarmament and arms control we have to take into account several factors. Contemporary peace research and the work of other social scientists suggests that the causes of the seemingly unstoppable arms race – like the causes of its almost inevitable outcome, war – are many and inter-related. Some of the difficulties have been known for a long time and others are of a more recent nature or have become more prominent.

An important factor has to be recognized right at the beginning. In the general framework in which disarmament negotiations take place, one does not negotiate in isolation but with one or more other parties; negotiations are multilateral. It is the insistence on the need for multilateral negotiations, leading to the simultaneous and balanced reduction of military forces of all participants, which has characterized the approach in this field.

Of course not *all* disarmament decisions are like this. The parliaments of Sweden and Canada decided unilaterally not to produce or acquire nuclear weapons, and some countries are relatively strict in applying arms export policies, again on a unilateral basis.

Multilateral disarmament is, in a sense, the ideal approach: nations arm because they are insecure and want to protect their independence and sovereignty (among other reasons). If all agree to limit armaments, the security of all might be maintained at lower cost. If

The Unmaking of Mankind: *3 million years of evolution to produce . . . the short haircut*

just one state does not participate in negotiations then others may be unwilling to proceed, believing partial disarmament to jeopardize their security.

John Garnett has written that,

Without question, the basic conceptual apparatus for thinking about disarmament was articulated well before the Second World War; and although a few new interesting ideas have emerged since 1945, it is quite remarkable how much of the post-war thinking was foreshadowed in that earlier period.

This was the period, between the wars, when unsuccessful negotiations took place under the auspices of the League of Nations; one can even find parallels with modern attitudes in the 19th century. A leading advocate of peace and disarmament, Elihu Burritt, argued in 1861 for the 'simultaneous and proportionate disarmament of nations'. Exactly 100 years later the Soviet-American McCloy-Zorin Agreement on Principles for Disarmament stated that 'All measures of general and complete disarmament should be balanced so that at no stage . . . could any state or group of states gain military advantage, and that security is ensured equally for all'.

The concepts of mutuality, reciprocity, simultaneity, balance and proportionality occur again and again, and offer one explanation for the poor results achieved in disarmament negotiations.

We indicated earlier that the SALT process was delayed by disputes over the nature of 'strategic' weapons, these difficulties leading to the issuing of a separate protocol and accounting for the 'understandings' and promises which accompany the Treaty and made it possible to regard certain weapons as belonging to one category (e.g. tactical) rather than another (e.g. strategic). If such difficulties arise in *bilateral* treaties, then much greater problems can be expected at the multilateral level.

Thus the negotiations for Mutual and Balanced Force Reductions (MBFR) in Europe, held in Vienna since 1973, and involving nineteen NATO and WTO countries, accepted in principle the limiting of the size of ground forces to 700,000 for each side, but could not reach agreement on the present size of WTO troops! After eight years an agreement on basic facts and figures is still lacking.

When such a relatively simple agreement cannot be obtained, what hope is there of reaching agreements on limiting highly sophisticated weapons, such as in SALT, where qualitative characteristics are becoming increasingly important. SALT seems to suggest the answer – numerical ceilings *can* be agreed precisely because of their relative irrelevance in the face of qualitative improvements, the control of which hardly figures on the agenda.

What is true of the SALT negotiations between the

USA and the Soviet Union is even more true of the two alliances – they both possess enormous military strength but this strength is composed of different elements so that there are major asymmetries in the character of their weaponry and manpower. With the maintenance of equal and present security an apparent prerequisite, the problems of resolving these disparities are immense.

It is therefore sobering to reflect on the opportunities for disarmament in the past with less sophisticated weapons, fewer states and more homogeneity in both. Even then, though, progress was virtually non-existent. Thus these problems suggest, even by themselves, good reasons for the failure of recent disarmament negotiations to achieve worthwhile results. There are, though, more fundamental problems, but before discussing them we should mention another major obstacle, that of verification.

Mutual hostility and mistrust make it inevitable that verification and inspection must have high priority – without adequate safeguards to ensure that the contracting parties abide by the decisions no agreements will be possible. Many negotiations since 1945 have broken down on the issue of verification and it is difficult to tell whether one or both parties could, in particular circumstances, be blamed for taking up unreasonable positions, or whether differences were genuine. There have certainly been accusations of deliberate creation of difficulties to prevent agreements being reached.

'Verification' is always available to shipwreck an agreement at the last stage – by pursuing or insisting on an absolutely perfect verification system, rather than accepting a merely adequate and satisfactory one – blame being placed on the other side.

On-site inspection as a means of verification has never been popular with the Soviet Union and the tendency now is towards using 'national technical means of verification' such as remote sensing by satellite. While such techniques are remarkably sophisticated, new weapons developments are such that they can not now be verified by such means. However competent the remote sensing, it would be difficult to determine the number of warheads in a MIRV system, for example.

Thus while technological innovation, in the form of introduction of satellites, may have appeared to be of use in decreasing the need for on-site inspection, a whole range of other technological innovations are making this much more difficult. They also further undermine arms control agreements by leading to the development of multi-purpose weapons which do not fit into the normal categories, presenting difficulties of an entirely new order, as was apparent in the SALT negotiations.

The cruise missile is a very good example of such a weapon. It can carry conventional or nuclear warheads and in the latter form can have tactical or strategic functions. It can be launched from many different kinds of platform (vehicle, plane, submarine etc.) and, furthermore, its specific mission can be decided at very short notice because of the very flexible information and guidance systems with which it is equipped. One can imagine it appearing in different kinds of arms control arenas.

These various formidable problems of individual negotiations have, on occasions, led to other approaches, especially attempts to develop *comprehensive* disarmament negotiations as a means of overcoming individual difficulties relating to particular systems. Such comprehensive approaches have experienced other difficulties, especially the requirement of major commitments by participants. Thus problems inherent in each approach have resulted in a fluctuation, within the UN in particular, between specific and general negotiations.

TECHNOLOGICAL MOMENTUM

Another way in which technological progress hampers arms control and disarmament is that, at the same time that negotiators are trying to control certain existing weapons, more advanced versions and completely new ones are being developed and even prepared for deployment. *Any arms control agenda is out of date by the time it is drawn up*, and eventual agreement may be of only antiquarian interest – one step forward and two steps back!

One possible approach, suggested by Christoph Bertram of IISS, is to negotiate in terms of missions rather than weapons. Instead of worrying about military *inputs* such as troops, tanks, missiles or warheads, arms control concentrates on *outputs* such as abilities to make pre-emptive strikes. In other words, numerical symmetry is replaced by option symmetry, resulting in agreements more resistant to technological pressure.

Yet no approach is promising unless the political will for success in arms control is present. Far from restraining technological momentum, arms control talks often have the opposite effect with states being unwilling to go 'naked into the conference chamber', preferring to negotiate from a position of strength. Thus it is proclaimed that participation is not a sign of weakness, rather the threat of arms escalation is made unless agreement is reached.

A new development becomes a bargaining chip, but if the negotiations fail that chip becomes a reality and this process can be repeated continually. This kind of negotiating from strength, wanting to commence discussions from a position of superiority rather than equality, hides the reality of wanting to dictate terms to the opponent and thereby *leave* the conference chamber still in a position of strength! In current jargon this is the 'dual track' approach – talking disarmament but at the same time introducing new weapons with the avowed aim of making the negotiations more successful.

The peculiar logic of the traditional dictum 'if you want peace, prepare for war', has thus been transferred to the arms control arena – 'if you want disarmament, build up your armaments' – and may well help to explain the failure to achieve peace and disarmament.

More significantly such an approach has powerful support within negotiating countries, giving a momentum to the particular attitude which may override, as an explanation of the failure of arms control, the more specific reasons which we have outlined so far. An examination of the causes of the arms race itself does suggest that the armaments industry in its widest sense has a crucial role, the convenient shorthand of the 'military-industrial complex', first used by Eisenhower in his farewell address twenty years ago, being appropriate. (In any discussion on this subject a reference to Eisenhower is now virtually obligatory – his impeccable credentials as a president and ex-general ensure that this notion can no longer easily be dismissed as existing only in the minds of dupes or left-wing radicals!)

Whilst recognizing 'the imperative need' for the development which had led to 'this conjunction of an immense military establishment and a large arms industry', he drew attention to its grave implications:

In the councils of government, we must guard against the acquisition of unwarranted influence, whether sought or unsought, by the military-industrial complex. The potential for the disastrous rise of misplaced power exists and will persist.

Eisenhower went on to warn of a subtler and perhaps more fundamental alteration which had occurred in American society – 'Akin to, and largely responsible for the sweeping changes in our industrial-military posture, has been the technological revolution during recent decades'. He spoke of the 'danger that public policy could itself become the captive of a scientific-technological elite'.

This is precisely what has happened, as has been persuasively argued most recently by Lord Zuckerman, formerly Chief Scientific Adviser to the British Government and, from 1964 to 1971, head of the Government's Scientific Civil Service. The scientists, technologists and

engineers, in stimulating change and promoting new techniques, have not simply been acting as the servants of politicians and military chiefs, the main argument runs, but

. . . were themselves the ones who initiated the new developments, who created the new demands. . . . They were the ones who, at base, were determining the social, economic and political future of the world.

Hence

The nuclear world, with all its hazards, is the scientists' creation; it is certainly not a world that came about in response to any external demand. . . . So is the world of missiles. So is the unending arms race by which we are all now threatened.

This phenomenon – 'the unplanned and unrestrained technological exploitation of new scientific knowledge' – constitutes the root of the problem. In the field of armaments and defence policy, the relationship between the politician, the military adviser and the scientist – traditionally thought of as forming a hierarchy in that order in the decision-making process – has been turned upside down. Zuckerman argues that 'military chiefs, who by convention are the official advisers on national security, merely serve as a channel through which the men in the laboratories transmit their views'. And he goes on to say that it is he, the technician, and not the commander in the field, let alone the minister, who starts the process of formulating the so-called military need. As a result,

. . . the men in the nuclear weapons laboratories of both sides have succeeded in creating a world with an irrational foundation, on which a new set of political realities has in turn had to be built. They have become the alchemists of our times.

In the industrial societies of East and West, and most prominently in the United States and the Soviet Union, this development, so authoritatively described by Zuckerman and confirmed in the writings of many other prominent science advisers, especially in the United States, has to be recognized and tackled in any attempt to halt the arms race and start a process of genuine arms control and disarmament.

Focussing attention on the technological impetus of the arms race brings out its self-generated momentum. It is, in part, a race to keep up with and put into practice the technical developments and breakthroughs achieved in one's own laboratories and weapons research establishments; it is a race to turn the possible into the actual. To that extent the arms race contributes to and exacerbates international political tensions which themselves generated the arms race in the first place.

These tensions are all too easily exacerbated in a climate of different perceptions. Most people in Western society perceive of the Soviet Union as a monolithic political force of immense power which successfully imposes its political will on the Warsaw pact states and has sufficient power to weld them into a coherent force which greatly outnumbers the NATO military capability. The Soviet Union is perceived as having an overwhelming superiority in conventional forces of all kinds and has now acquired a nuclear superiority as well.

Such a perception is extremely difficult to break down even though, as we have seen, the nuclear superiority is highly questionable. Moreover, examination of data from Western sources shows that, for example, NATO forces actually outnumber those of the WTO by 4.9 million to 4.8 million, and a far smaller proportion of NATO forces are inexperienced conscripts. NATO and China together outnumber the WTO forces by 2:1! Warsaw Pact superiority in tanks becomes less a threat when one remembers that NATO countries have produced well over half a million rounds for precision-guided anti-tank weapons, ten times the number of WTO tanks.

But the Soviet perception of the situation is also worth examining. From *their* position they are surrounded by powerful and increasingly aggressive countries, especially China and the NATO group. They are faced with an economically powerful Japan in the east and a highly volatile Islamic world to the south with the ever-present threat of dissension spilling over into the large Muslim population of the southern Soviet Union. At least one result of this is very high levels of commitment to military

---

'They [Soviets] don't want nuclear war any more than we do. In fact, in many ways they – this generation has been through hell. They lost 20 million people. They talk to you about it all the time. They don't want to see their children go through the hell that they went through. And anybody that thinks that they want to bring war to their territory just doesn't understand this generation of Russian leaders, including Mr Brezhnev.'

US Ambassador Averell Harriman
20 April 1977

developments, aided no doubt by the Soviet equivalent of the military-industrial complex.

The armaments policies of a state are determined, in the first place, by those of other states, particularly those it regards as its greatest rivals, but stimulated by the internal factors we have considered. *Each fuels the other*. In a world of independent states, where no international or supranational authority exists to settle peacefully situations of conflict and, if need be, forcefully implement any decisions made, all states rely on their own military force to safeguard their security and survival. As long as this international disorder persists, individual states will maintain and strengthen their capacity to survive and compete in this 'anarchic' world society. Mutual suspicion and hostility are endemic in this society; tensions may rise, conflicts resulting in war may become inevitable.

To prevent this from happening and to ensure that if such an eventuality occurs the country will be victorious, its armed might is of paramount importance. In such a system total disarmament is out of the question. Salvador de Madariaga, one of this century's greatest thinkers on disarmament, was right in saying that 'the problem of disarmament is not the problem of disarmament. It really is the problem of the organization of the world community.'

Advocating disarmament and, more modestly, genuine and effective arms control, need not imply an ignorance or denial of these ultimate realities. If realism is to be measured by comparing intentions and results, the arms policies of the superpowers have been far from realistic – their, and the world's, security and survival have never before been threatened as they are now. Their 'realistic' disarmament policies have utterly failed; the ideal of multilateral disarmament has led nowhere.

Given the massive overkill capacities and the many trends leading us to nuclear war, we have to propose solutions which are not consequent on an effective re-ordering of the world political system, although movement towards the solutions may also be a step towards approaching the wider issues.

Unilateral initiatives should now be considered as complementary to, if not *in lieu* of, multilateral negotiations as a way of contributing to breaking the deadlock which has characterized the latter. Such stimulation, aided by greater pressure for genuine multilateral commitments, inevitably coming largely from the West, must be formulated rapidly.

At the same time the defence and security debate should be taken out of the narrow framework to which it has traditionally been confined. There is much more to defence than weapons and brute force; indeed the nuclear age has brought us to the stage where they are no longer compatible. In the next chapter we will make some general suggestions for the paths which might be followed for curbing the nuclear arms race in a realistic way and we will also indicate some of the alternative possibilities for non-nuclear defence.

Here, though, we would say finally that to believe that the failure of disarmament and arms control thus far is only to be expected, and that the future will not be much different, is a counsel of despair which is neither morally nor intellectually justifiable.

REFERENCES

Garnett, J. (1979). 'Disarmament and Arms Control Since 1945' in Martin, L. (Ed.) *Strategic Thought in the Nuclear Age*. Heinemann, London.

Lord Zuckerman (1980). *Science Advisers, Scientific Advisers and Nuclear Weapons*. The Menard Press, London.

Hickman, M. B. (Ed.) (1971). *The Military and American Society*. Glencoe Press, Beverly Hills.

International Institute for Strategic Studies (1980). *The Military Balance 1980–81*. IISS, London.

Part 4

What Has to
be Done

12

Effective Disarmament

In this book so far we have endeavoured to provide information about nuclear weapons and nuclear war. We have presented the latest information on the nuclear arsenals of the superpowers and have also described the extent and significance of the smaller nuclear arsenals of countries such as Britain, France and China. It is evident that current arsenals are far in excess of anything that could be warranted by any conceivable theory of deterrence, that the numbers and types of nuclear weapons are increasing rapidly and that new nuclear states will come into being in the next decade.

We have placed some emphasis on the disturbing way in which nuclear weapons are now integrated into the organization and structure of the armed forces of the superpowers and we have concentrated especially on the huge dangers of the new strategic weapons as well as the accompanying attitudes towards fighting a nuclear war. We have attempted to give you some idea about what that war might be like and the effects it would have on us. Finally we have described the protracted negotiations on nuclear disarmament, their failure to achieve anything that is really substantive and some of the reasons for that failure.

If you feel that this is a picture of unremitting gloom then there is some comfort to be drawn from the fact that, over the past two years, and in many different countries, there has developed a remarkable grass-roots concern for the problems posed by nuclear weapons, a concern so widespread that it is beginning to give real hope for the future. We will draw your attention to some of the approaches being adopted in Britain by a diversity of organizations and in so doing we hope to suggest action that *you* might take to help the process of effective nuclear disarmament. First, though, we would like to indicate the developments that need to be seen over the next few years if we are to curb the nuclear arms race.

The phenomena of escalation, proliferation and new weaponry all serve to make the point that time is short and we would insist that very substantial progress *must* be achieved by the end of the 1980s if there is to be much hope of avoiding nuclear conflict. Yet it is difficult to put forward realistic disarmament proposals in the context of the admitted failure of many attempts to curb the increase in nuclear weapons. To propose rapid moves towards strategic nuclear disarmament, for example, is to invite accusations of idealism. While we would by no means reject the need for some idealism, we would claim that such proposals are fundamentally realistic too.

Initially, support must be gained for two modest but significant steps. One is the realization of a comprehensive test ban treaty, preceded by a moratorium on testing until the details can be negotiated. The other is an agreement on non-first use of nuclear weapons. The rapid conclusion of such processes, especially if accompanied by ratification of SALT II would be a valuable first step which could be accomplished readily. By themselves, though, they will not remove the danger of further developments, indeed they will not even curb it, and so we must make realistic suggestions which can acquire sufficient support to encourage immediate progress. As just one example of the kind of thinking which is now necessary we would propose a series of three steps towards strategic nuclear disarmament which, taken with other negotiations, really would have a fundamental impact on the nuclear arms race. We must emphasize that these proposals are made to indicate the scale of the task which has to be completed. To those who are familiar with the sad litany of failed disarmament negotiations, it will be all too easy to dismiss these ideas. But there is a completely different constituency, large in numbers and growing rapidly, which *will* be prepared to work for such proposals, or others like them.

The three linked international treaties could be introduced at approximately three-year intervals during the course of the 1980s and would aim to achieve a step-by-step reduction in strategic nuclear arsenals. There would inevitably be strong opposition to them, perhaps expressed in terms of fears over imbalances or problems of verification but why should such problems not be overcome if the necessary political will can be induced?

The overall aim would be the phasing out of all strategic nuclear weapons through the medium of these treaties, this being accompanied by parallel negotiations on theatre and tactical weapons and problems of proliferation.

PHASE I ('SALT III')

The accompanying table shows the relative dispositions of strategic nuclear forces for the United States and the Soviet Union on 18 June 1979, the date of the initial signing of the SALT II agreement in Vienna. These dispositions have changed slightly in the past two years but serve as an appropriate base for further proposals.

The first step would be set hopefully for some time in the mid 1980s and would involve a reduction in all major categories of strategic weapons on both sides, representing a decrease of approximately one third compared to 1979 figures. While the American decrease would be slightly higher than that of the Soviet Union, the latter would undertake a major reduction in its MIRVed missile

Strategic nuclear disarmament

Category	United States			Soviet Union		
	June 1979	SALT III 1983/84	SALT IV 1986/7	June 1979	SALT III 1983/4	SALT IV 1986/7
ICBM – MIRV	550	350	150	608	400	200
– non-MIRV	504	400	200	790	600	250
ICBM total	1,054	750	350	1,398	1,000	450
SLBM – MIRV	496	400	200	114	112	80
– non-MIRV	160	128	48	806	518	144
SLBM total	656	528	248	950	630	224
Bombers	573	200	0	156	100	0
Total MIRV-launchers	1,046	750	350	752	512	280
% change in 1979		−28	−67		−32	−63
Total weapons systems	2,283	1,478	598	2,504	1,730	674
% change on 1979		−35	−74		−31	−73

forces, 32 per cent against 28 per cent for the United States. The US would undertake a major reduction of its strategic bomber force but would retain most of its submarine-launched systems. The Soviet Union would reduce its non-MIRVed ICBMs and SLBMs considerably.

Such total reductions would represent a huge breakthrough in the current nuclear arms race, but of much greater significance would be the other aspect of the agreement, a decision to halt development and deployment of new systems. In every sense this would be of fundamental significance. Without it, the reduction in current strategic weapons would be almost meaningless.

As we have already seen, one of the basic problems with the nuclear arms race has been the ability of the technological momentum of new weapons developments to proceed much faster than disarmament negotiations, thus largely nullifying any chance of success. This system has to be broken by political pressure codified in a treaty. Thus SALT III must incorporate the following.

For the Soviet Union

– Halt to all ABM developments including current improvements to the Galosh system. Withdrawal of the Galosh system.
– Cancellation of development and deployment of all four new ICBM programmes.
– Ban on mobile basing of ICBMs.
– Cancellation of new strategic bomber programmes.
– Ban on deployment of long-range versions of the Backfire bomber.
– No deployment of Typhoon-class ballistic missile submarines.

> 'We must either learn to live together as brothers or we are going to perish together as fools.'
> Martin Luther King

For the United States

– Halt to all ABM developments.
– Cancellation of the development of the M-X and SICBM programmes.
– Ban on mobile basing of ICBMs.
– Cancellation of air-launched cruise missile and the B1 strategic bomber and halt to development of further strategic bombers.
– Withdrawal of existing Trident-class submarines (*USS Ohio* and *USS Michigan*). No further deployment of Trident missiles on Poseidon-type submarines.
– Cancellation of Trident II missile.

These would be the major provisions but there would be others of lesser importance. The formidable task of controlling weapons in space would have to be faced, possibly in a separate series of negotiations. Allied to this SALT III proposal would be the involvement of the lesser nuclear powers. We will argue a number of options for the United Kingdom later in this chapter, but would suggest, in this context, that minimum demands would be

– No replacement of the British Polaris missiles with Trident missiles.
– No MIRVing of French submarine-launched missiles and cancellation of new French medium-range missile.
– No deployment of new Chinese ICBMs and SLBMs.

The broad effects of such a treaty would be threefold. First and most important would be control over the current nuclear arms race involving the Soviet Union and the United States, effected by the ban on the development and deployment of new strategic systems. This control would be fundamental and of immense significance.

The second effect would appear to be more modest, namely the one third reduction in numbers of strategic nuclear weapons systems. Even though apparently modest, this too would be of considerable significance, representing a reversal of the current overwhelming trend towards increased numbers of warheads.

The third effect would be to curb the entry of the three lesser nuclear powers into the major strategic arms race. Again this may appear relatively modest but, as we have already seen, any of the three countries in that category will, on present trends, be a truly significant strategic nuclear power within a decade.

PHASE 2 ('SALT IV')

A further step towards strategic nuclear disarmament would come within three years of this initial treaty and would represent a much greater reduction in strategic arsenals, taking them down to little more than one quarter of 1979 levels. Once again the suggested details are given in the table on p 254.

This treaty would involve the total withdrawal of all manned bombers and substantial further decreases in ICBM and SLBM numbers. The United States would have fewer total nuclear delivery systems, but a higher proportion would have multiple warheads. The lesser nuclear powers would be involved in the negotiations, and the final outcome would be a decrease in the numbers of their long-range nuclear arsenals.

While these negotiations would involve a real and very substantial reversal of the strategic nuclear arms race, the manner in which it could be negotiated would ensure that each of the major nuclear powers could avoid a feeling of vulnerability, primarily because the design calls for a phased reduction of numbers of weapons, based on deployment of weapons available in 1981.

This is a crucial point; as we would now be talking about disarmament of current weapons systems, not a new generation, neither of the superpowers need consider itself to be at risk from a disarming first strike. Supposing that the US ICBM force was said to be at risk from the remaining 200 MIRVed Soviet ICBMs, it could be stressed that the United States would still have a substantial SLBM force. Similarly the Soviet SLBM force might be very limited and vulnerable to US anti-submarine warfare tactics, but the force of 150 MIRVed ICBMs at the disposal of the United States, even if including the latest of the 1981 upgraded Minuteman missiles, would be insufficient to threaten the 450 Soviet ICBMs.

It may seem unfortunate to have to talk in terms of such careful balances, but such negotiations as we are suggesting do involve a basic change in political and military outlooks. It would be naïve to expect anything else than mistrust and open opposition from the military.

PHASE 3 ('SALT V')

Finally we proceed to a follow-up treaty with perhaps just the smallest shade of idealism creeping in. This would be reached by the end of the 1980s and would be a treaty designed to ban all long-range nuclear delivery systems. It would involve the five major nuclear powers but would be open to other countries as well, allied to the parallel development of more effective non-proliferation legislation.

GENERAL NUCLEAR DISARMAMENT

The proposal which we have sketched out here is concerned with the highly destructive long-range strategic nuclear weapons. It would do virtually nothing to control the tens of thousands of theatre and tactical nuclear weapons which are currently deployed throughout the world in perhaps twenty countries.

Were we to experience negotiations leading to the kinds of agreements which have been described, then attempts to achieve some degree of disarmament at a lower level would receive a considerable boost. Nevertheless such attempts would have to have a firm basis in the reality of current dispositions, and the most significant direction in which to move would most likely involve the concept of the nuclear-free zone.

Such zones would be extensions of the treaties already in operation and would have the major aim of creating further such zones in major regions of the world, especially those in which nuclear conflict at a tactical or theatre level is most likely. There is little doubt that Europe is the most significant such area, both in terms of potential conflict and also the very high concentration of nuclear weapons. Proposals for European nuclear disarmament are gaining in popularity at an impressive speed and there are a number of different approaches which can be adopted.

One is to seek a general European nuclear-free zone; but this raises the immediate problem of what we mean by Europe. If it is every country of Europe except European Russia then nuclear disarmament in such a zone will be criticized strongly by the military of the West. They will say that it will be grossly unbalanced, that it will involve removal of all NATO tactical and theatre weapons *and* the much longer-range French, British and American systems which are essentially part of the strategic arsenals, while leaving Soviet weapons untouched. Thus 'Poland to Portugal' does raise some problems, although it has the significant aspect of focussing on the Europe that is locked in between the two superpowers. An alternative is to take in European Russia involving a nuclear-free zone from 'the Atlantic to the Urals'. But that region contains perhaps 40 per cent of all Soviet ICBMs and the base for around 60 per cent of their missile-carrying submarines. In this case the balance, such as it is, has swung the other way and Soviet opposition will be fierce.

The second approach is to seek a European nuclear-free zone evolving out of controls of particular categories of weapons systems. These might be nuclear-capable artillery, or missiles with a particular range, or classes of aircraft. This approach has the advantage of avoiding the geographical problems but presents us with formidably complex negotiations.

Finally one might suggest a piecemeal geographical approach, with small groups of nations taking what amounts to unilateral action, perhaps involving Scandinavian or Balkan states. In terms of the development of nuclear disarmament movements in Europe this approach is now quite likely, but it is, at best, an incomplete solution. The major pressure would come from smaller European states, mainly in Western Europe, and the opposition would probably come primarily from the more powerful members of NATO.

On the other hand there is clearly a rapidly increasing demand for European nuclear disarmament, and this must occasion a political response. Perhaps the most significant point of all is that some kind of European nuclear-free zone will, in practice, be much easier to negotiate if it is done in a climate of strategic nuclear disarmament. Thus the problem of the location of long-range missiles in Europe becomes much less central to European nuclear disarmament if those very weapons are themselves subject to strategic arms limitation negotiations. *The two approaches make far more sense when linked than they do separately.*

The major advantage of the nuclear-free zone approach is that it succeeds in coming to terms with the major problem of the integration of tactical nuclear weapons into military organization. Because of this integration, and the problems of verification that it raises, it is highly unlikely that disarmament negotiations at this level could be conducted in a similar way to those for strategic weapons – the geographical approach is more realistic.

' . . . mere praise of peace is easy, but ineffective. What is needed is active participation in the fight against war and everything that leads to it.'
Albert Einstein, 1953

We should recognize the relationship between strategic and regional disarmament approaches, on the one hand, and the problems of proliferation on the other. We have already discussed the nature of the problem of proliferation and its likely extent over the next decade or so. Although the Non-Proliferation Treaty exists, it can be argued that it is far too weak to counteract the pressures for proliferation. A more effective series of agreements is necessary, especially in terms of the connection between nuclear power programmes and nuclear weapons production.

Such a process of agreement, involving many countries of the world, is only likely to have any chance of success in the context of genuine moves towards disarmament from the major nuclear powers. Any move to impose proliferation control in the present circumstances would stimulate formidable opposition throughout the non-nuclear world and might well be counter-productive. It would be a very different matter if the nuclear states were moving towards disarmament. Under those circumstances, far stronger action would be possible, maybe under UN control, for effective steps to prevent proliferation.

PROBLEMS OF GENERAL NUCLEAR DISARMAMENT

It is all too easy to dismiss the suggestions which have been made here as being irrelevant and far-fetched, but the alternative must be stressed. That is of a continuing arms race with the development of counterforce weapons and the trend towards nuclear war-fighting, the further integration of nuclear weapons into conventional defence systems and the prospects for formidable escalation and proliferation over the next decade.

To have put forward such proposals only two years ago would have been to invite ridicule, but there is sufficient evidence of an awakening concern over the current dangers to indicate that such proposals must now be made. They are, of course, far from complete and more detailed plans are being developed, especially in connection with the UN Special Session on Disarmament scheduled for 1982.

We also have to take into account chemical and biological weapons as well as the huge increase in spending on conventional weapons. Proposals for general nuclear disarmament do not necessarily address themselves to the immense problems of the third world, and say little about the basic political conflicts in the world. Many would argue, for example, that the nuclear arms race is a fundamental aspect of our existing political systems and these must be changed if we are to achieve nuclear disarmament.

Unfortunately this involves the difficult problem of timescales. The nuclear arms race is likely to ensure our destruction before much progress can be made towards improvements in the human political system. To put it bluntly, in order to face up to the conflicts between states and between peoples it is necessary that we still have states and peoples in existence! The nature of the nuclear arms race is such that we have to control it *as an initial step* towards approaching more general problems of conflict. In doing so, though, we may well be commencing the more general task.

BRITAIN AND NUCLEAR DISARMAMENT

It is not the purpose of this book to argue one particular policy for Britain, but, in the context of our concern over the risks of nuclear war, and the suggestions for disarmament which have been put forward, it is appropriate to indicate some positive options for Britain and also to suggest alternative defence policies which might be pursued in an era of nuclear disarmament.

In the context of the proposals made, an initial demand

must be that Britain mounts a major diplomatic initiative to encourage action for strategic and European nuclear disarmament and to discourage proliferation. This initiative should be accompanied by a national and international campaign on the dangers of the nuclear arms race. Such an initiative, though, would only have credibility if Britain itself commenced an immediate process of initiating nuclear disarmament.

Such a commitment could take a number of forms. It might involve the cancellation of the replacement of Polaris missiles by the Trident system, followed by the phasing out of the Polaris missiles themselves. That alone would be an historic event – the first major decision by any country to commence independent nuclear disarmament. It would certainly have a remarkable effect on the non-nuclear and non-aligned countries and would have a major impact on arms control negotiations and disarmament campaigns throughout the world. We should not underestimate this impact. It is very easy to say that a country like Britain is of little or no consequence in terms of nuclear armaments and that independent nuclear disarmament would be irrelevant. This is nonsense. As we have seen, Britain has a large range of nuclear weapons, it is expanding its nuclear arsenal considerably and for the country to accept the principle of *decreasing* its nuclear commitment *would* have a considerable impact especially when accompanied by a general diplomatic initiative.

The United Nations includes over 140 countries which do not have nuclear weapons. As recent initiatives within the UN have shown, many of those countries have governments which are becoming greatly concerned over the nuclear arms race. The effect on these, and on people concerned with disarmament, could be remarkable.

A further development by Britain could be the withdrawal of a theatre nuclear capacity, both by the country itself and in relation to American weapons in Britain. This policy could certainly be consistent with remaining a signatory of the North Atlantic Treaty and also with remaining in the NATO unified military command. It could be followed by a more general commitment to full independent nuclear disarmament by Britain.

We would ourselves argue that this is the policy to consider and we would further argue that such a process may be an essential prerequisite for a change in the international climate of opinion towards effective *multilateral* nuclear disarmament.

The programme which was sketched out earlier in this chapter was done in the context of the terrible dangers of the nuclear arms race. Those dangers are not yet generally appreciated and avoiding them will take, as a minimum, a massive swing in international opinion. One important catalyst would be a nuclear power acting as pace-maker. Indeed the minimum we would argue for is that Britain is an appropriate country to take a lead in making a series of decisions, constantly keeping ahead of international disarmament trends, and helping to maintain the impetus to enhance those trends.

ALTERNATIVE APPROACHES
TO DEFENCE

If Britain were to opt for nuclear disarmament, whether or not this was part of a general international trend, then there would be three broad options open for alternative defence policies, the most obvious being reliance on effective conventional defence forces. This is the kind of path that Sweden and, to a lesser extent, Switzerland, have taken and it is one which is immensely enhanced by recent developments in conventional defence munitions.

The principle is still one of deterrence, but to make it *too costly* for a potential aggressor to attempt to over-run a country rather than to threaten that aggressor with nuclear destruction, while risking such destruction for yourself. Sweden, remember, could certainly develop nuclear weapons if it so decided, but it chooses to follow a different path. It has total armed forces of just 66,000 including over 45,000 conscripts, but can mobilize to about 800,000 (nearly ten per cent of the total population and more than twice the size of the total UK armed forces) within 72 hours. Even so it spends a much smaller proportion of its gross national product on defence than does Britain, the United States or any of the major Warsaw Pact countries. It relies on highly mobile and efficient defensive naval and air forces and an army strongly supported by modern defensive weapons.

Switzerland, with a slightly smaller population than Sweden, spends even less on defence and has armed forces totalling only 3500 regular troops together with 15,000 recruits on 17-week training courses who then become reservists. Some 300,000 reservists do refresher training each year and the armed forces can be mobilized to 625,000 in just 48 hours.

Countries such as Sweden and Switzerland orientate their armed forces to defence, and in doing so they are aided by developments in precision-guided munitions. By this we mean the wide range of modern guided missiles which can be used for anti-aircraft and anti-tank defence. These developments have been quite extraordinary and they look like altering the whole balance of conventional warfare, making things more difficult for the attacker and easier for the defender. Even as long ago as 1973, during the Arab-Israeli conflict, some of these methods were starting to be used, and current developments have gone well beyond the weapons then available. During that conflict for example, a total of 58 Maverick anti-tank missiles were used, which destroyed 52 tanks. The advantage of precision-guided munitions is that if a country pursues a policy of deterrence based on conventional forces, then these munitions greatly enhance that deterrent effect.

A second option is to adopt tactics of territorial defence, with the intention of making it extremely difficult for an opponent to occupy a country. Tactics involve use of direct military confrontation by small, highly mobile units equipped with light precision-guided munitions, the use of electronic counter-warfare and the adoption of guerilla tactics backed up by civilian militia. Swedish and Yugoslav policies both embody aspects of this approach, with the latter placing some reliance on partisan resistance.

Such an option can be adopted along with the earlier methods of frontier defence, and together these can provide a very high degree of potential deterrence. A third option goes considerably further, aiming to meet a potential occupying power with civilian non-cooperation and passive resistance rather than with armed opposition. There are many different strategies which could be employed and these include use of selective and general strikes, boycotts, acts of civil disobedience and obstruction. Bureaucratic delaying tactics, rigorous working to rule, careful but persistent non-cooperation, deliberate but covert errors and many other tactics can collectively make a country uncontrollable.

Such strategies are not nearly as far-fetched as might be supposed and there is a wealth of experience from India, Czechoslovakia, Norway and Denmark under German occupation, many ex-colonies and other countries. The fundamental approach may be different but passive resistance has an undeniable relevance in the nuclear age in that it side-steps military confrontation.

It would be folly to suggest that workable strategies could be developed overnight. Any realistic possibility of passive resistance requires an educated and largely united people, skilled in the methods and united in their commitment. We would argue, though, that this and other alternatives which have been sketched out here, *could* give rise to thoroughly realistic policies in the context of independent nuclear disarmament.

What is quite incredible is the almost total lack of consideration given to such policies in Britain. Unlike Sweden and Holland, research on alternative defence policies in Britain has been limited to very few writers, notably Stephen King-Hall in the 1950s and, more recently, Adam Roberts and April Carter. In the autumn of 1980, however, an Alternative Defence Commission was established by the Lansbury House Trust and the Bradford University School of Peace Studies and will publish a major report on alternative defence policies for Britain in 1982.

But this is an exception, and the general rule in Britain is one of almost no interest in anything but the existing military policies. Britain is well endowed with defence colleges and defence research centres. Considerable funding goes towards research in strategic studies yet there is almost no funding for peace research. Small research groups at the Universities of Lancaster and Sussex and a small number of researchers in other colleges together with just one full department of peace studies at Bradford University make up the total. Most Western European and North American countries have a number of such centres but this is not the case in Britain. The reader will perhaps forgive a slight trace of bitterness when we say that our own department is, at the time of writing (July 1981), threatened by the recently announced cuts in university finance.

We believe there are viable alternatives to the increasingly insane reliance on nuclear weapons. We further believe that Britain can take a lead in moves towards general nuclear disarmament and that this represents a view which is gathering strength rapidly at present. It is particularly interesting to see that some retired military officers and, indeed, some serving officers are now questioning existing policies. What we have yet to see is a Government which is alive to these developments. No doubt that will come.

'If my soldiers began to think, not one would remain in the ranks.'
Frederick the Great

REFERENCES

Barnaby, F. (1981). *The Nuclear Arms Race*, Peace Studies Papers No. 4. School of Peace Studies, University of Bradford.

Carter, A. (1981). 'Alternatives to the Bomb', *Peace News*, Nottingham, 3 April 1981.

Geeraerts, G. (Editor) (1977). *Possibilities of Civilian Defence in Western Europe*. Swets and Zeitlinger, Amsterdam and Lisse.

Sims, N.A. (1979). *Approaches to Disarmament*. Quaker Peace and Service, London.

13
What You can Do

We would not pretend that the suggestions that have been made here for nuclear disarmament are the only options. We would, however, insist that a massive move towards nuclear disarmament is the most urgent task that faces us all. We are also convinced that this can only be achieved if there is much greater public knowledge about the issues and much greater activity by ordinary people to force the issues to the forefront of the political arena.

We would suggest that you can do two things. One is to make it your immediate concern to become well informed on the issues, and to aid this we have included comments on a number of useful books and other sources of information at the end of this chapter. The other is that you can act yourself, and join with others to help prevent nuclear destruction, by stimulating moves towards disarmament.

The inevitable response is a feeling of impotence. 'What difference can I make?' is a common reaction. But it goes without saying that movements for change *can* be effective by virtue of the sum total of many individual actions. You can discuss, argue with and convince your family and friends at home, at work, in your neighbour-

---

'Nobody made a greater mistake than he who did nothing because he could do only a little.'
Edmund Burke

hood and elsewhere. Do not despise the traditional tasks of writing to your local paper and your MP, but include local councillors, constituency committees and other relevant organizations. You should certainly be able to find other like-minded people. Get together with them and arrange a public meeting – a showing of *The War Game* or a debate. Above all, be aware of the many organizations now active in this field and join in with them.

Remember that changes in attitude can and do come about because ordinary people want them to, and work for them. Twenty-five years ago a few individuals managed to awaken the conscience of millions of people to the plight of war-refugees still living in refugee camps in Central Europe, more than a decade after the end of the Second World War. World Refugee Year followed with conspicuous success.

More recently there have been some remarkable changes in public attitude to environmental issues. Ten years ago subjects like solar and wind power were considered to be weird and cranky, but now they are taken seriously. Urban motorways, new airports and other major projects can now only go forward after much more careful attention to the needs of local communities. In many countries even the whole development of nuclear power is being called into question. Perhaps you do not necessarily agree with those particular changes, but the point is that significant changes in attitude *can* occur and ultimately governments *have* to respond to them.

More importantly, there is ample evidence that a major shift in public opinion is now commencing, a realization that negotiated nuclear disarmament is a mainstream concern and is an integral part of future progress.

THE RE-BIRTH OF THE NUCLEAR DISARMAMENT MOVEMENT

Until the late autumn of 1979, concern over nuclear weapons in Britain, and indeed in much of Europe, was minimal. Yet in less than two years it has become one of the major political issues. Several factors have combined to bring about this change.

One was the decision by NATO member states, announced in December 1979, to deploy a range of new theatre weapons, the ground-launched cruise missile and the Pershing II ballistic missile, in Western Europe. The cruise missile would be located in Italy, West Germany, Belgium, Holland and Britain and the Pershing II missile would be located in West Germany. Opposition to this move developed initially in Holland but later in West Germany and Britain.

The Soviet invasion of Afghanistan and a notable increase in East-West tension gave cause for concern over future conflict, and the fear of nuclear war was heightened by reports of false alarms affecting missile early-warning systems in November 1979 and again early in 1980, and by the growing awareness that a considerable escalation in numbers and capabilities of strategic missiles and other weapons was in progress.

Early in 1980 the British Government came under some pressure to issue guidelines on Civil Defence for nuclear attack and, rather hastily, published a booklet called *Protect and Survive*. This had the reverse effect to that intended. It appeared to be a remarkably complacent document, designed to reassure people, but by virtue of its manifestly simplistic and misleading statements it was subject to ridicule.

At about the same time a series of articles by the historian E. P. Thompson, coupled with public meetings involving him and other disarmament campaigners, helped to stimulate considerable public interest. In many cities audiences of 600 to 1000 assembled and during the course of the summer of 1980, and especially around the anniversaries of Hiroshima and Nagasaki days, vigils and other demonstrations took place throughout Britain.

The decision to deploy the Trident missile system gave further stimulus to nuclear disarmers, as did information about the 'Square Leg' home defence exercise in September 1980. The following month the Campaign for Nuclear Disarmament was able to hold a very large public meeting in Central London, involving around 80,000 people, the largest such meeting since the early 1960s. Also that month the Labour Party adopted a unilateral nuclear disarmament platform at its annual conference.

Although press, radio and television coverage of the nuclear disarmament debate was very limited there was evidence that by the summer of 1981 it was beginning to

---

'Our future on this planet, exposed as it is to nuclear annihilation, depends upon one single factor: humanity must make a moral about-turn.'

Pope John-Paul II at Hiroshima
25 February 1981

occupy a central place in the political life of the country. One remarkable development was that many local authorities were adopting nuclear-free zone policies. By mid-June 1981 some 70 local authorities covering 13 million people had followed this particular path, with many more likely to adopt such policies by the end of the year.

The current nuclear disarmament campaigns have a number of characteristics which make them somewhat different from the previous period of campaigning twenty years ago. One is that there are large numbers of people in their thirties and forties who have been involved in nuclear disarmament campaigning before. They are experienced and many are involved in local politics. They have been joined, especially in 1981, by large numbers of much younger people, a veritable second generation. The combination of numbers and experience is significant.

A second feature is that the disarmers tend to be much more knowledgeable about the issues, including specific policies and even weapons. This is allied to a particularly interesting feature, the rise of local campaigns, often geared to particular issues, especially in the areas which have air bases and where cruise missiles are likely to be deployed.

Perhaps most significant of all is the exceptionally rapid growth of interest in nuclear disarmament and the broad spectrum of opinion apparent within that growth. While there is still a tendency for support to come from the left of centre this is no longer a dominant feature. The involvement of church members as well as that of the medical profession is most apparent and support is now coming from all parts of the political spectrum, especially in the campaigns for multilateral disarmament and also campaigns focussing on local issues.

There are many different groups involved in Britain but the three most important are the World Disarmament Campaign, European Nuclear Disarmament and the Campaign for Nuclear Disarmament. They may well have a joint membership larger than any of the political parties. This itself is significant because there appears to be a 'credibility gap' in that the media and Government still appear to be unaware of the extent of this support.

World Disarmament Campaign (WDC, 21 Little Russell Street, London WC1)

This aims primarily at supporting United Nations initiatives for multilateral disarmament. It was formed at a large rally in London in April 1980 and two of its most significant sponsors are the Nobel Peace Laureate, Lord Noel-Baker, and Lord Fenner Brockway. WDC is particularly concerned with preparing for the second UN General Assembly Special Session on Disarmament to be held in 1982. In Britain, the WDC is headed by Michael Harbottle, a former Chief-of-Staff of UN Forces in Cyprus.

WDC is noteworthy in two particular ways. One is that it has, in the space of just over a year, seen the creation of some 350 local affiliated groups. Strongest support appears to come from Methodists, Quakers and local United Nations Associations. The second is that WDC is attracting support from members of all the major political parties.

WDC works closely with other disarmament groups and as well as concentrating on gathering mass support for a petition on disarmament it is focusing attention on issues such as the link between disarmament and development and the critical need for confidence-building measures between states, especially the Eastern and Western blocs.

European Nuclear Disarmament (END, 6 Endsleigh Street, London WC2)

END developed partly as a response to the NATO decision to deploy cruise missiles and the Pershing II, an appeal for European Nuclear Disarmament being launched in April 1980. END is not an organization in the sense of having a large national membership but is perhaps better described as a leaning or orientation. Work has been co-ordinated by a small group of about ten people and contact is maintained by a quarterly END Bulletin (published from the Bertrand Russell Peace Foundation, Gamble Street, Nottingham) and by a small London office.

Such a description should not underestimate the support for END which is particularly apparent from two directions. The idea of some kind of European nuclear-free zone is now becoming very popular in Britain, interest coming from established disarmament organizations and from a number of local peace groups. European nuclear disarmament is also attracting immense support and interest from many European countries. The END appeal, for example, has attracted signatories from twenty-two European countries *including five countries of Eastern Europe*.

The extent of interest was demonstrated by the first major international rally in Brussels in April 1981 and the indications are that European action is likely to be the major growth area during 1982.

Campaign for Nuclear Disarmament
(11 Goodwin Street, London N4)

CND was established in 1959. It was the main vehicle for disarmament campaigning in the early 1960s but for fifteen years had no more than 3000 national members and, at most, 200 local groups, many of which were inactive. Even so it persisted with campaigning and providing information on nuclear disarmament and its members were partly responsible for stimulating the new wave of interest in the late 1970s when CND began to attract new members.

Its growth over the past two years has been remarkable. By July 1981 the national membership had risen to 25,000 and there were around 900 local groups having a local membership of around 250,000. By then CND was selling 30,000 pamphlets every month and attracting new national members at well over 200 a week. A half-page advertisement for CND in one national newspaper attracted over 3000 enquiries.

A significant trend in 1981 was its increasing support from trade unions, with 13 national unions affiliating, including the TGWU, ASLEF, ASTMS and the Civil and Public Servants Association. There was also strong support coming from parties such as Plaid Cymru and the Scottish Nationalists and support within the Liberal Party was rising rapidly. Although the Social Democratic Party does not, as a party, support unilateral nuclear disarmament, there is a wing of such opinion within the party.

CND is sometimes represented as an organization concerned solely with unilateral nuclear disarmament, but it is actually committed strongly to multilateral disarmament (including chemical and biological weapons) and supports European Nuclear Disarmament and WDC. Its members frequently say that unilateral and multilateral disarmament are parts of a single solution to the problem of nuclear weapons and that 'unilateralists are multilateralists who mean it'!

CND has been criticized as a left-wing front and some politicians have even represented it as an arm of the KGB. This ignores the very wide support which CND now has with a major role being played by the Churches, especially Quakers, Methodists and Catholics (the General Secretary, Bruce Kent, is a Catholic priest). What is very revealing is that such criticisms demonstrate that those making them are seriously out of touch with the general concern over the risk of nuclear war.

Other peace organizations

In addition to the large organizations already mentioned there are several rather smaller and often more specialist groups that are very active on nuclear disarmament as well as other issues. The Peace Pledge Union (6 Endsleigh

Street, London WC1H 0DX) is a pacifist group which has organized a very valuable campaign against militarism, questioning many of the military orientations within society that are so easily taken for granted. Pax Christi (Blackfriars Hall, Southampton Road, London NW5) is largely but by no means entirely, Roman Catholic and has strong links with other European countries. The Fellowship of Reconciliation (9 Coombe Road, New Malden, Surrey) tends to draw support particularly from the Anglican and Free Churches. It organized a remarkable cycling pilgrimage for peace early in 1981 which covered 900 miles from Iona to Canterbury. More specialist groups which are concerned primarily with nuclear war include Scientists Against Nuclear Arms (SANA, 11 Chapel Street, Woburn Sands, Milton Keynes MK17 8PG) and the Medical Campaign Against Nuclear Weapons (120 Edith Road, London W14).

Sources of information

The major sources of information used in this book have been listed at the end of each chapter, but we are also including a general list of books and journals together with a few comments on them. In addition there is a short list of peace and conflict study centres.

BOOKS

John Cox (1981) *Overkill*. Penguin Books, London

A basic yet comprehensive study of nuclear weapons including a useful description of nuclear energy, the workings of nuclear weapons and the nature and extent of current arsenals.

> 'Lead me from death to life, from falsehood to truth.
> Lead me from despair to hope, from fear to trust.
> Lead me from hate to love, from war to peace.
> Let peace fill our heart, our world, our universe . . .'
> Prayer for Peace, 1981

Robert Neild (1981) *How to Make Your Mind Up About the Bomb*. Andre Deutsch, London

A thoughtful, logical and readable examination of British nuclear defence policy in which the author reaches the conclusion that nuclear disarmament is in Britain's interest.

E. P. Thompson and Dan Smith (1980) *Protest and Survive*. Penguin Books, London.

This includes a revised version of Thompson's best-selling pamphlet 'Protest and Survive', together with several useful essays, including David Holloway's discussion of Soviet militarism and Alva Myrdal's piece on disarmament negotiations.

Dan Smith (1980) *The Defence of the Realm in the 1980s*. Croom Helm, London.

Dan Smith's book is a rarity – an independent and critical discussion of British defence policies, placed in the context of East-West strategic relationships, Britain's role within NATO and the problems of technological complexity and costs of modern weapons systems.

Peace Studies Papers. University of Bradford, Bradford, BD7 1DP, West Yorkshire and Housmans, 5 Caledonian Road, London N1.

The School of Peace Studies is the only such department in any British university or college. It was established, with considerable Quaker support, in 1973 and runs undergraduate and postgraduate degree courses in peace studies. It started a series of *Peace Studies Papers* in 1980 and these are published jointly with Housmans. The first five papers are:
1 Peter van den Dungen (1980) *Foundations of Peace Research*.
2 Bob Overy (1980) *How Effective are Peace Movements?*
3 Nigel Young (1980) *Problems and Possibilities in the Study of Peace*.
4 Frank Barnaby (1981) *The Nuclear Arms Race*.
5 Paul Rogers (1981) *A Guide to Nuclear Weapons*.

S. Glasstone and P. J. Dolan (1980) *The Effects of Nuclear Weapons*. Castle House, Tunbridge Wells.

The best book on the effects of nuclear weapons. It has gone through a number of revisions and reprintings since first publication and is comprehensive and up-to-date. It has a simple and clear main text backed up by detailed authoritative technical sections.

Office of Technology Assessment (1980) *The Effects of Nuclear War*. Congress of the United States (published by Croom Helm, London).

A recent and invaluable contribution to the literature on nuclear weapons, involving a series of carefully assessed case studies of nuclear attack.

Report of the Secretary-General (1980) *General and Complete Disarmament: Comprehensive study on nuclear weapons*. Publication A/35/392, United Nations.

A key work of reference – comprehensive, well-balanced, accurate and concise. It has a good set of references which will take you into the literature should you wish to study further. Probably the best single souce of material on the subject.

Alva Myrdal *et al* (1981) *The Dynamics of European Nuclear Disarmament*. Spokesman University Paperbacks

A recent, important book on the background to nuclear weapons in Europe with a discussion of policies and programmes directed towards achieving disarmament. Includes contributions from Eastern Europe.

Alva Myrdal (1977), *The Game of Disarmament*. Manchester University Press and Spokesman Books.

A basic text, from a person experienced in disarmament negotiations, which seeks to explain the repeated failure of such negotiations.

F. Barnaby and R. Huisken (1975) *Arms Uncontrolled*. Stockholm International Peace Research Institute (published by Harvard University Press).

An older but still topical book which presents an overview of problems of nuclear weapons and includes consideration of issues such as chemical and biological warfare.

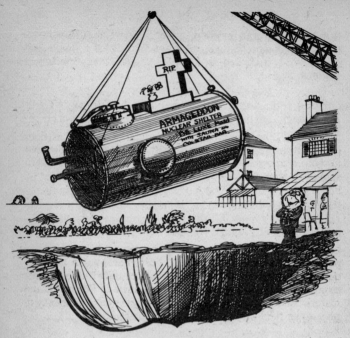

Safe at last.

P. Goodwin (1981) *Nuclear War: The Facts on our Survival*. Ash and Grant, London.

This is well written and well illustrated. Peter Goodwin is a physicist by training and he concentrates on the technical matters concerned with nuclear weapons and their effects but also includes detailed descriptions of what attacks on Britain would be like.

Protect and Survive (1980). HMSO, London.

This should have been given a golden award for services to CND. Prepared originally for distribution in the 'run up' to a nuclear attack as part of the Government's information package, it was released last year presumably in an ill-judged effort to meet criticism of the Home Office reticence about Civil Defence for nuclear war. The general response of the public appears to have been to regard the instructions in the booklet as an absurd response to the scale of the threat. However, the book is by no means completely inaccurate – the problem lies more with the Civil Defence policy on which it is based.

Domestic Nuclear Shelters (1981). HMSO, London.

After its success with *Protect and Survive* the Home Office followed up with this gem. There is a technical manual but you are more likely to see the short popular version. This does contain what we might charitably call errors of simplification – *no* fall-out from air bursts, fall-out dust only remaining radioactive for a few days and so on. Should war come you might be better off in a shelter. You might be better off working *now* to try to stop war happening.

Nuclear Weapons (1980). HMSO, London.

Intended primarily for those 'who are involved in home defence planning, but it may be of interest to others,' this is the frequently updated standard Home Office guide. It compares unfavourably with books such as Glasstone and Dolan and the material should be treated with caution as it has a tendency to play down the likely effects of a nuclear attack.

The Home Office Circulars on Civil Defence.

If you read nothing else you should take advantage of all the studies that *your* taxes have paid for. Write to the Home Office in London and ask for a set of the ES/memoranda from 1973 to 1981. When you get your set, pour yourself a large drink and take a deep breath before you start to read – *and just hope it never happens*.

Home Office and Air Ministry (1946), *The Effects of the Atomic Bombs at Hiroshima and Nagasaki*. Report of the British Mission to Japan, HMSO, London.

The official report of the British survey, with a tone markedly different to more recent government publications on the effects of nuclear weapons.

Journal of Radiation Research, supplement (1975). 'A review of thirty years' study of Hiroshima and Nagasaki atomic bomb survivors.' Japan Radiation Research Society.

The literature on the medical effects of the atomic bombing is vast and often technically difficult, but these papers form a very useful and comprehensive recent summary.

JOURNALS

The best monthly journal is probably *Bulletin of the Atomic Scientists* which covers almost all the issues we have dealt with. It is a balanced journal which is widely read and endeavours to produce articles easily understandable to the non-scientist. The British weekly, *New Scientist*, has frequent articles on nuclear weapons and related matters and the more specialized American weekly, *Science*, is worth looking at in the library. *Flight International* covers the weaponry in all its gory detail and *NATO Review* (available from the Ministry of Defence) occasionally lets slip some interesting information and views. A less conventional source of information is *New Statesman* with one of the most efficient 'detectives' in the business, Duncan Campbell, on its staff. *Peace News* is a pacifist-orientated fortnightly with a good coverage of disarmament campaigns. Finally, the reader will probably expect a mention of *Protect and Survive Monthly*. To our minds this has many of the features of the American reaction to the problem during the worst part of the cold war. It appears to be accepted that nuclear war must come about sooner or later. The problem having been defined in this manner, a variety of more or less cranky technical solutions are offered. Worth borrowing one or two issues (it is widely on sale) just to see what the alternative to political action looks like.

INSTITUTES

Stockholm International Peace Research Institute Bergsrama S-17173, Solna, Sweden.

SIPRI is an independent institute for research into problems of peace and conflict, especially those of disarmament and arms regulations. It was established in 1966 to commemorate 150 years of peace in Sweden. The Institute is financed from the Swedish Parliament but has an international governing board and staff. Its major publication is the SIPRI Yearbook: World Armaments and Disarmament, which is possibly the best source book of information on nuclear weapons and strategic trends.

SIPRI also publishes several books each year, recent examples including books on chemical weapons, tactical nuclear weapons and nuclear energy and nuclear weapons proliferation.

International Institute for Strategic Studies 23 Tavistock Street, London WC2.

IISS is the major applied research institute for strategic studies in Western Europe. Its orientation is strongly pro-NATO although it does, on occasions, distance itself somewhat from policies of particular NATO member states. It publishes a bi-monthly journal, *Survival*, and two important annual surveys. *Strategic Survey* is a detailed assessment of strategic trends throughout the year and is published in May each year. *Military Balance*, normally published in the early autumn, makes an assessment of military strengths of all countries and also includes analyses of major strategic developments. Its publications are regarded as reasonably authoritative but by no means infallible.

Armaments and Disarmament Information Unit Mantell Building, University of Sussex, Falmer, Brighton, Sussex.

ADIU is a small but very active unit intended to provide information for anyone interested in armaments and disarmament. It has tended to concentrate on nuclear issues and produces a bi-monthly bulletin. This is especially useful for a detailed listing of papers and articles published in newspapers and general academic journals.

Center for Defense Information 122 Maryland Avenue N.E., Washington D.C. 20002.

The CDI is a useful independent source of information on US defence policy and weapons developments. It publishes the monthly *Defense Monitor*, each issue concentrating on a single topic.

Conclusions

'I like to believe that people in the long run
are going to do more to promote peace than
are governments. Indeed, I think that
people want peace so much that one of
these days governments had better get out
of their way and let them have it.'

Dwight D. Eisenhower
6 September 1959

Our concern has been with the problem of nuclear
weapons and the nuclear arms race. Although we are led
to believe that nuclear weapons have kept the peace since
World War II and that deterrence is still a workable idea,
it is apparent that several factors are combining to make
this little more than an illusion.

Both the superpowers now have a strategic nuclear
arsenal vastly greater than that required for any kind of
deterrence. A single American submarine or a few Soviet
ICBMs can destroy all its enemy's major cities, yet we
now have the largest *increase* in strategic nuclear weapons
that there has ever been – something approaching 50 per
cent over barely five years. It makes utter nonsense of
protestations about a desire for disarmament and shows

that the military-industrial interests are still firmly in control of government defence policies.

Quite apart from the superpowers there are three highly significant nuclear states – Britain, France and China – each able to inflict catastrophic damage and each vigorously expanding its capability. Britain is replacing its submarine-launched missiles with a larger and much more advanced system; the French are doing likewise, just as they, like the British, are expanding the means of delivery for tactical nuclear weapons. China is developing its own effective ICBM as well as a submarine-launched missile.

For those who take the view that the Russians cannot be trusted and that no amount of weaponry is too much to keep them in check, it is appropriate at least to see this from Moscow's point of view. These developments represent a frightening trend for (the Soviet Union) which not only faces the United States, but also Britain, a second nuclear country in the NATO military command structure. It also faces a more independent France and, most worrying of all, an intractable China with its expanding nuclear arsenal and increasingly close links with the United States.

At the very least, this outlook for the Soviet Union is one of potential conflict on many of its frontiers and gives it further justification for expanding its own nuclear capability. In addition to the four major nuclear weapons states, the Soviet Union needs to worry about India, Israel, South Africa and a number of potential nuclear weapons states such as Pakistan, South Korea and Argentina – all non-communist states.

The prospect of fifteen – even twenty-five – nuclear weapons states within a decade is hardly less than traumatic to all of us, including the superpowers, yet control of proliferation is simply not credible without a lead from the existing possessors of nuclear weapons. The principal route to a nuclear weapons capability is likely to be via a civil nuclear power programme and efforts to sell the technology world-wide raise major problems.

In addition to the size and expansion of nuclear arsenals we have the subtle yet fundamental changes in weapons technology which are accelerating the slide towards nuclear conflict. For the present it is clear enough that the United States is ahead with its efforts to develop counter-silo weapons, although the Soviet Union is putting considerable resources into similar programmes.

Allied to the new technology of strategic weapons we have the highly dangerous integration of nuclear weapons throughout the armed services. There are now over 40,000 tactical and theatre warheads existing in a wide variety of forms and for many different purposes, but they have become so much a fundamental tool of the armed forces that it will be well-nigh impossible to imagine a major conflict not involving their use. The situation is made even more fraught by the development of immensely destructive conventional munitions and chemical weapons. All in all, these developments effectively demolish the existence of any threshold between different levels of destructiveness.

We also have the race to bring in new forms of effective anti-submarine warfare, ballistic missile defences and space weapons such as high-energy lasers and particle beams. Major developments in these areas simply add to instability.

But, most importantly, whichever 'side' is ahead does not increase its security, as a counterforce ability does little more than pressurize an opposing country to adopt launch-on-warning tactics or *even strike first while it can*.

The prospect of nuclear war must not be unthinkable in the sense that we ignore it, but neither must it become acceptable. One of the most disturbing trends of all is the insidious tendency in some quarters to minimize the effects of a strategic nuclear war. It would be simply catastrophic and Britain would be one of the worst casualties of the first few minutes of that war. To talk of rapid recovery and a return to normality is utter nonsense – 'radioactive stone age' is probably closer to reality. There is little doubt that whether or not one believes that Britain should bristle with nuclear weapons, the price for this would be annihilation. This seems an unintelligent option and a much more intelligent course would be to survive first and *then* to resist by other means any attempt at occupation, if that were to happen.

It is the sheer scale of the nuclear devastation that has to be understood. A single ICBM could easily kill 500,000 people and injure a million more in a major city whereas in World War II all the bombs that dropped on London killed 30,000. There are well over 40,000 nuclear warheads in the world with a total destructive capacity a million times greater than the Hiroshima bomb. One really large warhead is more destructive than all the non-nuclear explosives made since gunpowder was invented.

It is in this context that the Civil Defence programme, as presently proposed, has been shown to be little more than a confidence trick in that it cannot afford any significant protection for the mass of the population. Even enormously expensive deep shelters could be countered by the use of different kinds of nuclear attack.

The scale of the arms race also needs to be understood. About *half* the world's physicists are engaged in research and development programmes concerned with defence. The United States and the Soviet Union spend over £50 million *a day* on nuclear warheads and associated delivery systems. The world cannot afford this insane use of resources, both material and human.

Yet we have looked at the attempts at nuclear disarmament and have seen that they have achieved scarcely anything. True there has been some limited progress, but this is greatly outweighed by the international trends towards escalation and proliferation.

Against this broad background we have to say that the prospects for avoiding nuclear conflict are bleak. Unless the existing trends can be curbed, halted and then reversed in the space of a decade *we doubt that a nuclear holocaust can be avoided in the lifetime of most of us*. It is quite conceivable that any one of a variety of events, including accidents, could trigger a nuclear conflict at any time.

Some initial ideas on how to pull back from the abyss have been put forward and we have concentrated, perhaps unusually, on the strategic arms race and how it might be controlled. We have also discussed alternative defence strategies for Britain, including passive resistance. This would obviously require education and training on a large scale but it would be small in cost compared with existing commitments in defence.

We also propose a strong emphasis on disarmament in Britain or Europe, including the creation of more nuclear-free zones, for we see the three levels of action, national, continental and global, as necessarily integrated. To some people our suggestions may appear unrealistic but we are convinced that such proposals, or others like them, are *essential*. The nuclear arms race *has* to be brought under control. How precisely it happens is rather less important than that it happens soon.

The growth of public concern in the past two years over the increasing likelihood of nuclear war is easily the most hopeful sign for the future. It is all too easy to dismiss this development by pointing out that only in the West do you have such a growing awareness since it is not possible in the Soviet bloc. Such condemnation usually talks of the need for the Soviet bloc to make the first move. But surely the fact that there is more freedom of debate in the West is precisely the reason why we have such an immense responsibility and a greater possibility for action. With two massive blocs locked into a single system, one of them has to start breaking out. In an era of extreme overkill, with massive excesses of nuclear arms, major concessions can be made with confidence; concessions sufficient even to start a process of disarmament.

The problems are formidable and, with the pressure of nuclear arms developments, time is now very short. Whilst the *governments* of East and West are drifting further apart there is unmistakable and growing evidence that *people* within these countries are reacting against the threat of destruction.

Until recently we would have had few grounds for any optimism. Yet times *are* changing, people *are* becoming aware of the problems and *are* starting to take action. We hope this report will contribute to these developments.

THE CAMPAIGN FOR SURVIVAL

This is a campaign in which everyone can play a part. Its object is to distribute information leaflets on nuclear war to every household in Britain.

These leaflets contain, in simple question and answer form, a summary of the material contained in this book. By helping to distribute them to your friends, your workmates and your community you will be making people aware of the facts. This in turn will help to create pressure on government to engage in positive negotiations on disarmament now, as well as to examine alternative defence policies. It will also find more people like you, who will join in the distribution.

Just fill in the form below (or send a letter if you prefer) and send it with a cheque or postal order for the amount stated, and you will be sent the leaflets post free.

Tick
here

1   100 leaflets and free collecting box   £2.50   └─
        or
2   200 leaflets and free collecting box   £3.50   └─
        or
3   100 leaflets, one copy of
        this book and free collecting box   £3.50   └─
        Additional lots of 100 leaflets   £1.00   └─

Total: £ . . . .

Tick your requirements on the right and enter the total at the bottom. Send a cheque or postal order for this amount and your name and address to *Campaign for Survival, P.O. Box 11, Godalming, Surrey.*

If you can spare more than the stated sum the money will be used to provide material for those who cannot afford to buy it.